Charles A. Ward is Assistant Professor of Slavic Languages at the University of Wisconsin-Milwaukee. A graduate of Harvard, he studied for a year at Moscow University before taking his Ph.D. at Chicago. He has led many groups to Russia.

Maps, illustrations and typography by F. Randolph Helms Associates

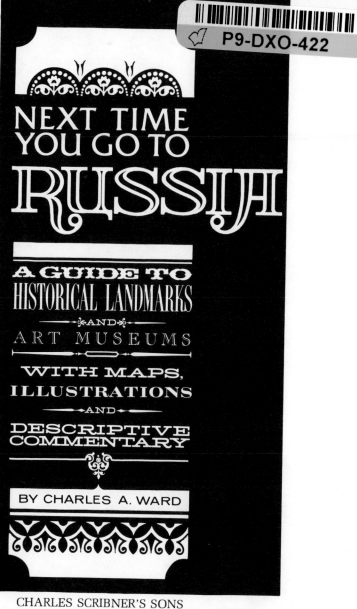

NEXT TIME YOU GO TO RUSSIA

A GUIDE TO HISTORICAL LANDMARKS AND ART MUSEUMS WITH MAPS, ILLUSTRATIONS AND DESCRIPTIVE COMMENTARY

BY CHARLES A. WARD

CHARLES SCRIBNER'S SONS
NEW YORK

Library of Congress Catalog Card Number 79-66593 ISBN 0-684-16455-8
This edition published 1980 by Charles Scribner's Sons Copyright © 1977, 1980 Charles A. Ward

First edition published 1977 by Academic Travel Books, division of Academic Travel Abroad, Washington, D.C.

Printed in the United States of America.
3 5 7 9 11 13 15 17 19 Q/P 20 18 16 14 12 10 8 6 4

FOREWORD

Since the mid-1960's foreign travel to the Soviet Union has grown at an increasingly rapid rate, for travelers have discovered a wealth and diversity of sights there, and the Soviet tour industry has greatly expanded its accommodations and services. Yet while tourism to Russia has increased rapidly, there is still only a small amount of travel literature about the Soviet Union. Most guidebooks lack useful city maps, even of Moscow and Leningrad; almost none has plans or reference material on the collections of the great museums, or identification of the country's many architectural treasures. This guide book supplies such material.

The travel information in **Next Time You Go to Russia** was first gathered for members of the University of Wisconsin Soviet Seminar. It was then expanded for use by the Smithsonian Associates tours, and other groups associated with Academic Travel Abroad, a Washington, D.C., travel agency. The organizing principle behind the book was to provide a guide to the main cities of central Russia, with additional sections on Tallinn in Estonia, Kiev in the Ukraine, and Uzbekistan, or Soviet Central Asia. In its present form the book fills the gap between a stereotyped "tourguide" and a text reference too bulky to be easily transported. Detailed maps and plans, relevant dates, concise background information, and brief descriptions of the major sights make this book a useful aid to the traveler and a handy reference for the student of the history, arts, and architecture of Russia. Since travelers can spend only a week in Leningrad and Moscow, description of these cities is generally limited to attractions near the center of town. A more complete description is given of the remaining towns, most of which can be surveyed in a day or two of diligent touring.

The maps and plans are numbered consecutively in bold type so that any map can be readily located. A key system has been provided to facilitate easy reference to the location of any specific sight on a map, or to its location in the text. Two numbers, in parentheses, follow the name of each sight in the text. The first number, in bold-face type, refers to the number of the map, and the second number, in regular type, refers to the number of that sight on the map. In addition, the sequence of numbers on each map corresponds to the order of presentation in the text, so that the description of an item noted on a map can be readily located in the text. The book has four appendices. The Glossary of Architectural terms illustrates and defines the main features of old Russian churches and neoclassical buildings described in the book. The other appendices — background reference material on government leaders and architects mentioned in the text — expand the usefulness of the book for both traveler and student.

It is hoped that this guide will contribute to the traveler's appreciation of the Soviet Union by presenting basic background information on buildings to be seen and by providing the location and identification of many sights which otherwise might be overlooked. I wish to extend my special thanks to F. Randolph Helms for the extraordinary job he did on the maps, illustrations, and typography.

Charles A. Ward

To Karen

CONTENTS

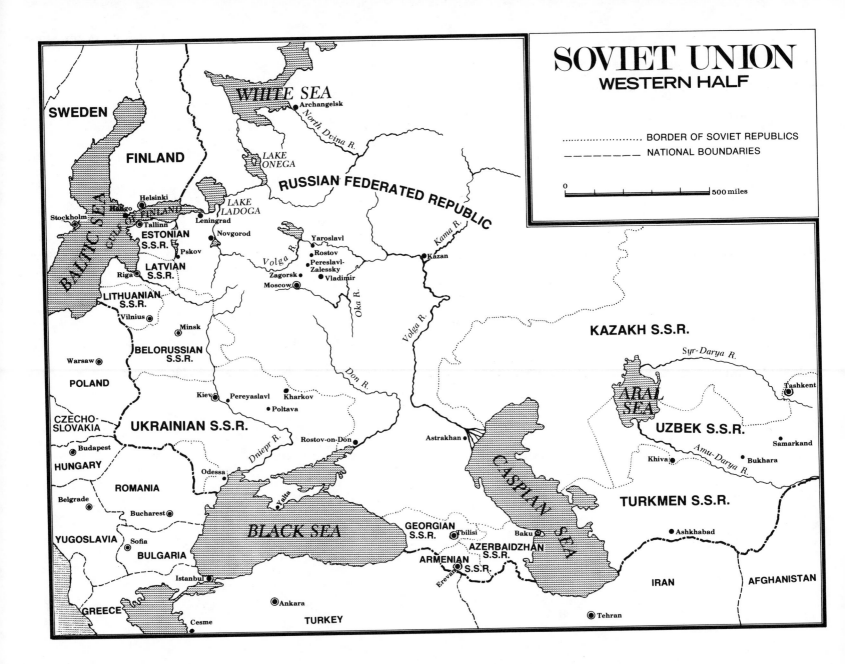

SOVIET UNION
WESTERN HALF

.... BORDER OF SOVIET REPUBLICS

– – – – – – – – NATIONAL BOUNDARIES

0 _____ 500 miles

SWEDEN

FINLAND

WHITE SEA

• Archangelsk

North Dvina R.

LAKE ONEGA

RUSSIAN FEDERATED REPUBLIC

BALTIC SEA

Helsinki •
Hango ●
GULF OF FINLAND
Stockholm ●
● Tallinn
ESTONIAN S.S.R.
● Pskov

● Leningrad

LAKE LADOGA

Novgorod •

Yaroslavl •
● Rostov
Pereslavl-Zalessky •
● Vladimir
Volga R.
Zagorsk •
Moscow ●

Oka R.

Kama R.

● Kazan

Volga R.

LATVIAN S.S.R.
Riga ●

LITHUANIAN S.S.R.
Vilnius ●

● Minsk

BELORUSSIAN S.S.R.

Warsaw ●

POLAND

KAZAKH S.S.R.

Syr-Darya R.

ARAL SEA

● Tashkent

UZBEK S.S.R.

● Samarkand

Amu-Darya R.
Khiva ● ● Bukhara

CZECHO-SLOVAKIA

UKRAINIAN S.S.R.

Kiev ●
● Pereyaslavl
● Kharkov
● Poltava

Dniepr R.

Don R.

Rostov-on-Don ●

Astrakhan ●

CASPIAN SEA

TURKMEN S.S.R.

● Ashkhabad

● Budapest

HUNGARY

Odessa ●

Yalta •

ROMANIA

Belgrade ●

Bucharest ●

BLACK SEA

GEORGIAN S.S.R.
● Tbilisi
Baku ●

AZERBAIDZHAN S.S.R.

ARMENIAN S.S.R.
Erevan ●

IRAN

AFGHANISTAN

YUGOSLAVIA

Sofia ●

BULGARIA

Istanbul ●

GREECE

Cesme •

● Ankara

TURKEY

● Tehran

LENINGRAD

Winter Palace: Hermitage

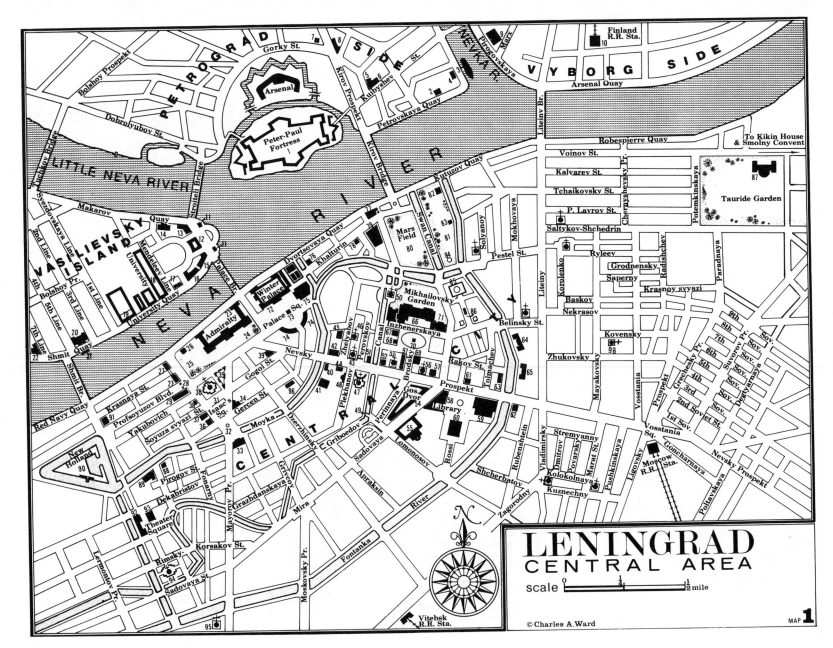

LENINGRAD
CENTRAL AREA

scale 0 ¼ ½ mile

© Charles A. Ward

MAP 1

VYBORG SIDE

PETROGRAD SIDE

VASILEVSKY ISLAND

CENTER

Peter-Paul Fortress

Arsenal

Tauride Garden

Mars Field

Mikhailovsky Garden

Winter Palace

Admiralty

New Holland

Theater Square

Finland R.R. Sta.

Vitebsk R.R. Sta.

Moscow R.R. Sta.

To Kikin House & Smolny Convent

2

Key to Map 1

1. Peter-Paul Fortress
2. Peter's House (#5 Petrovskaya Quay)
3. Aurora Battleship
4. 5-story military school
5. Gorky St. #½, 1906, by Van Hohen
6. #4 Kuibyshev St. for lumber industrialist Brandt
7. Momument to Gorky
8. #1 Kirov Prospekt, Lidval House
9. Intourist Hotel "Leningrad"
10. Finland R.R. Station
11. Rostral Columns (Pushkin Sq.)
12. Naval Museum
13. Geological Museum
14. Museum of Russian Literary History
15. Zoological Museum
16. Anthropological & Ethnographical Museum
17. Academy of Sciences Bldg.
18. Leningrad State University
19. Menshikov Palace
20. Academy of Fine Arts
21. Boat Landing w/ Sphinx
22. Academic's House
23. Admiralty
24. Gorky Gardens
25. Decembrist's Sq.
26. Statue of Peter
27. Senate & Synod Bldgs.
28. Ionic Columns at Profsoyuzov St.
29. Horse Guards Riding School
30. St. Isaac's Cathedral
31. St. Isaac's Square
32. Nicholas I Monument
33. City Soviet (former Mariinsky Palace)
34. Astoria Hotel
35. Lobanov-Rostovsky Palace
36. Headquarters Intourist (#11 Isaac's Sq.)
37. Myatlev Palace
38. Museum of Musical Instruments
39. Office Bldg.
40. Stroganov Palace
41. Razumovsky Palace
42. Dutch Church & Dutch House
43. Lutheran Church of Peter & Paul
44. Four-story Fur Merchant Bldg.
45. DLT
46. St. Mary's Church
47. Kazan Cathedral
48. Small Park
49. Bank Bridge
50. Church of the Resurrection
51. Dom Knigi Bookstore
52. Small Hall of the Philharmonia
53. St. Catherine Church
54. Gostiny Dvor
55. Page Corps (now Suvorov Mil. Sch.)
56. Armenian Church of St. Catherine
57. "Passage" Womens' Store
58. Saltykov-Shchedrin Public Library
59. Pioneer's Palace
60. Pushkin Drama Theater
61. Gastronom #1
62. Beloselsky-Belozersky Palace
63. Leningrad House of Friendship
64. Arctic Institute
65. Catherine Institute
66. Russian Museum
67. Maly Theater
68. Brodsky Home
69. State Philharmonic
70. Pushkin Statue
71. Museum of Ethnography of the Peoples of the USSR
72. Winter Palace
73. Alexander Column
74. General Staff Hdqtrs.
75. Guard Corps Hdqtrs. Bldg.
76. Preobrazhensky Barracks
77. Marble Palace
78. Main Pharmacy
79. Pavlov Regiment Barracks
80. Mars Field
81. Summer Garden
82. Summer Palace of Peter
83. Coffee House Pavilion
84. Red Porphyry Vase
85. Engineer's Castle
86. Parade Ground
87. Tauride Palace
88. Architect Montferrand's Home
89. House of Culture
90. Arch of the New Holland
91. Palace of Labor
92. Kirov Opera and Ballet Theater
93. National Conservatory
94. St. Nikola Cathedral
95. Trinity Cathedral
96. "Beriozka" Shop at #26 Gercen St.
97. Europe Hotel on Brodsky St.
98. Roman Catholic Church

Kazan Cathedral: Leningrad

4

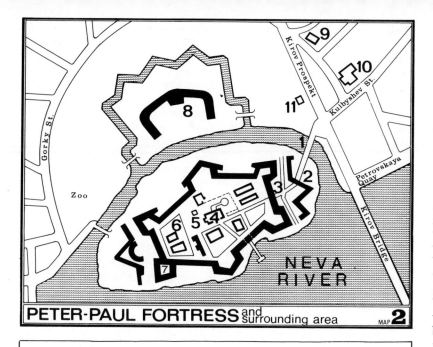

PETER-PAUL FORTRESS and surrounding area

MAP 2

1. Bridge
2. St. John Gate
3. St. Peter Gate
4. Peter-Paul Cathedral
5. "Boat House"
6. Mint
7. Trubetskoy Bastion
8. Arsenal Military Museum
9. Mosque
10. Museum of Revolution
11. Monument to Sailors of Steregushchy destroyer

LENINGRAD
(Map 1)

Leningrad is the second largest city in the Soviet Union, with a population of about four million. The city, founded as St. Petersburg by Peter the Great, was built on marshy land won from the Swedes in 1703 during the Northern War (1700-1721). Petersburg became Russia's main port providing direct sea access to the West and replacing the ice-locked port of Archangelsk on the White Sea, which could be used only a few months of the year. The city was officially founded by a cannon shot from the embryonic fortress on May 16, 1703. It was the capital of the Russian Empire from 1712-1918.

The establishment of Petersburg altered the Russian Empire in innumerable ways. As the new capital, and the scene of feverish building for more than a century, Petersburg caused a drain of wealth and talent from central Russia. As a new port it caused trade patterns to shift to the West, affecting the economy of the cities on the former upper Volga trade routes to Archangelsk. The architecture and very conception of Petersburg was Western in its origin, its street plan rational, geometrical, and designed by foreign architects, and its buildings in Western European style, breaking with the native Russian architectural traditions. The regularized street plan and neoclassicism of the Petersburg architecture spread, by the end of the century, to Moscow and the provinces, and was but one of the visible signs of the "modernization" which appeared in Russia after Peter the Great.

Leningrad is laid out on both sides of the Neva River as it completes its short flow from Lake Ladoga to the Gulf of Finland. The main four divisions of the city are the *Vyborg Side* and *Petrograd Side*, on the right bank (north side) of the river; *Vasilievsky Island* in the river, and the *Central City* on the left bank of the Neva.

PETROGRAD SIDE

The Petrograd Side, originally called Berezovy Island, is the oldest part of Leningrad, and is located between the Little Neva and Nevka Rivers. The name of this section has changed several times over the centuries. (It was the "Petersburg Side" in nineteenth-century Russian novels.) It is here that Peter began his new city with the Peter-Paul Fortress (1-1), the first large structure built in the city.

PETER-PAUL FORTRESS (Map 2). The main entrance to the fortress is from Kirov Prospekt by a bridge over the moat (2-1). The *St. John Gate* (2-2) leads through the first bastion. The fortress proper is entered through *St. Peter's Gate* (2-3), built in 1717-1718 by the Swiss-born architect Domenico Tressini. The gate is in the form of a triumphal arch with statues of Bellona and Minerva in the niches. The two-headed

Imperial eagle over the archway was done in 1722 by F. Vassu, and the large bas-relief above it is by Konrad Osner (it depicts the return to earth of the fortune teller Simon, achieved by St. Peter's prayers, an allegory of Russia's defeat of Sweden during the Northern War).

The masonry walls of the fortress (now up to 28 feet tall and 60 feet wide) were begun in 1706 by Tressini and were sheathed in granite in the 1780's. The fortress soon lost its military importance and became a prison for those considered to be a threat to the state. Peter had his son Aleksey tortured to death in the fortress, and numerous 19th-century writers and social critics spent time here. The prison was converted to a museum in 1924, with major restoration in 1956-1958. Cells in the *Trubetskoy Bastion* (2-7) are open for view.

The **PETER-PAUL CHURCH** (2-4 and Plan 3) was designed by Tressini and built between 1713-1732. It is in a western style unknown in Russia till then, a long rectangular church with ten columns, an immensely tall steeple in front, and a relatively modest drum and dome at the rear of the church. The church was somewhat remodeled in 1766. The building's dimensions are 98 by 210 feet, and the spire is 400 feet high, topped by an angel holding a cross.

The interior is light and airy, with an opulent gilt baroque iconostasis designed by Moscow architect I.P. Zarudny, and carved between 1722-1726. The church also contains the tombs of Russian rulers from Peter the Great through Alexander III. All are of white marble except those of Alexander II (green jasper) and his wife, Maria Alexandrovna (pink quartz).

At the entrance to the church (north-west corner) is a small building called the *"Boat House"* (2-5), built in 1761 to house the skiff which Peter sailed in his childhood. (The skiff itself is now in the Naval Museum.) Opposite the cathedral and boat house is the *Mint* (2-6), (*Monetny dvor*), built 1800-1806, where Soviet coins and medals are still struck.

To the north of the Fortress is the *Arsenal* (2-8), or *Kronwerk*, 1850-1860, which has housed a military (artillery) museum since 1872.

The Petrovskaya Quay, along the Neva, leads to *Peter's house* (1-2) of 1703 (#5 Petrovskaya Quay), a two-room log cabin now inside a brick structure built to preserve it in 1784. It is open as a museum with some memorabilia of Peter's time.

Anchored off the quay is the *Aurora Battleship* (1-3), which fired a shot signaling the storming of the Winter Palace in 1917, at the start of the October Revolution. It was mothballed in 1947 and became a museum in 1956. The five-story building opposite it, in an early architectural style, is a *military school* (1-4) built in 1910.

Gorky Street begins near the shore and forms a partial circle around the *Arsenal* (2-8). The first building, Gorky St. #1/2 (1-5), was built in 1906 by Van Hohen and was given by Nicholas II to his favorite, a ballerina named Kshesinskaya. The adjacent building, around the corner at #4 Kuibyshev St. (1-6), was built for lumber industrialist Brandt. Both houses were used by the Bolsheviks in 1917, and now house the *Museum of the October Revolution*.

The writer Maxim Gorky lived from 1914-1921 in the house at #23 Gorky Street.

At the intersection of Gorky St. and Kirov Prospekt is the *Leningrad Mosque* (2-9), 1912, designed by Vasilev, Van Hohen, and Krichinsky, and roughly modeled on the tomb of Tamerlane in Samarkand.

The building at #1 Kirov Prospekt (1-8) was built in 1902-1904 by the architect F.I. Lidval as his own residence. It is an early example of the "style moderne" which began to affect Russian architecture at the beginning of the 20th century.

VYBORG SIDE

The Vyborg Side developed as a workers district, and therefore has few buildings of architectural note or historic significance. The new *Intourist hotel "Leningrad"* (1-9) is at #7 Pirogovskaya Quay, across from the Aurora Battleship, so more and more foreign tourists are in this area. The main sights are the Samsonievsky Church (outside of Map 1), at #41 Prospekt Karl Marx, built 1728-1740. The Vyborg Factory-Kitchen (outside of Map 1), #45 Prospekt Karl Marx, built 1928-1930, is a good example of Leningrad "Constructivist" architecture. The *Finland Railroad Station* (1-10), to which Lenin returned to Russia in 1917, was totally rebuilt in 1960.

VASILIEVSKY ISLAND

This is Leningrad's largest island, located in the Neva River in the central part of the city. From its eastern point, or "Strelka," is one of the finest views of the city: the Winter Palace, Hermitage, Admiralty, and St. Isaac's Cathedral to the south; the Peter-Paul Fortress to the north.

In the 1720's Vasilievsky Island began to be developed as the administrative center of the city. The island was often isolated by inclement weather, so it was decided, in the 1730's, to make the left bank area the main focus of the city. Industry developed on the island in the 19th century, and by the 20th century many cultural institutions had moved into old buildings along the shore of the island.

Pushkin Square is at the point of the island. Prominent are the two *"Rostral Columns* (1-11), by Thomas de Thomon, 1809. These 100-foot tall towers with oil flares on top served as lighthouses for guiding ships on foggy days. The statues at the base represent the rivers Neva, Volga, Dniepr, and Volkhov. This area of the island served as the Port of Petersburg until 1880.

The *Naval Museum* (**1-12**), #4 Pushkin Square, was built as the Stock Exchange, 1805-1810, by Thomon and A.D. Zakharov, in the form of a Greek Doric temple. The Naval Museum was moved here from the Admiralty in 1940. The museum prominently features a huge collection of ship models.

Makarov Quay runs along the north side of the island. The *Geological Museum* (**1-13**) is at #2 Makarov Quay, and is in a former warehouse building, 1826-1832, designed by Luchini. Next door, at #4, is the *Museum of Russian Literary History* (**1-14**) (the "Pushkinsky dom"), in the former Customs House, 1829-1832, by Luchini.

University Quay runs along the south side of the island:

#1 - *Zoological Museum* (**1-15**), in a former port building, 1826-1832 by Luchini. The museum exhibits a large collection of stuffed animals, including mastadons from the Siberian permafrost.

#3 - *Anthropological and Ethnographical Museum* (**1-16**), built in 1718-1722 by a German architect, Mattarnovi; restored 1947-1949. This museum was formerly the "Kunstkammer" of Peter the Great, and still contains his collection of "curiosities and oddities" as well as ethnographical displays, particularly strong on peoples of the Orient and Africa.

#5 - *The Academy of Sciences Building* (**1-17**), 1784-1787 by G. Quarenghi.

#7 - *Leningrad State University* (**1-18**), designed by Tressini, 1722-1742, as the "Twelve Colleges" building for the Senate and Ministries in the 18th century. It was the home of a pedagogical institute from 1804, then of the University, which was founded in 1819.

#15 - *The Menshikov Palace* (**1-19**), by G. Schaedel and Fontana, 1710-1727, one of the earliest large houses built in Petersburg. It was in part reconstructed in the 1760's, and restoration has been going on since 1960.

#17 - *Academy of Fine Arts* (**1-20**), 1764-1788 by Kokorinov and Vallin de la Mothe. Its students and teachers included artists Kramskoy, Surikov, Serov, Repin, and architects Bazhenov and Voronikhin. Since 1947 it has housed the Research-Museum of the Academy of Arts. On the quay in front is a *boat landing* (**1-21**) by K. Thon, 1832-1834, including an Egyptian sphinx depicting Amenhotep III (1400-1376 BC).

The Lt. Shmit Quay is a continuation of University Quay. The first building (corner of 7th Line) is the *Academic's House* (**1-22**), 1808-1809 by Bazhenov and Zakharov, with 26 memorial plaques on the facade. Among them is one to the psychologist Ivan Pavlov, whose apartment in the building is now a museum.

At #17 Shmit Quay is the *Frunze Naval Academy* (outside of map 1), in a building with a ten-column portico built 1796-1809 by Volkov.

#45 Shmit Quay is the *Institute of Mining* (outside of map 1), 1806-1809 by Voronikhin, modeled on the temple of Poseidon at Paestrum. The Institute contains a Museum of Mining.

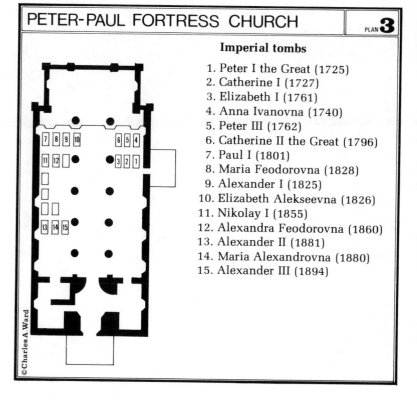

PETER-PAUL FORTRESS CHURCH — PLAN 3

Imperial tombs

1. Peter I the Great (1725)
2. Catherine I (1727)
3. Elizabeth I (1761)
4. Anna Ivanovna (1740)
5. Peter III (1762)
6. Catherine II the Great (1796)
7. Paul I (1801)
8. Maria Feodorovna (1828)
9. Alexander I (1825)
10. Elizabeth Alekseevna (1826)
11. Nikolay I (1855)
12. Alexandra Feodorovna (1860)
13. Alexander II (1881)
14. Maria Alexandrovna (1880)
15. Alexander III (1894)

©Charles A.Ward

CENTRAL CITY — LEFT BANK OF THE NEVA RIVER

The street pattern of the left bank was laid out with three main radial roads which center on the tower of the Admiralty building, the ship building yards of the 18th century. These three streets, Nevsky Prospekt, Dzerzhinsky Street, and Prospekt Mayorov, are transected by numerous streets and three channels, the Moyka River, the Griboedov Canal, and the Fontanka River.

The *Admiralty* (**1-23**) was begun in 1704, but achieved its present form after the remodeling by A.D. Zakharov, 1806-1823. The building is 458 yards long, with a central tower 230 feet high, topped by a weathervane in the form of a ship. The inner courts, where the boats were constructed, have been built up since 1871 when shipbuilding was transferred downriver. The building faces south on the *Gorky Gardens* (**1-24**), which were laid out in 1874. The main decorations are sculptures of nymphs holding a globe, on either side of the entrance pas-

Admiralty: Leningrad

sageway of the tower, and the statues and columns of the tower's superstructure. The Admiralty building now houses the Leningrad Naval College.

Decembrists Square (**1**-25) is to the west of the Admiralty. In its center is the famous *Statue of Peter* (**1**-26) by Falconet, cast in 1775 and unveiled in 1782. The statue is 16.5 feet tall, mounted on a giant granite boulder 46 feet long, 20 feet wide, and 16 feet tall. Peter is dressed simply in a robe, without pomp, looking toward Sweden. His horse is treading on a snake (a symbol of opposition to Peter's reforms).

The *Senate and Synod Buildings* (**1**-27), to the west of the square, were built in 1829-1834 by Carlo Rossi, replacing former Senate buildings on that site. The buildings are joined by an arch over Krasnaya St., and were constructed to give a unity to the west side of the square to match the recently completed Admiralty wing on the east. The buildings now house the Historical Archives. Just to the south is Profsoyuzov Boulevard, created in 1845 by enclosing a canal. The two granite *Ionic columns* (**1**-28) at the beginning of the street are topped by winged statues of Victory, a gift of the Prussian prince in exchange for a copy of the horse statues on the Anichkov bridge which Nicholas I sent to Berlin. On the other side of Profsoyuzov St. is the former *Horse Guards Riding School* (**1**-29), 1804-1807, by Quarenghi. The end facing Decembrists Square has a double column portico protecting wall relief sculptures of a Roman hippodrome. The two sculptures of horses before the building are by Italian sculptor P. Triscorni, and were brought to Russia in 1817. The building is now used as an exhibition hall.

St. Isaac's Cathedral (**1**-30), 1818-1849, was designed by French architect Auguste Ricard de Montferrand. The cathedral is named for St. Isaac of Dalmatia whose Saint's Day (May 30) coincides with Peter the Great's birthday. The church is the largest in Leningrad and, with its tall gilt dome, is one of the focal points and landmarks of the city. The church was completed in 1858, but many of the interior paintings were then replaced by mosaics, a job which continued till 1914.

The church was built on the site of a smaller church of the same name by Rinaldi and Brenna, 1768-1802. The mixture of old and new foundations caused the cathedral to settle unevenly, resulting in extensive repairs from 1873-1898. All 48 columns of the porticoes were realigned and a number of the marble veneer panels of the walls had to be replaced. A perfect color match could not be found, so now the church has a mottled effect on the outside. The church "worked" until 1928, when it was converted into a museum which opened in 1931. The interior suffered extensive frost and moisture damage during World War Two, and was restored from 1947-1963.

The church is somewhat squat and its lower mass does not lead naturally to the large dome above. But the individual details of the exterior are notable. The church is cross-plan, 364 feet long, 315 feet wide, and 330 feet to the top of the dome. The four porticoes are modeled on the Pantheon in Rome, and feature monolithic columns of red Finnish granite 54 feet tall and 7 feet in diameter at the base. The walls are 15 feet thick, of brick and alternate courses of granite, faced with a marble veneer. Pediments, more than 100 feet long, are highly articulated bronze reliefs. The west pediment portrays the "Meeting of St. Isaac with Emperor Theodosius" by Vitali (a reclining Montferrand in a toga is depicted on the left, holding a model of the cathedral). The south pediment represents the "Adoration of the Magi" by Vitali. East: "St. Isaac foretelling his death to Emperor Valentinian" by LeMaire. North: "Resurrection of Christ" by LeMaire.

The sober exterior of the cathedral is offset by the opulence of the interior, all in marble and rare minerals. The iconostasis is 223 feet long of white marble, with gilding and mosaic icons. The central iconostasis door is 23 feet high, cast in bronze (Vitali's design), flanked by two lapis lazuli columns 16 feet tall, and ten columns of malachite 30 feet tall (the columns are iron inside, with a mineral veneer). The central iconostasis door is open, revealing a stained glass window of the Ascension, an architectural detail from the Roman Catholic West rather than the Russian Orthodox tradition. The side chapels at the ends of the iconostasis, dedicated to St. Catherine and St. Alexander Nevsky, are finished in white marble with malachite panels. The altars are topped by gilded sculptures of the "Resurrection" and "Transfiguration" by Pimenov. The icons in the church are of 19th-century design, far from the classic icon designs of ancient Russia, but are executed in a virtuoso mosaic technique, with stones of thousands of tints laid in such a smooth manner that from only a short distance the mosaics appear to be paintings.

The three sets of massive entrance doors are of oak covered with bronze reliefs by Vitali. The North door depicts scenes of the life of Isaac of Dalmatia. The south door: events from Old Russian history. West door: scenes from the lives of Saints Peter and Paul.

The interior of the dome, painted by K. Bryullov, depicts the "Virgin surrounded by Saints." The interior of the dome is 269 feet above the floor, and now supports a Foucault pendulum installed in 1931.

The decor of the church was most expensive. In addition to the lapis lazuli, malachite, and Carrara marble of the iconostasis, the walls have Russian rose marble, grey marble from Finland, green from Genoa, yellow from Sienna, red "griotto" from France. For gilding of the dome and interior detail, nearly 900 pounds of gold were used.

A stairway by the south entrance leads to an observation gallery outside the base of the dome, from which there is an excellent panorama of the city.

St. Isaac's Square (1-31) is bounded on the north by the Cathedral. In the center of the square is a 49-foot tall *monument to Nicholas I* (1-32), 1859, designed by Montferrand. The sculpture is by P. Klodt, an equestrian statue of Nicholas on a rearing horse balanced on its two back legs. The pedestal of the statue is surrounded by four allegorical figures with the features of Nicholas's wife and three daughters, representing Faith, Wisdom, Force, and Justice. Lower down are four bronze reliefs of highlights of Nicholas's reign. The two buildings flanking the statue are former ministries built in 1844-1853 by architect N.E. Efimov. Behind the statue, at the south end of the square, is the *City Soviet* (1-33), the former Mariinsky Palace, 1839-1844 by A. Stakenschneider, a rebuilding of an older palace for Nicholas's elder daughter, Maria.

On the east side of the square, at the corner of Mayorov and Gercen Streets, is the *Astoria Hotel* (1-34), 1910-1912, by Lidval. North of it, across Mayorov Street, is the three-sided *Lobanov-Rostovsky Palace* (1-35) by Montferrand, 1817-1820, which housed the War Office until 1917. The eight-column portico facing Gorky Garden is flanked by two statues of lions.

On the west side of the square is the *Headquarters of Intourist* (1-36), at #11 Isaac's Square, in the former German Embassy, 1910-1912, designed by Peter Behrens. Next to it, at #9, is the former *"Myatlev Palace"* (1-37), from the 1760's, built for N. Naryshkin. The French philosopher Diderot stayed there in 1773-1774. The building at #5 Isaac's Square houses the *Museum of Musical Instruments* (1-38).

NEVSKY PROSPEKT is the main thoroughfare of Leningrad, and a street which has figured prominently in Russian history and Russian literature. The street, 2 1/2 miles long, leads from the Admiralty to the *Alexander Nevsky Monastery* (Plan 5). Odd numbers are on the right going away from the Admiralty.

#9 (corner of Gogol St.), an *office building* built in 1912 as a bank by architect Peretyakovich, in grey granite (1-39).

#17 (at Moyka River), the *Stroganov Palace* (1-40), 1752-1754, a baroque palace by Rastrelli, now an administrative office building. The sphinxes at the entrance are by Voronikhin. [Behind the palace, at #48 Moyka Quay, is the former *Razumovsky Palace* (1-41), 1770, by Kokorinov and Vallin de la Mothe. It was rebuilt in 1830 and now houses a pedagogical institute. Next door at #50 Moyka is another section of the institute, in a building by Rastrelli, 1750-1753, but rebuilt at the end of the century.]

#20 Nevsky (at Moyka River), the former *Dutch Church house* (1-42), 1834-1837 by Jacquot, a three-story building with a four-column portico. The original facade has been preserved, though the building now houses a library.

#22-24, the former *Lutheran Church of Peter & Paul* (1-43), 1833-1838, by A. Bryullov, is set back somewhat from the street. The church was remodeled in the 1950's to house a swimming pool.

#21 (opposite Zhelyabov St.) is a *modern building of 1912* with three large glassed-in arches four stories high, built for a fur merchant (1-44). [At Zhelyabov St. #21-23 is *DLT* (1-45), the second largest Department Store in Leningrad. At #6a Zhelyabov is *St. Mary's Church* (1-46) (former Finnish Church), remodeled in present form in late 1800's.]

The *Kazan Cathedral* (1-47) (at Griboedov Canal), was built 1801-1811 by A. Voronikhin on the site of a smaller church from the 1730's. The church faces Nevsky Prospekt with a large curved colonnade of 96 columns. The cathedral is basically crossplan, 180 by 236 feet, with columned porticoes on each face. The dome, 65 feet in diameter, was the first cast-iron reinforced dome in Russia, and rises to 285 feet. The columns and church veneer are finished in a yellow limestone quarried south of Leningrad. The north doors, facing Nevsky Prospekt, are a copy of Ghiberti's doors of the Bapistry in Florence. The interior of the cathedral is notable for its 56 monolithic Finnish granite columns 35 feet tall, a mosaic floor of colored marble, and numerous relief sculptures. The tomb of General Kutuzov, hero of the Napoleonic wars, is to the right of the entrance.

The cathedral now houses the *Museum of the History of Religion and Atheism*, founded in 1932, with exhibits exposing the anti-scientific basis of all world religions and showing the role of science in establishing a materialistic world view. The 150,000 items on display are divided into departments dealing with: Prehistoric and early Tribal origins of Religion; Greek gods; Origin of Christianity and Rome; Medieval Christianity, Crusades, Inquisition, and Reformation; Modern Catholicism and the role of the Vatican in world politics and economy; Religions of the East; History of the Russian Orthodox Church; and Atheism and Religion in present-day USSR.

In front of the cathedral are statues of 1812 War generals Kutuzov and Barclay de Tolli. To the west across Plekhanov Street is a small *park* (1-48) with a massive cast-iron fence by Voronikhin, 1811, and a fountain by Thomas de Thomon, 1809, moved here from a Tsarist summer palace in 1935.

On Griboedov Canal, to the south, is the *"Bank Bridge"* (1-49), a suspension bridge supported by gilt-winged griffins, and named for the Imperial Bank Building, 1783-1789 by Quarenghi, now the Leningrad Institute of Finances and Economy. The fence along the canal here, designed by L. Rusca, was built in 1817.

On the Griboedov Canal to the north of Nevsky prospekt is the *Church of the Resurrection "on blood"* (1-50), 1883-1907 by Alfred Parland and others. The church, designed in a pseudo-Old Russian style, is built on the site of the bomb-assassination of Tsar Alexander II on March 1, 1881. Mosaics on the pediments and on the inside were designed by artists Nesterov and V. Vasnetsov. The elaborate fence opposite the church at the end of Mikhailovsky Gardens, from 1907, is attributed to Parland.

#28 Nevsky (corner Griboedov Canal), the *Dom Knigi bookstore* (1-51), built as the Singer Sewing Machine Co. building, 1902-1904. Singer wanted it to be eleven stories high, but no private building could be higher than the Winter Palace. Nonetheless it stands out on Nevsky. Note the metal sculpture on top, and art nouveau door hardware and elevator cage inside. The building is the first steel-frame building constructed in Russia.

#30, the *Small Hall of the Philharmonia* (1-52), built by Rastrelli in mid-1700's, but entirely reconstructed in 1829 by Jacquot.

#32, *St. Catherine Church* (1-53), 1763-1783 by Vallin de la Mothe, remodeled 1828-1830 and restored in 1947. The church was the burial place of the last Polish king, Stanislas Poniatowski (died 1798), and of French General J.V. Moreau (died 1813).

#35, *Gostiny Dvor* (1-54), Leningrad's largest and most famous department store. Built 1761-1785 by Vallin de la Mothe, it was reconstructed several times over the centuries. The original facade was restored in 1947-1948.

At Sadovaya St. #26, opposite the back of Gostiny dvor, is the former *Page Corps* (1-55), originally built for Count Vorontsov by Rastrelli, 1749-1757. The building now houses the Suvorov Military School.

#40-42 Nevsky, former *Armenian Church of St. Catherine* (1-56), 1771-1780, designed by Yury Velten.

#48, the *"Passage" Women's Department Store* (1-57), 1846-1848; rebuilt in 1900.

#37, (at Sadovaya St.), *Saltykov-Shchedrin Public Library* (1-58), 1796-1801 by Sokolov, with additions 1828-1834 by Rossi.

#39 (at Fontanka), *Pioneer's Palace* (1-59), former Anichkov Palace, from the 1740's, with numerous later additions and remodelling. The main facade faces the Fontanka River. The palace was the home of the heirs - apparent during the 19th century and still has vestibule, staircase, meeting hall, and four drawing rooms in their 19th-century style.

The *Pushkin Drama Theater* (1-60), set back from Nevsky Prospekt, is between the Public Library and Pioneer Palace. It was designed by Rossi and built 1828-1832. Before it is a small square with a statue of Catherine II in the center, by M.O. Mikeshin, unveiled in 1873. The east side of the square has two pavilions by Rossi, constructed 1816-1818 during his remodeling of the Anichkov Palace.

#56, *Gastronom #1* (1-61), former Eliseev Food Store, built 1903-1907 by Baranovsky in the modern style. The food store has an

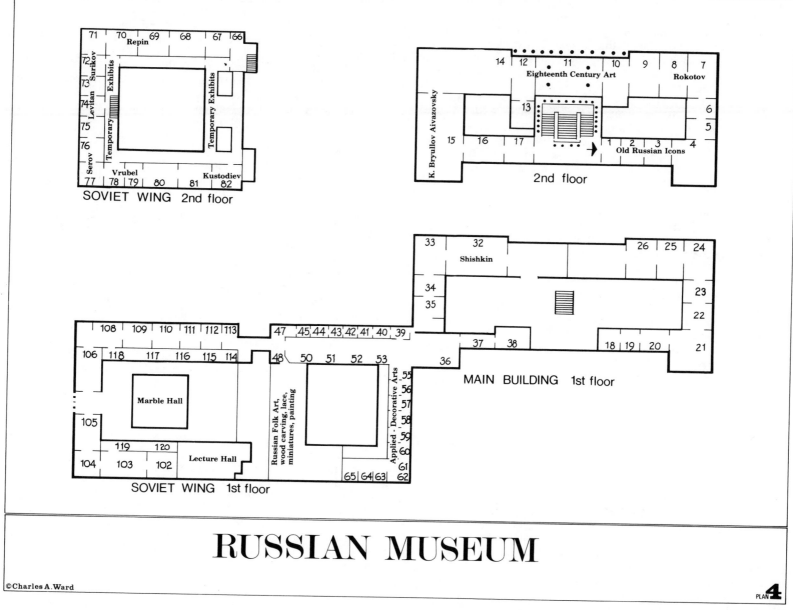

SOVIET WING 2nd floor

2nd floor

MAIN BUILDING 1st floor

SOVIET WING 1st floor

RUSSIAN MUSEUM

©Charles A.Ward

PLAN **4**

11

interesting "art nouveau" interior. The second floor houses the Comedy Theater. The Anichkov Bridge over the Fontanka River is marked by four statues of rearing horses done between 1841-1850 by P. Klodt.

#41 (across the Fontanka), the former *Beloselsky-Belozersky Palace* (**1-62**), 1846-1848 by Stakenschneider, an enlargement and re-building of a former palace by Thomon. It now houses a Leningrad district Party Headquarters.

To the left, at #21 Fontanka Quay, is the *Leningrad House of Friendship* (**1-63**), built in the 1820's for D.L. Naryshkin, with a renaissance facade added in 1848 by Efimov. Notable is the Columned Hall, with ceiling designed by G. Scotti, restored in 1948-1949 after destruction during World War II. The building was reconstructed as the House of Friendship in 1965, and preserves rooms in Gothic, Renaissance, Baroque, and Neoclassical style, as redone in the mid-1800's by Bernard Simon.

At #34 Fontanka is the *Arctic Institute* (**1-64**), in the former Sheremetev Palace, 1750-1755 by S. Chevakinsky, later rebuilt and expanded. At #36 is the *"Catherine Institute"* (**1-65**), 1804-1807 by Quarenghi, now a branch of the Public Library.

Arts Square is on the left side of Nevsky Prospekt and is reached by the short Brodsky Street. The square was designed by Rossi, who projected uniform facades for all the buildings on the square to harmonize with the Michael Palace (now the *Russian Museum*) (**1-66**) which he built there, 1819-1825.

#1 Arts Sq., the *Maly Theater* (**1-67**), 1831-1833 by A. Bryullov, remodeled by A. Kavos in 1859.

#3, former *home of Soviet painter L. Brodsky* (**1-68**) (from 1924-1939). His apartment is now a museum with a good small collection of late 19th-early 20th century paintings, as well as works by Brodsky himself.

The *State Philharmonic* (**1-69**) (south-east corner of square at Brodsky St.), 1834-1839 by Jacquot, formerly the Aristocrat's Club (Dvoryanskoe sobranie).

In the center of the square is a *statue of the poet Pushkin* (1799-1837) done in 1957 by Anikushkin (**1-70**).

The **RUSSIAN MUSEUM (Plan 4)**, along with the Tretyakov Gallery in Moscow, is the main repository of Russian art. The building is the former "New Michael Palace", 1819-1825 by Rossi, built by Alexander I for his younger brother. Rossi designed not only the building, but the furniture, floor parquets, chandeliers, and the fence railing outside. The building was redone as a museum in 1895, opened in 1898, and was further restored after World War II. Some of the rooms still retain their elaborate neoclassical decor, the most outstanding being the "White Hall" (No. 11 on the plan), decorated with Rossi's furniture, sculpture by Kozlovsky, reliefs by Pimenov, and wall murals by Vighi. Many of the gallery ceilings on the second floor, overlooking the Mikhailovsky Gardens, are excellent examples of room decoration of the time.

A tour of the collection begins on the second floor with Russian Icons, rooms 1-4. Rooms 5-12 display works of the 18th century with the remainder of the second floor devoted to early 19th century. The remainder of the 19th-century collection is on the first floor of the main palace, and in halls 39-48, and the second floor of the wing added to the museum in 1911. Soviet art is on the first floor of this wing.

To the right of the Russian Museum is the *Museum of Ethnography of the Peoples of the USSR* (**1-71**), in a building constructed in 1911. The exhibits are devoted to daily life, costumes and applied art of Soviet nationality groups from the Baltic Sea to Central Asia to the Pacific.

The **ALEXANDER NEVSKY LAVRA MONASTERY (Plan 5)** is at the end of Nevsky Prospekt. It was founded by Peter the Great in 1710, designed by Tressini, and built on the purported site of Alexander Nevsky's defeat of the Swedes in 1240.

The monastery area is entered through a *passage gate* over which is a small *chapel* by I.E. Starov, 1783-1785, in neoclassic style (**5-11**). The entrance roadway leads between two cemeteries. On the left is the *18th-century Necropolis* (formerly the Lazarevskoe Cemetery) (**5-7**), begun when Peter's sister Natalya was buried there in 1716. It also contains the graves of writers M. Lomonosov and D. Fonvizen; architects Voronikhin, Rossi, Starov, Zakharov, Thomas de Thomon, and Quarenghi; sculptors Kozlovski, Martos, Shchedrin, and others.

To the right is the *19th-century Necropolis* (**5-8**) (formerly the Tikhvin Cemetery), begun in 1823. It contains graves of writers Karamzin, Krylov, Dostoevsky; composers Glinka, Mussorgsky, Rimsky-Korsakov, Borodin, Tchaikovsky, and A. Rubenstein; painters Kramskoy, Shishkin; sculptors Demut-Malinovsky, Pimenov, Orlovsky, Vitali, and Klodt.

The monastery proper is entered after crossing a bridge over a narrow canal. To the left is the two-story *Church of Alexander Nevsky (upper) and Annunciation (lower)* (**5-1**), built 1717-1722 by Tressini. Both house a *Museum of Urban Sculpture*, containing funereal sculpture. The Church of the Annunciation also contains tombs of General Suvorov (18th century), and members of the Tsar's family and statesmen of the 19th century, with stones carved mainly by Martos and Shchedrin.

The main church of the monastery is the *Trinity Cathedral* (**5-3**), 1776-1790 by Starov, on the site of an earlier church by Tressini. The cathedral is flanked by *monastery buildings* (**5-2** and **4**) which face the courtyard with large glassed-in arches. These auxillary buildings are by architect Rastorguev, built in 1750's-1760's. In the central area of the monastery is a cemetery with graves of Soviet military heroes. There is another large graveyard area behind the Trinity Cathedral. The cathedral still functions, and there is a Seminary in the Monastery.

PALACE SQUARE. The *Winter Palace* (**1-72**), 1754-1762, was designed by Rastrelli, the master of the baroque style in Russia. The interior was redone several times in later years by various architects. A three-day fire in December, 1837, totally gutted the palace, but it was restored in two years under the supervision of architects V. Stasov and A. Bryullov. The palace was the winter residence of the Tsars until the 20th century. Since the 1920's it has housed part of the Hermitage Art Collection.

In the center of the square rises the 154-foot *Alexander Column* (**1-73**), designed by Montferrand and constructed 1830-1834. The monolithic shaft of red Finnish granite is 82 feet tall, twelve feet thick at the base, and weighs 700 tons, but was raised vertical in one hour, twenty minutes by 2490 men with a complex pulley system. The column supports a statue of an angel with the face of Alexander I, and represents peace in Europe after the defeat of Napoleon. The 26-foot tall square pedestal, of one piece of granite, is decorated by four allegorical bronze bas-reliefs by Leppe and Svintsov. The column is not connected to the base and stands by its own weight.

Facing the palace is the *General Staff Headquarters* (**1-74**), 1819-1829 by Rossi, an open "U"-shaped building which forms the south side of the square. On top of its arch, which marks the beginning of Gercen St., is a bronze Victory and six-horse chariot by Demut-Malinovsky and Pimenov, in honor of the victory over Napoleon. The building now houses military administrative offices.

To the east side of the square is the former *Guard Corps Headquarters building* (**1-75**), 1840-1848 by A. Bryullov.

Khalturin Street leads east from Palace Square, parallel to the Neva River. In the early 19th century this was the residential area of rich foreign merchants and members of the royal family. The first building on the left past the Winter Canal was the *Preobrazhensky Barracks* (**1-76**) in the 19th century. At #5 Khalturin St. is the *"Marble Palace"* (**1-77**), 1768-1785 by Rinaldi, a gift of Catherine II to Count Orlov. It now houses a branch of the Lenin Museum (since 1937). The building is granite with pilasters and window frames of pink and blue marble from Finland and Siberia. Inside, note the harmony of the marble of the main staircase and of the former ballroom on the second floor.

The building at #4 Khalturin St., 1789-1796 by Quarenghi, was the *main pharmacy* of old Petersburg (**1-78**).

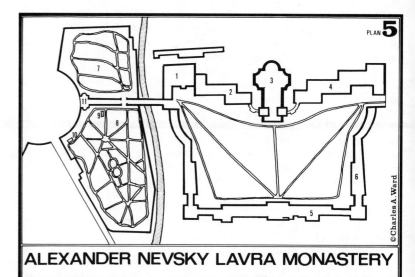

ALEXANDER NEVSKY LAVRA MONASTERY

1. Church of Alexander Nevsky (upper) and Church of Annunciation (lower)
2. Dukhovsky Corpus
3. Trinity Cathedral
4. Fedorovsky Corpus
5. Metropolitan's Palace
6. Seminary Corpus
7. 18th Century Necropolis
8. 19th Century Necropolis Cemetery
9. Dostoevsky's Grave
10. Tchaikovsky's Grave
11. Entrance Gate and Church

The long building at #2 Khalturin St., facing Mars Field, is the *barracks of the former Pavlov Regiment*, 1817-1820 by Stasov. It now houses the Len-energo Building (**1-79**).

Mars Field (**1-80**), at the end of Khalturin St., is the former military parade ground. Once a dusty, overgrown field, it was made into a park-like area by the Soviets. At the Neva end is Suvorov Square, with Kozlovsky's statue of General Suvorov as Mars, done in 1801.

The *Summer Garden* (**1-81**), Petersburg's first park, is bordered by the Neva, Fontanka, and Moyka Rivers, and the Swan Canal. It was laid out by Peter the Great and a Dutchman, Jan Roozen, in 1706-1712. The railing on the Neva side, by Velten and Yegorov, was erected 1770-1784. At the northeast corner of the park is the small two-story *Summer Palace of Peter* (**1-82**), 1710-1712, designed in the Dutch style by Tressini. Since 1934 it has housed a museum of decorative arts of the time of Peter the Great, including some of Peter's own furniture. The Summer Garden also has a *"Coffee House"* pavilion by Rossi, 1826, overlooking the Fontanka (**1-83**). In addition to many marble statues, there is a bronze of poet and fable writer Ivan Krylov, done in 1855 by P. Klodt. At the south end of the garden is a tall *red porphyry vase*, erected in the 1830's (**1-84**).

The *Engineer's Castle* is just to the south of the Summer Garden, and is the "Old Michael Palace," built 1797-1800 by Bazhenov and Brenna (**1-85**). It was constructed for Tsar Paul on the site of a wooden palace by Rastrelli which Paul had destroyed on taking the throne. The castle originally had drawbridges, moats, and so forth, since Paul was afraid of enemies who would plot against him. He was assassinated in the castle in 1801 soon after moving in. The parade ground to the south of the castle was made into a park by Rossi in the 1820's (**1-86**). In the center is a monument to Peter the Great, designed in 1719-1724 by Carlo Rastrelli (the architect's father), cast in 1746, but erected only in 1800. It was Russia's first equestrian statue. Bas-reliefs on the pediment represent battles at Poltava (1709) and Hango (1714), decisive Russian victories in the Northern War.

The castle stood vacant from 1801, for Alexander I, who was party to the plot to assassinate his father, did not want to live there. The Army Engineering Academy was established in the castle in 1819. Its most famous graduate was the writer Dostoevsky.

Voinov Street, which runs parallel to the Neva River, leads to Prince Potemkin's *Tauride Palace* (**1-87**), 1783-1789 (#47 Voinov St.), designed by Starov in severe neoclassic style. The palace served as the meeting place of the Duma, or Russian parliament, from 1906-1917. It now houses the regional school of the Leningrad Communist Party, and is also used as a conference center.

Two blocks further along the street, at Stavropolsky Lane (outside of Map 1), the *Kikin House*, 1714-1720, one of the oldest buildings in Leningrad. Though often rebuilt, its facade was restored to its original appearance in 1952-1953. It is now the House of Pioneers of the Smolny District.

THE SMOLNY. At the end of Voinov Street is the *Smolny Convent* (outside of Map 1), founded by Tsarina Elizabeth, and built by Rastrelli, 1748-1764. The cathedral, a five-cupola church with central dome 280 feet high, is one of the best examples of baroque style in the city. The interior was completed only in 1835, by V. Stasov, in neoclassic style. The "Smolny Institute," a boarding school for daughters of the nobility, established by Catherine the Great in 1764, was at first housed in the nuns cells south of the cathedral. In 1808 the Institute moved to a new building by Quarenghi, 1806-1808, adjacent to the convent. This three-story structure in neoclassical style extends 235 yards along the Neva, with wings at the ends, which form a sort of shallow courtyard. The Revolutionary government used this building in 1917, and Lenin lived there till the government moved to Moscow in 1918. His room is preserved as a museum. The building now is the Headquarters of the Regional Committee of the Communist Party. The five-column pavilions forming an entrance from the square were added in 1923-1924.

THE WESTERN SECTION OF THE CITY

The house at #86 Moyka Quay, to the west of St. Isaac's Square, was architect *Montferrand's home* (**1-88**) from the 1820's to 1850's. A little further along, at #94, is the *House of Culture* (**1-89**), a former home of the Yusupov family. The building was designed by Vallin de la Mothe in the 1760's, but was extensively remodeled and enlarged by Mikhailov in 1830. After Prince Yusupov emigrated in 1917, his collection of 1000 paintings and works of art was displayed in this building. In 1925 it was divided between the Hermitage and Moscow Museum of Fine Arts. In 1916 the monk Rasputin, one of the advisors to the royal family, was murdered in the basement of Yusupov's house.

At #103 Moyka is the *arch of the New Holland* (**1-90**), a triangular island between canals formerly used as a depot for naval stores. It was built in the 1760's by Chevakinsky, with its main architectural ornament, the Great Arch facing the Moyka, designed by Vallin de la Mothe.

The *Palace of Labor* (**1-91**) is at the back of the New Holland, at the end of Profsoyuzov Street. It was built 1853-1861 by Stakenschneider for Nicholas I's eldest son, Nicholas.

Theater Square contains the *Kirov Opera and Ballet Theater* (**1-92**), totally rebuilt in 1860 by Albert Kavos following a fire in the former theater. Across the street is the *National Conservatory* (**1-93**), 1891-1896. To the left of the Conservatory is a monument to the composer Rimsky-Korsakov, unveiled in 1952. To the right of the conservatory is a statue of Mikhail Glinka, from 1906.

St. Nikola Cathedral (**1-94**), south of Theater Square, was built in 1753-1762 by Chevakinsky, pupil of Rastrelli. This baroque style church has two stories. The dark lower level is open daily, but the magnificent upper church is generally open only on Sundays and Holy days.

The *Sovetskaya Hotel* (outside of Map **1**), #43 Lermontov Prospekt, at the Fontanka River, is one of the main new hotels in Leningrad.

Trinity Cathedral (**1**-95), near the Fontanka at Izmailovsky Prospekt, is a large five-dome church with projecting six-column porticos on each side built 1828-1835 by Stasov. Its exterior was restored after damage during World War II.

SHOPPING IN LENINGRAD

The best value and best selection of souvenirs is to be found in the foreign currency, or *"Beriozka"* shops. The main stores are at *#26 Gercen St.* (**1**-96), and in the *Sovetskaya Hotel* (Fontanka at Lermontovsky Prospekt). There are also shops in the Astoria Hotel and the *Europe (Evropeiskaya) Hotel* (**1**-97), on Brodsky St.

For window shopping and browsing in Russian stores, begin with the main department stores:

Gostiny Dvor - #35 Nevsky prospekt (**1**-54)
DLT - #21-23 Zhelyabov Street (**1**-45)
Passazh - #48 Nevsky prospekt (women's wear) (**1**-57)

Nevsky Prospekt itself is the main shopping street of Leningrad and is lined with numerous small specialty shops.

TRANSPORTATION

Most touring is done in Intourist buses. If you want to go on your own, follow the map of Leningrad. There is usually much walking involved, even if you use public transit. Below are the main buses, trams, and trolleys for sites not in the center of town. It should be noted that the "Leningrad" and "Sovetskaya" Hotels are not on convenient bus or trolley lines to anywhere. Bus 30 and Trolley 1 run from the point of Vasilievsky Island past the Hermitage along the whole length of Nevsky Prospekt to the Alexander Nevsky Monastery.

The Smolny can be reached from Nevsky Prospekt on Trolley 5 and Bus 6.

Theater Square can be reached from Nevsky Prospekt on Bus 3, 27, (via Gercen Street).

Tram 3 runs from Revolution Sq., opposite the Peter-Paul Fortress, across the Kirov Bridge, and along Sadovaya Street.

Tram 9, 20, trolleys 8, 19, 23 run from the Vyborg side along Liteiny Avenue as far as Nevsky Prospekt.

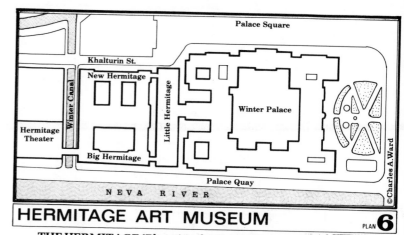

HERMITAGE ART MUSEUM — PLAN **6**

THE HERMITAGE (Plan 6) is the Soviet Union's largest museum of non-Russian art. It is strong in most areas, and has excellent collections of classical works, Flemish and Dutch schools, and French impressionists. It also has halls devoted to Russian culture and art from various republics of the Soviet Union. The famous "Scythian Gold Collection" is housed in rooms entered from Rm. 121 of the New Hermitage.

The museum is housed in four buildings: the *Winter Palace*, the *Little Hermitage*, the *Big and New Hermitage*, and the *Hermitage Theater*.

Winter Palace: 1754-1762, was designed by Rastrelli in the baroque style. Many of the rooms were redone in the neoclassic style by Quarenghi in the 1780's-1790's, and by Rossi and Montferrand in the first third of the 19th century. A fire in December, 1837, gutted the palace. It was reconstructed by Stasov and A. Bryullov. Some of the rooms were restored and others were redone in contemporary style.

Little Hermitage: 1764-1775, by Vallin de la Mothe (facade facing the river) and 1764-1765 (facade facing Palace Square, by Velten). Art was displayed in two galleries next to the "hanging gardens" (central section on the second floor level). The Pavilion Hall (Rm. 204) was built there in 1856 by Stakenschneider. It contains Italian mosaics of the 18th-19th centuries, and the "Peacock Clock" by James Cox, an 18th century Englishman.

Big Hermitage, 1771-1787, designed by Velten. **New Hermitage**, 1842-1851, by Leo von Klenze and others, built to exhibit part of the collection which was opened to the public in 1853. The entrance was from Khalturin St. under a porch roof supported by ten sculpted male figures 19 ft. tall, by Terebenev.

Hermitage Theater, 1783-1787, by Quarenghi, in Italian renaissance style. It is connected to the Museum by an archway over the Winter Canal.

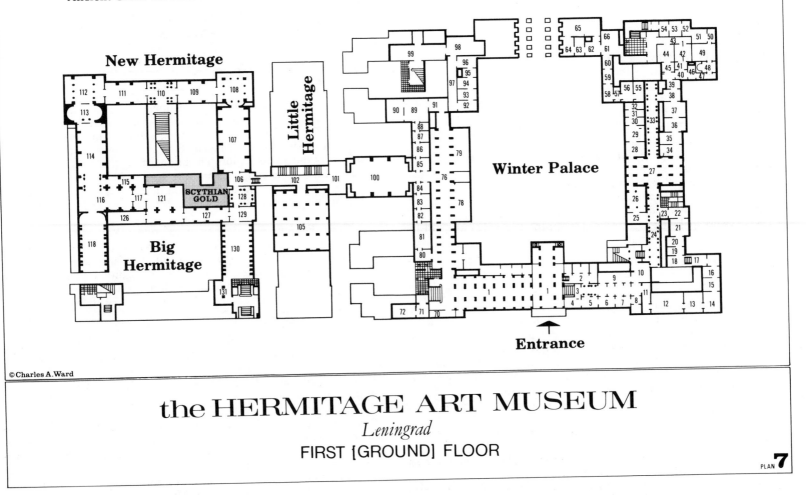

Classical World: Greece, Rome
Ancient Cities on Black Sea Coast

11-33: Prehistoric Art, Cultures
34-53: Central Asian Art
55-66: Culture of Caucasian Tribes
81-91: Egypt, 4000 BC to 700 AD
92-96: Babylon, Assyria

New Hermitage

Little Hermitage

Winter Palace

SCYTHIAN GOLD

Big Hermitage

Entrance

©Charles A.Ward

the HERMITAGE ART MUSEUM
Leningrad
FIRST [GROUND] FLOOR

PLAN **7**

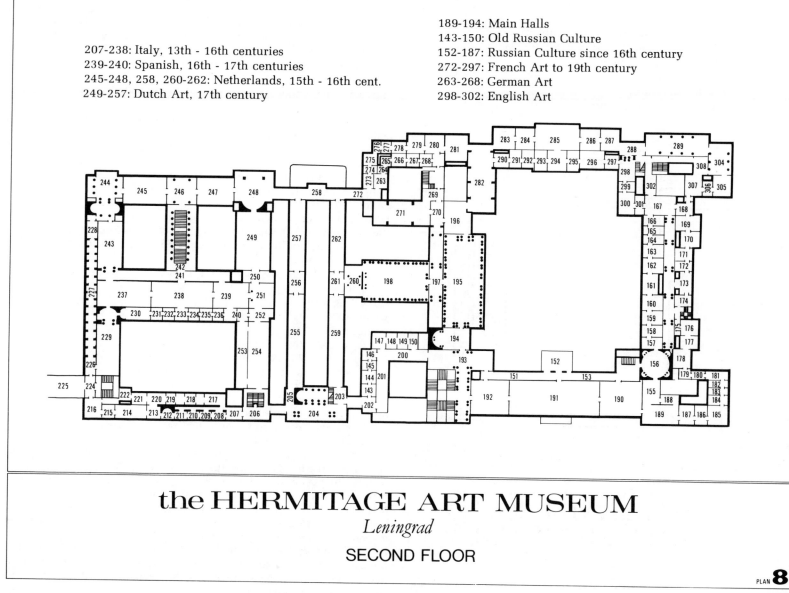

207-238: Italy, 13th - 16th centuries
239-240: Spanish, 16th - 17th centuries
245-248, 258, 260-262: Netherlands, 15th - 16th cent.
249-257: Dutch Art, 17th century

189-194: Main Halls
143-150: Old Russian Culture
152-187: Russian Culture since 16th century
272-297: French Art to 19th century
263-268: German Art
298-302: English Art

the HERMITAGE ART MUSEUM
Leningrad
SECOND FLOOR

314-333,343-350: French Art, 19th - 20th cent.
334-342: U.S. and European Art, 20th cent.
351-371: China, Mongolia
375-376: Japan
381-382: Byzantium
383-397: Near East, Central Asia, 8th - 20th cent.

the HERMITAGE
ART MUSEUM
Leningrad
THIRD FLOOR

PLAN **9**

THE HERMITAGE ART COLLECTION was begun in 1764 with the purchase of 225 pictures in Berlin. Collected by the Prussian patriot Joh. Gotzkowski, they had been intended for Frederick the Great, but he needed money after the Seven Years War, so sold them to Catherine the Great. In 1769 the gallery of Count Bruhl of Dresden was purchased. In 1772 the Crozat collection was purchased in France. In 1779 Sir Robert Walpole's collection was acquired in England, including famous Van Dyck's. From the start the collection was most broad, including engravings, sculpture, stone carving, money and medals, tapestries, jewelry, paintings.

The collection has grown steadily since its beginning. Some of the major acquisitions were:

1814 - 38 paintings and 4 statues of the Malmaison Collection, bought from ex-Empress Josephine.

1815 - collection of 67 paintings from Amsterdam banker Coesvelt.

1836 - 33 paintings from collection of Spanish minister Don Manuel Godoy.

1850 - collection of Venetian family Garbarigo.

1861 - purchase in Rome of classical art of the Marquise de Campana

1917 - nationalization of Yusupov, Morozov, Nashchokin, and other private collections.

The halls now display about 65,000 items from a collection of 2,700,000.

Plans 7, 8, and 9

Rooms with seats for resting are:

1st floor: 78, 109

2nd floor: 197, 282, 303, 337-339, 245-247, 251

3rd floor: 315-323, 325, 328, 333

The museum is generally open from 11-6, closed on Monday.

In addition to the collection, the design of some of the rooms of the Winter Palace are quite noteworthy, with elaborate parquet floors, wall-coverings, chandeliers, columns, and so forth. The second floor of the palace contained both the formal reception rooms and the living rooms of the tsar's family.

The "Jordan Staircase," to the left of the entrance, is the grand entrance to the formal rooms upstairs. It was designed by Rastrelli and restored by Stasov after the fire of 1837. At the top of the stairs are two rows of formal rooms, one to the south, one to the west.

8-192 The *Small Hall*, with four gold chandeliers, parquet floor, mid-wall frieze, and ceiling painting ("Sacrifice of Iphegenia") with an elaborate border; a neoclassic interior by Stasov.

8-191 *Grand (Ball) Hall*, 200 by 61 feet, a reworking of Quarenghi's design by Stasov, with 3/4 engaged Corinthian columns of imitation marble, eight chandeliers, and elaborate cornice and ceiling detail. The room is used for temporary exhibits.

8-190 *Concert Hall*, by Quarenghi, restored by Stasov, a smaller but more elaborate version of the Ball Room. It now exhibits Russian silverwork of 17th-20th centuries. The main exhibit is the tomb of Alexander Nevsky, covered with ornamental bas-relief in silver depicting scenes of Nevsky's life. The tomb, made in the mid-1800's by an unknown artist, contains more than 3,200 pounds of silver.

Beyond this row of formal rooms are the former living rooms of the royal family. Several of them are of note:

8-189 The *Malachite Hall*, designed in 1839 by A. Bryullov as a living room for Nicholas I's wife. The room has columns, pilasters, two fireplaces, and tables of malachite, over 5,500 pounds used in all the decor. The doors, ceiling molding, and capitals of the columns are in gold leaf, and harmonize with the elaborate floor parquet.

8-155 *Large Dining Room*, by Bryullov, a formal room with Doric columns of yellow imitation marble.

8-156 The *Rotunda Room*, by Montferrand, redone by Bryullov in 1839, a rotunda 50 feet in diameter supported by fluted Corinthian columns of white imitation marble. The floor and inside of the dome are of elaborate design.

The remaining rooms of the north-west corner lost their neoclassic decor at the end of the 19th century.

8-193 *Field Marshal's Room*, by Montferrand, restored by Stasov, in white imitation marble with paired Ionic pilasters along the walls.

8-194 *Peter's Room*, by Montferrand, restored and slightly altered by Stasov; decorative ceiling vault with double-headed eagle pattern, walls divided into panels by Corinthian pilasters with complex capitals; wall panels of red Lyons velvet with double-headed eagles embroidered in silver thread (now tarnished). A niche at the end of the room contains a throne carved in London and a picture of Peter I with Minerva, by Amigoni, an 18th-century Italian painter, in an elaborate "altar" frame with green jasper columns and open baroque pediment.

8-195 *"Coat of Arms" Hall*, 162 by 65 feet, by Stasov. The coats of arms of the Russian provinces are on the gilt chandeliers. The room has white walls accented by paired gilt Corinthian columns. The room was used for balls and receptions.

8-196 *New Hall*, by Stasov. It was designed as a guards room, hence the military frieze at the top of the wall and the reliefs in the wall panels formed by the pilasters of the walls.

8-271 former *Palace Chapel*, by Rastrelli, restored by Stasov.

8-197 *Military Portrait Gallery*, by Rossi, restored with some changes by Stasov. The Walls are covered by portraits of 300 generals who took part in the Napoleonic Wars. They were painted by George Dawe (1781-1829), an English painter who worked in the palace, 1819-1829, with two Russian assistants. The portraits were saved from burning during the fire of 1837.

8-198 *Georgievsky Hall* (Large Throne Room), 154 by 65 feet, by Quarenghi, redone by Stasov, in Carrara marble and gilt bronze. The floor parquet is made up of 16 varieties of wood and repeats the ceiling motif. A mosaic of semi-precious stones forming a map of the Soviet Union stands where the throne once was. The map consists of 45,000 pieces of stone, 29 square yards in area, with color-coded relief: green = valleys; white = mountain tops; blue = seas; brown = contours of mountain ranges. A diamond hammer and sickle on a ruby star marks Moscow.

8-260 *Apollo Hall*, by Quarenghi, restored by Efimov and Stasov, with exquisite parquet.

THE HERMITAGE COLLECTION

The description of the collection which follows is listed by subject area and hall. Use this description in conjunction with the floor plans (7, 8 and 9). (Halls are occasionally rearranged.)

Rooms 143-150: (Plan 8) OLD RUSSIAN CULTURE, 6-15th Cent.

143	excavation finds, 8th-10th centuries.
144	Old Russian village life.
145	City culture of Old Ladoga; 10th-12th century trade
146	Old Russian military armaments
147-149	Old Russian architecture, art, and writing, especially mosaics from Mikhailovsko-Zlatoverkhy Monastery in Kiev (early 12th century). Carved stone church ornaments; filigree and gold enameled jewelry. The Tmutorokhan stone; birch bark manuscripts from 12th century.
150	Novgorod and Pskov
151	MOSCOW CULTURE, 15th-17th centuries. Icons of Nikolay Zaraysky and Dmitry Voin (15th Century), Last Judgment (16th Century), John the Baptist, 1689; map of Siberia, 1698.

Rooms 152-161: (Plan 8) Russian Culture, first third, 19th Cent.

155	Peter the Great's lathes
156	Ivory chandelier (Peter worked on some of the details). Some of Peter's army uniforms.
157	Artifacts made in early Petersburg.
158	painting, sculpture, graphics; Rastrelli's bust of Peter (1723). Engravings of the city, 1716.
159	Furniture of first third of 18th century.

160   "Wax persona", Peter on throne, life-size, done by Rastrelli the elder; wax mask of Peter's face, hand, and foot; body of wood, wig of Peter's own hair; costume Peter wore at the coronation of his wife, Catherine I, in 1724.

Rooms 162-174: (Plan 8) Russian Culture, second half of 19th Cent.

163   Lomonosov room, includes his portrait of Peter.
165 & 170   Portraits
164 & 172   Water colors, engravings, sketches of 18th century Russian architecture (Rastrelli, Bazhenov, Kazakov, Starov).
169   "Egg-shaped clock" size of goose egg, with 400 parts; three mechanisms, for time, music, and moving gold figures. Built by Kulibin (1735-1818) over three years. The mechanisms still work, and have never been repaired.
167, 173, 174   Artifacts and folk art: silver, glass, metal, wood and bone carvings, porcelain.

Rooms 175-187: (Plan 8) Russian Culture, 1800-1860

175-177   General Social background of the period: costumes, classes, city views, portraits, Napoleonic invasion.
177   Decembrist uprising, 1825.
178   Period room, English Gothic walnut library (1894)
179-182   Development of progressive thought: literature, theater, science, technology, 1800-1860's. Bust of Pushkin by Vitali (1841), portraits of Turgenev, Gogol, others.
184   Architecture: sketches, engravings, city views, lithographs, etc. Architecture of Russian cities, 19th century.
185   Applied arts, especially glass and crystal (Rossi's designs). Faceted crystal with gilt bronze chandeliers, etc. Also chinaware, bone and horn carvings, etc.
186   Paintings and miniatures. Exhibition of interior of Winter Palace.
187   End of feudal system: Crimean War, end of serfdom. Also, a case with rare examples of Russian jewelry, 17-19th centuries.

Russian monumental carved stone urns

Malachite urns, halls 189, 192, 238, 241. **(Plan 8)**
Lapis Lazuli urns, hall 237, by Nalimov. **(Plan 8)**
Grey-violet porphyry, hall 249, by Strizhkov. **(Plan 8)**
The Kolyvanskaya vase (19 tons): 8 ft. high, bowl 16 ft. in diameter, of monolithic Jasper, carved 1829-1841: in hall 128. **(Plan 7)**

Rooms 11-33: (Plan 7) Prehistoric Cultures in Soviet Territory

These exhibits are from paleolithic and mesolithic to the time of the Scythians (7th to 3rd century BC). For the SCYTHIANS, see especially room 16, and 22-32 (excavations from the Altai mounds, preserved by the permafrost.)

Rooms 34-53: (Plan 7) Central Asian Art: Tadzhiks, Uzbeks, Kazaks, Kirgiz, Turkmen

38-40   Central Asia, 800-1000 AD; ceramics, bronze, silver, glass; architectural motifs.
48-49   Samarkand of Tamerlane; bronze kettle 5½ ft. tall, 8 ft. in diameter, two tons; used for holding water, a gift of Tamerlane to a mosque. Door of Gur Emir, the tomb of Tamerland in Samarkand.

Rooms 55-66: (Plan 7) Culture of Caucasian tribes, 1100 BC to 1900 AD

Rooms 81-91: (Plan 7) Culture of Ancient Egypt

82   Middle Kingdom (2100-1788 BC), black granite statue of Amenemhet II. Papyrus from 19th century BC.
83, 84   New Kingdom (1500-1050 BC)
85   Later period (1050-332 BC)
86, 87   Burial cults, sarcophagi, mummies
88, 91   Greco-Roman Egypt to Second century AD. Coptic Egypt, especially their linen, wool, and silk weavings, 4th-6th century AD.

Rooms 92-96: (Plan 7) Babylon, Assyria

Rooms 381, 381a, 382: (Plan 9) Byzantium, 5th-15th Century

Rooms 383-387, 391, 394: (Plan 9) Near and Mid-East, 3rd-19th Cent.

384   Persian ceramics, 12th-15th century
391-394   velvet and silk; oriental carpets, copper and bronze pieces; swords, Persian miniatures, etc.
388   Syria and Iraq, 8th-15th century
389-390   Islamic Egypt, 7th-15th century
395-397   Ottoman Turkey, 15th-18th century
368-371   India, 17th-20th century
351-371   CHINA
352   Exhibit from Hari-Hoto, dead city found under sands of Gobi desert.

CLASSICAL WORLD

Rooms 108, 109, 111-114, 121: (Plan 7) Greece 900-200 BC

Rooms 100, 115-117, 119, 120: Ancient cities of the northern Black Sea coast

7th century BC to Third Century AD. Vases, vessels from burial mounds, statuettes, gold masks. Superb collection of small Greek works: necklaces, rings, gold jewelry, terracotta, masks, toys.

102, 106, 107, 127-131: (Plan 7) Ancient Italy and Rome, 7th Century BC to 6th Century AD

ART OF WESTERN EUROPE
(Plan 8)

Rooms 207-222, 226-238, 241: (Plan 8) ITALY, 13th-18th Cent.

SPANISH SCHOOL (Plan 8)

239, 240   Morales, "Mater Dolorosa," "Madonna and child". El Greco, "Apostles Peter and Paul" (1614). Velasquez, "Luncheon" (1617), "Portrait of Olivares" (1638). Zurbaran, "St. Lawrence," "Virgin as a child." Murillo, "Blessing of Jacob by Isaac," "Rest on Flight to Europe," "Assumption of the Virgin." Goya, "Portrait of Actress Antonia Sarate" (ca. 1807).

Rooms 248, 258, 260-262: (Plan 8) NETHERLANDS, 15th-16th Cent.

261   Robert Campin, "Madonna and Child." Van der Weyden, "St. Luke painting The Virgin." Van der Goes, "Christ Weeping," "Adoration of the Magi."

260   Jan Provost, "Triumph of the Virgin."

262, 258   16th century, many artists including Pieter Breughel.

Rooms 245-247: (Plan 8) FLANDERS

247   Rubens: "Statue of Ceres," "Union of Earth and Water," "Descent From the Cross," "Jesus in house of Simon the Pharasee," "Lion Hunt," "Coronation of Marie Medici," "Perseus and Andromeda," and many others.

246   Anthony van Dyck, 25 paintings; portraits of early and Eng. period.

245   Jordaens, Snyders, Brouwer, Teniers (30).

Rooms 249-257: (Plan 8) DUTCH ART, 17th Century

249   Main Dutch Hall. Jan van Goyen, Salomon van Ruysdael. Jacob van Ruysdael "Swamp," "Peasant House," "Norwegian Waterfall," "Mountain Scene," and others. Frans Hals, "Portrait of a Young Man with Glove," "Portrait of a Man." Adrian Ostaade, six paintings. Jan Steen, nine works. Pieter de Hooch, "Mistress and Maid," Ger. Terborcht, three paintings.

251   van der Helst portraits.

254   REMBRANDT, 26 paintings, including "Adoration of Magi," "Portrait of young man with Lace Collar," "Portrait of an Old Soldier," "Flora," "Descent from the Cross," "Sacrifice of Abraham," "Danae," "Portrait of a Scholar," "Holy Family," "Portrait of Doomer," "Portrait of an Old Man in red," "Portrait of Old Man," "Return of Prodigal Son."

253   Rembrandt's students.

255-257   Galleries that border the "Hanging Gardens." Dutch art of 17th and early 18th century.

Rooms 263-268: (Plan 8) GERMAN ART

263   A. Holbein, "Portrait of a Young Man."

264   Durer and Hans Holbein the Younger, engravings. Lucas Cranach (5)

268   Mengs, Tischbein, et al.

Rooms 269-271: (Plan 8) European Porcelain, 18th-20th century

269   Dessert service given to Catherine II by Frederick the Great

Rooms 298-302: (Plan 8) ENGLISH ART, 17th-19th Cent.

298   17th, early 18th century. Robert Walker, Peter Lely, English silver.

299   18 century: Joshua Reynolds, "Young Heracles strangling the Snake," "Cupid untying Venus's Belt." George Romney, "Portrait of Mrs. Greer."

300   Gainsborough, "Portrait of Duchess of Beaufort." Henry Raeburn, George Morland. Wedgwood "Green Frog" china service, 1774, 952 pieces, prepared for Catherine II.

301   Early 19th century. Thomas Lawrence, George Dawe, Richard Bonington.

302   Later 19th century. "Adoration of Magi" by Ed. Burne-Jones.

Rooms 272-297: (Plan 8) FRANCE, 15th-18th Cent.

273   Limoge enamels

274   16th century Fontainebleau School, Clouet

275   Court art of Louis XVIII

276   Jacques Callot, Le Nain brothers

279   Poussin, several paintings

280   Claude Lorraine, "Morning," "Noon," "Evening," "Night," and others.

281   Charles LeBrun, and others.

282   17th and 18th century silverware.

290-297   French Applied Arts: furniture, tapestries, china, bronze, etc.

283	Portraiture, 1650-1700
284	Watteau
285-286	Rococo: Boucher (8), Falconet
287	Chardin. Houdon's statue of Voltaire
288	Fragonard, Vernet, and others

Rooms 314-333, 343-350: (Plan 9) FRENCH ART, 19th-20th Cent.

314	Revolutionary art and neoclassicism of First Empire
332	David, Antoine Gros, Gerard
331	Delacroix, "Lion Hunt in Morocco," "Moroccan saddling a Horse," Ingres, "Portrait of N.D. Guryev."
321, 322, 325, 329	T. Rousseau, George Duprez, Corot, Millet, Courbet
320	Renois, "Portrait of a Girl with a Fan," and others. Degas, Rodin, Maillot
319	Claude Monet
318	Pisarro, Cezanne (11), Degas
317	Van Gogh: "Arena in Arles," "Women of Arles," "Bush," "Huts." Henri Rousseau, "Tropical Forests," "Jardin de Luxembourg."
315	Gauguin, 15 works of Tahitian period
316	Cezanne
342	Daumier's graphics
343-345	Henri Matisse, 35 paintings done between 1900-1913, "Red Room," "Dance," "Family Portrait," etc.
346-347	Picasso, 36 works, 1900-1912, including: blue period, "Absinthe Lover," "Portrait of Soler," "Rendezvous." Rose period, "Boy with a Dog." Cubist period, "Woman with a Fan," "Three Women," "Flute and Violin"
348-349	Derain, Vuillard, Bonnard, et.al.
350	Survage, Fugeron, Leger

Rooms 334-342 **(Plan 9)** display art of the 19th and 20th centuries from Germany, Belgium, Finland, Spain, Italy (Renato Guttuzo), United States of America (Rockwell Kent, Morris Pass, Frank Kirk, Alfred Maurer, James Morris): Hungary, Poland, Rumania, Czechoslovakia.

398-400	Examples of medals and orders not found in other displays.
303	West European woven wall coverings, 15th-18th centuries.
304	West European stone carving, 12th-19th centuries.

Smolny Convent

SUMMER PALACES
ALONG THE
GULF OF FINLAND

PETRODVORETS
PUSHKIN
PAVLOVSK

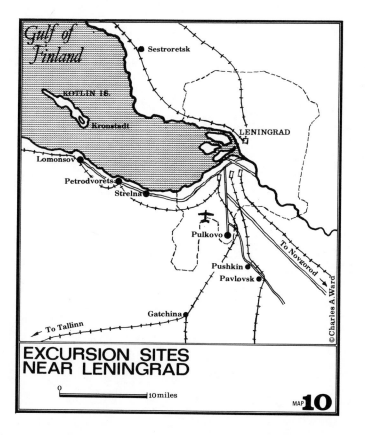

Gulf of Finland

Sestroretsk

KOTLIN IS.

Kronstadt

LENINGRAD

Lomonsov

Petrodvorets

Strelna

Pulkovo

To Novgorod

Pushkin

Pavlovsk

Gatchina

To Tallinn

©Charles A. Ward

EXCURSION SITES
NEAR LENINGRAD

0   10 miles

MAP **10**

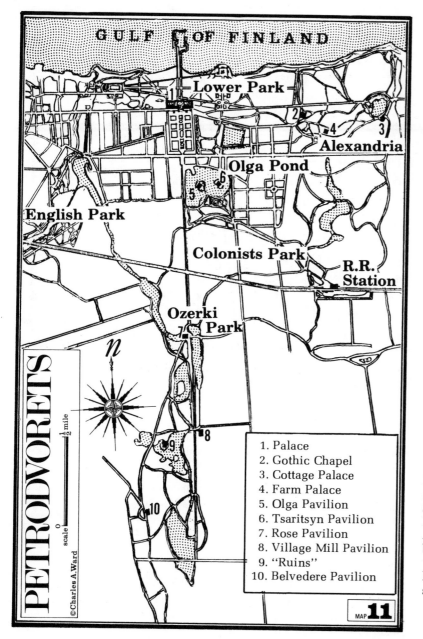

PETRODVORETS

GULF OF FINLAND

Lower Park

Alexandria

Olga Pond

English Park

Colonists Park

R.R. Station

Ozerki Park

N

½ mile

scale 0

©Charles A.Ward

1. Palace
2. Gothic Chapel
3. Cottage Palace
4. Farm Palace
5. Olga Pavilion
6. Tsaritsyn Pavilion
7. Rose Pavilion
8. Village Mill Pavilion
9. "Ruins"
10. Belvedere Pavilion

MAP **11**

SUMMER PALACES ALONG THE GULF OF FINLAND

(Map 10)

In 1703 Peter established a fortress and naval base at *Kronstadt* on *Kotlin Island* in the Gulf twenty miles west of Leningrad. During his trips back and forth to Kronstadt he would stop at a couple of places along the coast, at *Strelna*, twelve miles from the city, and Petergof (now *Petrodvorets*), 19 miles from the city. After defeating the Swedes at Poltava in 1709, Peter definitely secured the shore of the Gulf for Russia and was able to proceed in making Petersburg the new Russian capital. He planned a palace complex at Petergof to rival Versailles in splendor. At the same time his associate Menshikov began a palace at Oranienbaum (now *Lomonosov*) seven miles further down the coast. By the end of the century and during the 19th century the nobles of Petersburg built villas and palaces along the road between Petersburg and Petergof.

The coastal road leaves Leningrad from the west, along Gaz and Stachek Prospekts, passing the Narva Triumphal Arch (1814 by Quarenghi, remodeled in 1834 by Stasov), then past various former dachas of the nobility. Ten miles from Leningrad, on the right, are the yellow stucco buildings of the former Sergievsky Monastery, from 1743, now a police training academy. A mile or two further on the right is the shining baroque exterior of the Strelna Palace. Begun by Peter in 1716, then given to his daughter Elizabeth, the Palace was remodeled and expanded by various architects over the years. Its elaborate 18th-century exterior was restored after World War Two.

A mile or two beyond the palace are the grounds of the former Orlov estate, on which a gatekeeper's house, artificial "ruins" of the 19th century, and a decorative well (1840's by architect Charlemagne) have survived. Soon on the right is a green turreted building formerly belonging to Count Lvov. Several royal palaces are on the outskirts of Petrodvorets, including the Palace of Grand Duke Mark, which is scheduled for restoration, and Znamenka, an estate built by Prince Shuvalov in the 18th century, but taken over by the crown as a palace for Nicholas, eldest son of Nicholas I. The road then passes through the Alexandria Park of the Petrodvorets Estate, and past some neo-Gothic buildings, the most elaborate of which are the nine-tower Stables, 1847-1852 by N. Benois. Nearby are several neoGothic houses by Charlemagne, now a Rest Home, and the Gothic style Post Office on the main street, by Benois. (See Map **12**).

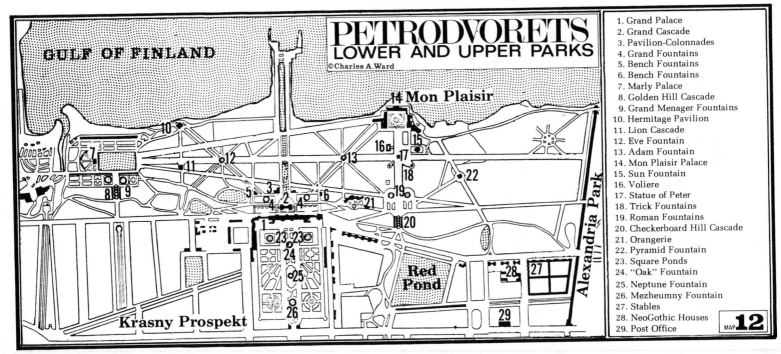

PETRODVORETS
LOWER AND UPPER PARKS
©Charles A. Ward

1. Grand Palace
2. Grand Cascade
3. Pavilion-Colonnades
4. Grand Fountains
5. Bench Fountains
6. Bench Fountains
7. Marly Palace
8. Golden Hill Cascade
9. Grand Menager Fountains
10. Hermitage Pavilion
11. Lion Cascade
12. Eve Fountain
13. Adam Fountain
14. Mon Plaisir Palace
15. Sun Fountain
16. Voliere
17. Statue of Peter
18. Trick Fountains
19. Roman Fountains
20. Checkerboard Hill Cascade
21. Orangerie
22. Pyramid Fountain
23. Square Ponds
24. "Oak" Fountain
25. Neptune Fountain
26. Mezheumny Fountain
27. Stables
28. NeoGothic Houses
29. Post Office

MAP **12**

GULF OF FINLAND
Mon Plaisir
Red Pond
Alexandria Park
Krasny Prospekt

PETRODVORETS
(Map 11)

Petrodvorets, the summer palace complex of Peter the Great, is located 19 miles west of Leningrad on the shore of the Gulf of Finland. Petrodvorets (called Petergof until 1944) was the first and most extensive of the summer palace complexes outside Leningrad, and should be seen in the summer when the fountains are working. It can be reached by road, by hydrofoil boat from the landing in front of the Hermitage, and by railroad from the Baltic Station. (The neoGothic Petrodvorets Train station, 1855, is by Benois).

The **LOWER PARK (Map 12)** of the estate is laid out on a natural terrace ⅓ mile wide, bounded on the north by the gulf and on the south by a 40-foot embankment as the land abruptly rises to a second natural terrace. The *Grand Palace* (**12**-1) was constructed at the edge of this second terrace and has a commanding view of the Lower Park and of the gulf beyond. Construction of the complex began in 1714, and from the beginning included numerous fountains and three cascades which descend the face of the terrace. The Lower Park also includes the pavilion-palaces *Marly* (**12**-7), *Hermitage* (**12**-10), and *Mon Plaisir*

(**12**-14). The fountains, which began operating in the 1720's, are naturally gravity fed from the Ropshinsky heights, an elevation 22 miles south and 300 feet above sea level. The fountains were engineered by Zemtsov and Michetti. The estate was almost totally occupied during the Second World War and the buildings and fountains were destroyed. While restoration continues, all the fountains now work and all exteriors have been restored. The description which follows is keyed to the numbers on the plans.

12-1. **GRAND PALACE (Plan 13)** built 1714-1721 by Braunstein and LeBlond. From 1746-1754 Elizabeth had Rastrelli lengthen the palace and add a third floor. The facade, including the two one-story wings and end pavilions (the Chapel and "Coat of Arms" pavilion) is almost 300 yards long. Rastrelli left the facade relatively plain, so as not to detract from the fountains below. In the 1780's Catherine the Great had Velten redesign some of the rooms of the palace. In the 1840's Stakenschneider remodeled a wing for Olga, daughter of Nicholas I (rooms c-f, and the east wing). The interior of the Palace is slowly being restored; some of the rooms are in Rastrelli's flamboyant baroque, others in later reworkings by Velten.

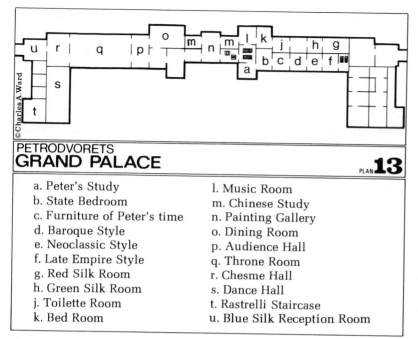

a. Peter's Study	l. Music Room
b. State Bedroom	m. Chinese Study
c. Furniture of Peter's time	n. Painting Gallery
d. Baroque Style	o. Dining Room
e. Neoclassic Style	p. Audience Hall
f. Late Empire Style	q. Throne Room
g. Red Silk Room	r. Chesme Hall
h. Green Silk Room	s. Dance Hall
j. Toilette Room	t. Rastrelli Staircase
k. Bed Room	u. Blue Silk Reception Room

13-a. *Oak Study*, in the style of Peter the Great (restored 1966), features intricate carved oak wall panels by French carver N. Pineau.

13-b. *Crown Bedroom*, designed by Velten, has Chinese silk wall coverings and a ceiling painting, "Venus and Adonis."

13-c. not restored; exhibits *furnishings of Peter's time* (early 1700's).

13-d. not restored, exhibits *furnishings of Elizabeth's time* (1740-1760), with inlaid furniture and moldings designed by Rastrelli.

13-e. not restored, *furnishings of Catherine's time* (1760-1796), works by Velten.

13-f. not restored; *furnishings of late Empire style* (1830's-1840's), works by Stakenschneider.

13-g. *Red Silk Drawing Room*

13-h. *Green Silk Drawing Room*

13-j. *Toilette Room*, with early 19th-century silk work and furniture.

13-k. *Turkish Divan Bedroom*, by Velten, with an oak and birch parquet of Rastrelli's design.

13-l. *Music Room*, walls with floral silk pattern.

13-m. *Chinese Study*, by Vallin de la Mothe, with a fancy parquet floor, and ceiling painting and wall paintings in Chinese style.

13-n. *Picture Gallery*, a two-story room in the center of the palace. The walls are completely covered by 368 canvases by P. Rotari. The ceiling painting is a reproduction of Tarsia's original of 1726, and the intricate door moldings are by Rastrelli.

13-o. *White Dining Hall*, 1770's by Velten; dinner service by Wedgwood.

13-p. *Audience Hall*, by Rastrelli, still under restoration in 1976.

13-q. *Throne Hall*, by Velten, a light airy room with windows on both sides, mirrors between the windows, and twelve crystal chandeliers.

13-r. *Chesme Hall*, by Velten. The ceiling painting has been restored as well as the large canvases of the battle of Chesme.

13-s. *Dance Hall*, or Mirror Hall, by Rastrelli, to be restored.

13-t. *Rastrelli's Grand Staircase*, to be restored.

The parks at Petrodvorets were laid out in relation to the Grand Palace. The Lower Park is in the formal style with three longitudinal paths emanating from the small Marly Palace. There are likewise three paths from the grand cascade, and three cascades along the edge of the terrace.

12-2. The *Grand Cascade*, 1714-1721, is the central focus of the Lower Park and the chief delight of the ensemble when the fountains are turned on. The whole complex is 130 feet wide, with two seven-step cascades on either side of a central grotto with a five-arch entrance. The water from a fountain in front of the grotto descends several steps and merges with water from the side cascades in a large lower basin. There is an island in the basin with a fountain of Samson forcing open the maw of a lion, out of which spurts a jet of water rising 65 feet. (The fountain is symbolic of Russia's defeat of Sweden; the battle of Poltava was on St. Samson's Day, and there is a lion on the Swedish coat of arms.) The cascades are lined with gilt statues of mythological figures. There are 36 large gilt statues around the cascade and innumerable jets of water spraying in various directions. The water from the basin flows to the Gulf of Finland through a canal lined by 22 fountains.

12-3. *Pavilion-Colonnades*, 1803 by Voronikhin, are on either side of the beginning of the canal beneath the cascade. The low domes at the canal end are covered by flowing water. The Colonnades were redone in marble by Stakenschneider in 1853-1854 and have 52 grey granite Doric columns, as well as ornamental lions at the ends. Behind the western colonnade is the "Favorita" fountain, with a mechanical dog chasing mechanical ducks.

12-4. The *Grand Fountains*, single jets rising from marble vases in the center of wide basins, are on either side of the grand cascade. The vases were designed by Stakenschneider in 1854 and are carved of Carrara marble left over from the decoration of St. Isaac's Cathedral in Leningrad. The five little four-step cascades on the edge of the terrace opposite were also redone in Carrara marble at this time.

12-5 At the beginning of the diagonal path leading from the Grand Fountains to the Hermitage is a *curved bench of Carrara marble*, 1854 by Stakenschneider, and behind it a *statue-fountain* of a nymph (statue a copy of a Greek original in the Hermitage collection).

12-6. Another *bench and statue-fountain of Dianida*, by Vitali, is at the beginning of the path leading to Mon Plaisir.

12-7. The *Marly Palace*, the focus of the western section of the Lower Park, is placed among artificial ponds originally used for breeding fish. The palace was designed by Braunstein and built 1719-1724. It was entirely reconstructed in 1898-1899 because of decrepitude, and was restored on the outside in 1954 after being blown up by the Nazis.

12-8. The *Golden Hill Cascade*, or Marly Cascade, 1721-1724 by Michetti and Zemtsov, is a 20-step cascade with water entering through three gilt lion masks below statues of Triton, Neptune, and Bacchus. In 1870 ten of the statues around the cascade were replaced with Carrara marble copies of ancient originals, carved in Italy. The gilt bronze decor of the faces of the steps of the cascade, which gave it its name, disappeared during the war.

12-9. The *Grand Menager Fountains*, 1721-1724, at the base of the cascade, each have one large jet 12″ in diameter rising to an impressive height. Beyond them are four small fountains in a row, with sculpted tritons as their bases.

12-10. The *Hermitage Pavilion*, 1721-1723 by Braunstein, built on an artificial island at the edge of the sea, is a small two-story building with large windows and Corinthian pilasters. On the second floor are 120 paintings of Flemish, Dutch, French, Italian, and German schools, hung again after the palace was rebuilt in 1952.

12-11. The *Lion Cascade*, 1857 by Stakenschneider, was a rectangular grey marble colonnade with a sculpture group in the center. It was largely destroyed during the war and has not been restored.

12-12. The *Eve Fountain*, 1726, is a statue by Bonazza surrounded by 16 jets of water.

12-13. The *Adam Fountain*, 1722 by Bonazza, in the eastern part of the park, is symmetrical to Eve in the western part. The two statues are copies of similar ones in the Doge's palace in Venice and symbolize Peter and his wife, the "first people" of the new Russian empire.

12-14. MON PLAISIR PALACE (Plan 14), 1714-1721, is the focus of the eastern part of the Lower Park, and was Peter's favorite palace. It is on a terrace at the edge of the sea and its large windows give a view of passing ships and, on a clear day, of Kronstadt and Leningrad. The central corpus has seven rooms flanked by long one-story galleries. The central *Grand Hall* (**14**-a) has an elaborate ceiling depicting Apollo surrounded by other figures, floral designs, and arabesques. At the corners are paired figures representing the seasons of the year. The palace is basically in oak paneling with checkerboard marble floors. In the central hall Peter installed 200 Dutch and Flemish paintings in 1722, Russia's first art gallery. The palace was preserved as a monument to Peter and remained intact until gutted in 1943.

The *Chinese Room* (**14**-g) restored by Palekh artists, has 94 lacquered panels in oriental style, and some porcelain pieces as well. The panel between the windows is the only original one to survive. The *kitchen and pantry* (**14**-e-f) are finished in blue Delft tiles. The *bedroom* (**14**-c) has an elaborate carved stucco fireplace designed by Michetti. The ceilings of the *Secretariat* (**14**-d), bedroom, and *study* (**14**-b) are painted in the "medallion" style. Later in the 18th century, wings were built at right angles to the Palace, the "Bath Wing" to the east, a series of six or seven rooms for various purposes. In 1747-1748 Rastrelli built the "Catherine Corpus" on the west. The exterior of these wings has been restored.

The wings surround a Dutch Garden, which contains the Crown Fountain, a 24-jet fountain in the center of the garden, and statue-fountains in the four quadrants (bronzes by Martos, 1817). Beyond the east wing is the "Chinese Garden" and the "Shell Fountain."

12-15. The *Sun Fountain*, 1770's, in the Menagerie Pond, is a rotating vertical column with two bronze discs sending out "rays" of water. The column, on a stone base with sixteen gold dolphins, was reconstructed in 1957.

12-16. A *Voliere* (aviary) is to the west of the Sun Fountain. Built in 1721 by Michetti, it was restored in 1959.

12-17. The *Statue of Peter*, 1883 by Antokolsky, is a new statue cast from the original mold to replace the original which disappeared in 1943.

12-18. *Chinese Umbrella, Little Oak Tree Fountains, etc. Trick fountains*.

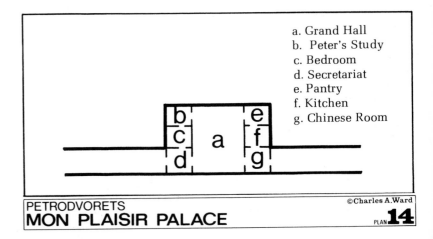

a. Grand Hall
b. Peter's Study
c. Bedroom
d. Secretariat
e. Pantry
f. Kitchen
g. Chinese Room

PETRODVORETS
MON PLAISIR PALACE

©Charles A. Ward

PLAN **14**

12-19. The *Roman Fountains*, 1800, were built according to a design by Rastrelli.

12-20. The *Checkerboard Hill Cascade*, or Dragon Cascade, 1739 by Zemtsov, is in the form of four sloping checkerboard surfaces with water coming from the mouths of three dragons at the top. There are grottos at the top and bottom, ten statues of mythological figures along the sides of the cascade, and an eagle above the top grotto, added in 1855. Totally destroyed in the war, the cascade was reconstructed in 1954.

12-21. The *Orangerie*, 1722, has a two-story central area flanked by curving wings. In front is a fountain representing a triton with tortoises, recreated in 1956 from original sketches of 1726.

12-22. *Pyramid Fountain*, 1721-1724 by Michetti and Zemtsov. The "pyramid" of water comes from 505 pipes which send the water as high as 30 feet. The balustrade around the fountain was added in 1771.

The **UPPER PARK** was begun in 1715, but attained its present form in 1754 when Rastrelli rebuilt it and added the fence and the gates at the south end.

12-23. The *Square Ponds* are nearest the palace and contain anonymous 18th-century marble statues representing Spring and Summer.

12-24. The *"Oak" Fountain* contained an artificial oak tree until 1929 when it was replaced by a marble cupid and eight dolphins.

12-25. The *Neptune Fountain*, in the center of the Park, has a sculpture group of Neptune with his trident surrounded by 32 figures. The sculpture was done in Nuremberg by Ritter and Schweiger in the 1650's and was purchased by Tsar Paul in 1797.

A statue of Apollo Belvedere, a bronze copy of 1798, stands facing the fountain on the south.

12-26. The *Mezheumny Fountain*, from the 1730's, contains a dragon and four dolphins as decoration.

OTHER PARKS

In the 19th century the areas to the east and south of the original ensemble were laid out for Nicholas I and his family. The **ALEXANDRIA PARK (Map 11)** (named for Nicholas' wife Alexandra) was laid out in 1826-1829 by Menelaws, an English architect, and was given a few structures in neoGothic style. Among them are the *Cottage Palace* (**11**-3), 1826-1829 by Menelaws, an eclectic mixture of neoGothic and rural English, which was Nicholas I's residence at Petrodvorets. The *Gothic Chapel* (**11**-2), or "Church of Alexander Nevsky," 1831-1833 by Schinkel and Menelaws, is a tall turreted church with neoGothic stucco molding and statues on the exterior. The *Farm (Fermersky) Palace* (**11**-4) 1829-1831 by Menelaws, was rebuilt in mid-century by Stakenschneider, but was severely damaged during the war.

The **COLONISTS PARK (Map 11)** was laid out along the Samson Canal south of the Upper Park in 1837 when the *Olga Pond* (named for Nicholas's daughter, Olga) was dug. Stakenschneider built pavilions on the islands in the pond. The *Tsaritsyn Pavilion* (**11**-6), 1842-1844, on the eastern island, follows the lines of a Pompeian Villa, but each facade has a different architectural resolution. The *Olga Pavilion* (**11**-5), 1847, on the western island, is a square tower at the water's edge.

The LUGOVOY, or **OZERKI PARK**, is further south, beyond the railroad line. Stakenschneider built several more pavilions in this 1500-acre area. The *Rose Pavilion* (**11**-7), 1845-1848, is a three-story "observation" tower surrounded by one-story wings somewhat in the Greek manner, and a portico with 16 grey marble figures by Terebenev. The *Belvedere Pavilion* (**11**-10) 1852-1857, is in the form of a Greek Temple with an Ionic colonnade on the second floor — 28 grey granite columns with white marble capitals. The entrance has large granite caryatids by Terebenev and an imposing staircase. The pavilion is elevated and on a clear day Leningrad is plainly visible. In the summer the pavilion is used as a Pioneer Youth Camp. Stakenschneider also built a *Village Mill Pavilion* (**11**-8) and some *"Ruins"* (**11**-9) on an island in the park.

The **ENGLISH PARK** occupies the western part of the estate and was created for Catherine the Great by Quarenghi in the 1780's. The Grand Palace which Quarenghi built there was the center of the park. The front lines in the Second World War went right through the English park, and the palace was totally destroyed, having suffered some 9,000 direct artillery hits.

LOMONOSOV (Map 10)

The estate at Lomonosov (Oranienbaum until 1944) was begun by A.D. Menshikov, Peter's closest associate, on the coast of the gulf seven miles west of Petrodvorets. The estate reverted to the crown and was used by Catherine the Great. This was the only summer palace complex not occupied and destroyed during World War Two. Menshikov's original palace, 1710-1725 by Schaedel and Fontana, was redone by Rastrelli in mid-century. It was used as a hospital and naval cadet school before reverting to the royal family in the 19th century, and its original interiors have not survived.

The main buildings at the estate are by Rinaldi. His first work was a palace for Peter III, 1758-1762, an eight-room, two story pavilion. His "Chinese Palace," 1762-1768 (named for some rooms with Chinese-style decor), was built for Catherine and is a modest (17-room) palace with exquisite interiors. Rinaldi's other main structure is the "Sledding Hill" Pavilion, done in the 1760's.

Lomonosov is just beyond the 25-mile travel limitation for foreigners with visas for Leningrad, and Intourist does not as a rule take visitors to the estate.

PALACES SOUTH OF LENINGRAD

Moscow Prospekt is the main road going south from Leningrad. It leads past the Moscow Triumphal Gates, 1835 by Stasov, and past the Victory Park to the city limits, now marked by a War Memorial consisting of an obelisk and sculpture groups surrounded by a low circular wall with a section missing on the north, symbolizing the broken ring of the blockade at the end of the siege of Leningrad. The monument was unveiled May 9, 1975. The road continues south between rows of greenhouses and heads directly for the Pulkovo Observatory on a hill ten miles south of the city. Along the way there is a turn-off road to the Leningrad Airport. Here and there in the median strip of the road are some of the milestones, of grey and pink marble and granite, designed by Rinaldi in the 1770's.

PUSHKIN (Map 15)

The town of Pushkin (called Tsarskoe selo, "Tsar's Village," until 1918) is located 15 miles south of Leningrad and is entered by passing between the pylons of the "Egyptian Gates" (15-27) 1828, by Menelaws. [The town can also be reached by commuter train from the Vitebsk Railroad Station.]

The *palace ensemble at Pushkin* (Plan **16**) began with a small palace, 1718-1724 by Braunstein, built for Peter's wife, Catherine. Expansion of the palace for Elizabeth was begun in 1743 by various architects, but was completed by Rastrelli, 1752-1756, in his full-blown baroque style, with doubled columns and statuary on the 326-yard long exterior. More than 200 lbs of gold were used to gild the original palace, something which has not been feasible in restoring the palace, which was gutted in 1943.

Catherine the Great used the palace every summer and had Scottish architect Charles Cameron remodel some of the rooms in neoclassic style. Since there was little time to evacuate the palace before the Second World War, many items were lost and the restoration is going slowly. The restored rooms on the second floor are reached by a Grand Staircase, at the top of which is the so-called *White Vestibule* (**16**-a), designed by Monighetti in 1860 in a neo-baroque style. The white-on-white ornamentation is relieved only by the red curtains and blue oriental vases on the wall.

The room to the south is the *Cavalier's Dining Room* (**16**-b), 1750 by Rastrelli, with gilt stucco molding, a tall Dutch stove, a ceiling painting of Apollo, and table setting of German porcelain. Beyond it is Rastrelli's *Grand Hall* (**16**-c), 250 feet long, tentatively scheduled to be reopened in 1978.

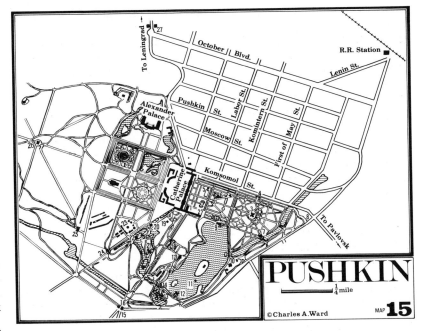

From the stairway a series of rooms (d-h on Plan 16) display the process and history of the restoration of the palace. The *Picture Gallery* (**16**-i) has 130 western European paintings of the 17th and 18th centuries, a parquet floor of several woods, impressive Dutch tile stoves as tall as the walls, and an Italian 18th-century ceiling painting. The four elaborate doors of the hall are by Rastrelli. The next two rooms display furnishings from unrestored halls in the palace. Turkish memorabilia is from the former Chesme Hall. The *Stasov Room* (**16**-j), done by Stasov in 1840, is in pink and green artificial marble with malachite ornaments.

The north wing of the palace was redesigned for Catherine by Cameron and seven of his rooms have been restored. His famous *Green Dining Room* (**16**-k) is considered one of his best. Its green walls are broken by white stucco figures by Martos, stucco garlands, and pink medallions. Cameron also designed the chairs and the bronze fireplace set. Note too the ivory bureau of carved walrus tusk. The parquet is of mahogany, oak, and maple.

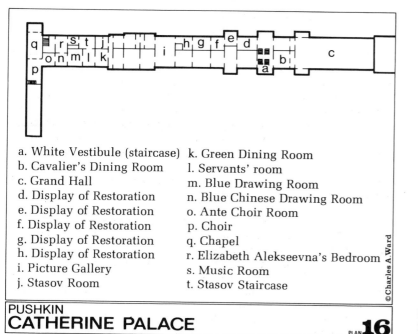

a. White Vestibule (staircase)
b. Cavalier's Dining Room
c. Grand Hall
d. Display of Restoration
e. Display of Restoration
f. Display of Restoration
g. Display of Restoration
h. Display of Restoration
i. Picture Gallery
j. Stasov Room
k. Green Dining Room
l. Servants' room
m. Blue Drawing Room
n. Blue Chinese Drawing Room
o. Ante Choir Room
p. Choir
q. Chapel
r. Elizabeth Alekseevna's Bedroom
s. Music Room
t. Stasov Staircase

©Charles A. Ward

PUSHKIN
CATHERINE PALACE

PLAN **16**

The *Blue Drawing Room* (**16**-m) has curtains, upholstery, and wall coverings of a blue and white floral pattern silk. The wall frieze-cornice has 88 small medallions set in gilded patterned molding, and the ceiling design is reflected in the fine large-pattern parquet. There are two fireplaces of Carrara marble and portraits of members of the royal family.

The *Blue Chinese Drawing Room* (**16**-n) gets its name from the blue-green silk walls painted with scenes of Chinese life. This room, too, has an elaborate wall frieze and cornice, and a medallion-style ceiling.

The *Ante Choir Room* (**16**-o) has golden silk wall coverings with peacocks and other birds, and furniture designed by Cameron.

Windows in the Choir Room overlook the *Chapel* (**16**-q), which was originally designed by Chevakinsky and is finished in dark blue with gilt ornamentation.

Elizabeth Alekseevna's Bedroom (**16**-r) has 50 slender ceramic columns set off against plain green walls. The door panels are intricately painted, and there is a pleasing parquet.

Cameron's living quarters for Catherine at the south end of the palace are being prepared for restoration.

At the north end of the palace, beyond the chapel, an archway over the road connects the palace to the former Lyceum Building, 1789-1791 by I. Neelov. Pushkin, Russia's greatest poet, studied at the Lyceum from 1811-1817.

From 1780-1795 Cameron remodeled existing buildings to construct the *"Cameron Gallery"* (**15**-2), a two-story belvedere wing extending into the park at right angles to the Palace. The gallery on the upper floor is lined with bronze busts and provides an excellent view of the park and the pond. The main approach is from the east where an impressive staircase with statues of Hercules and Flora leads up to the gallery. Between the gallery and the palace, opposite Catherine's suite of rooms, are the *Hanging Gardens and Agate Chambers* (**15**-1), a bathhouse with a rotunda entrance and rooms finished in agate, jasper, and marble on the upper floor. The Agate Chambers are open during the summer, as is the lower level of the gallery, which houses an exhibition. A large descent ramp leads southwest into the park from the Hanging Gardens.

The Parks in Pushkin were mainly planned by V. Neelov, who worked here from 1748 till his death in 1782. His sons I. Neelov and P. Neelov also contributed to the ensemble.

The section of the Park due east of the palace was laid out in the formal style in the early 18th century. A central path leads 550 yards from the palace to the *Hermitage Pavilion* (**15**-3), 1744-1756, completed by Rastrelli, a two-story central plan pavilion which was restored on the outside in 1954. The *"Hermitage Kitchen"* (**15**-4) at the edge of the park is a one-story brick building, 1775, by V. Neelov.

Nearer the palace is the *Upper Bathhouse* (**15**-5), 1777-1779 by I. Neelov, reconstructed in 1953 as a summer reading room. The *Lower Bathhouse* (**15**-6), in the second terrace of the park, 1777-1779 by I. Neelov, has a central round hall surrounded by six chambers. The pavilion is now a refreshment stand in the summer.

The grey marble *Morea Column* (**15**-7), 1770, is at the end of the park on a dam between two of the "Cascade Ponds." It memorializes a Russian victory over the Turks in the Mediterranean. Beyond it is the *Alexander Triumphal Arch* (**15**-8), 1818 by Stasov, a cast iron Doric colonnade erected by Alexander I in honor of those who served with him in the Napoleonic War.

The *Grotto* (**15**-9), 1753-1757 by Rastrelli, is on the shore of the Grand Pond and is decorated with stucco molding depicting dolphins, sea monsters, shells, etc.

The southern section of the Park was rebuilt by Catherine the Great in the "picturesque" style popular at the end of the century. The Grand Pond is thirty-five acres in size and was dug in its free-form contour in the 1770's.

The *Admiralty* (**15**-10), 1773 by Neelov, is a group of three buildings done in decorative brick with crenellations and towers. This was the boat house for the pond.

The island in the pond had a pavilion which had been redesigned by numerous architects. Destroyed in the war, it is scheduled for restoration according to Quarenghi's version of the late 1700's.

The *Chesme Column* (**15**-11), 1771-1778 by Rinaldi (restored in 1953) rises from the water near the end of the pond. The square granite base supports a marble and granite column rising 80 feet above the lake. The column is decorated with prows of ships and on the top has a bronze eagle breaking a crescent moon, symbolic of the Russian victory over the Turks at the battle of Chesme (Cesme) in the Aegean in 1770. The base of the column is decorated with bronze reliefs depicting sea battles.

The *Turkish Bath* (**15**-12), 1852 by Monighetti, at the south end of the pond, is a two-cupola structure with a minaret-like tower, built in memory of the Russo-Turkish war of 1829. The exterior was restored in 1958.

A small *Pyramid* (**15**-13), 1780's by Cameron, contains the graves of some of Catherine's pet dogs.

The *Marble Bridge* (**15**-14), 1770-1776 by V. Neelov, is one of the nicest structures along the pond. Reflections of the harmonious lines of its covered colonnade are visible from many angles.

At the south edge of the park are the *Gatchina Gates* (**15**-15), or Orlov Gates, a triumphal arch, 1778-1782 by Rinaldi, in multi-colored marble. Near it, inside the park, is the *Tower Ruins* (**15**-16), 1771 by Velten, a broad, short cylindrical tower topped by a small pergola.

Further around the pond is the *"Girl with a Pitcher"* fountain (**15**-17), a bronze statue of 1810 by Sokolov, inspired by LaFontaine's fable of the girl with a milk pitcher going to market. Uphill from the statue is the *Granite Terrace* (**15**-18), 1808-1810 by Rusca, in grey and rose granite, an overlook point along the central park path which begins at the ramp descending to the south of the Cameron Gallery.

To the west of this central path, near the palace is the *Kagulsky Obelisk* (**15**-19), 1770 by Rinaldi, the first of the Turkish War monuments in the park. Later a garden was built around it, including a fountain, pergola, and statuary.

The *Evening Hall* (**15**-20), 1796-1809 by P. Neelov, is a small building with an entrance marked by four Ionic columns. It is now used for exhibitions.

The *Concert Hall* (**15**-21), 1782-1786 by Quarenghi, on an island in the park, is a rectangular building with a rotunda portico at the main entrance. Nearby are the "Kitchen Ruins" by Quarenghi, an octagonal pergola made of classical architectural fragments from Italy.

The *Chinese Pergola* (**15**-22), 1778-1786 by Velten, is a decorative pavilion with patterned walls and exotic exterior details. It was restored 1954-1956 after severe war damage.

The *Alexander Park* occupies all the area from the northwest to southwest of the Palace. The area directly west of the palace was laid out in four large quadrants surrounded by a canal, designed by Rastrelli and others. The remainder of the park is in the picturesque style and has pavilions of a later date. The formal part of the park was worked on by several architects. The southeast quadrant has radial paths intersected by two concentric circles. The southwest quadrant was built around a "Chinese" Theater, 1777-1789 by I. Neelov, destroyed in the war. Restoration is planned. Ozerki, the northeast quadrant, contains two free-form ponds dug during Catherine's reign. The northwest quadrant contains "Mt. Parnassus," an artificial hill with a spiral pathway leading to the top.

The canal surrounding the quadrants is crossed by numerous bridges. The central one from the palace is a "Chinese Bridge" by Cameron. At the southeast corner is the Bridge-Pergola by Neelov.

South of the Formal Park is the *Chinese Village* (**15**-23), 1782-1796 by Cameron and V. Neelov, a series of small houses around a central rotunda. Stasov made some additions in the early 19th century. The village has not been restored.

South of the village is the *Grand Caprice* (**15**-24), a sort of tunnel surmounted by a Chinese pergola between the Catherine Park and the Alexander Park. It was begun in 1779 by V. Neelov and reworked by Quarenghi in 1786.

Further west is the *"Chapelle"* (**15**-25), 1827 by Menelaws, a tall square, neoGothic tower with a pyramid roof and with certain "ruined" features built in.

Near the west end of the park is the *Arsenal* (**15**-26) 1830-1835 by Menelaws, a brick neoGothic structure with four crenellated towers, which originally housed a weapons collection.

To the north of the formal gardens is the *Alexander Palace* (Map **15**) 1792-1796 by Quarenghi. It houses administrative offices and is not open for view.

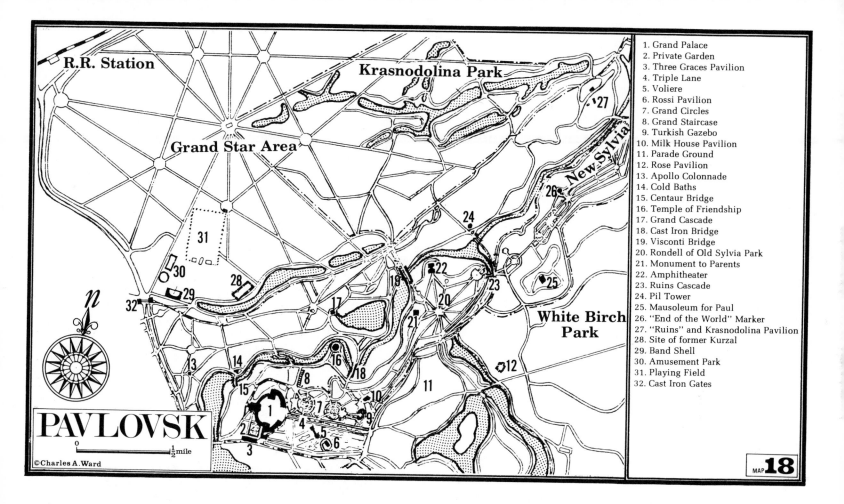

PAVLOVSK

R.R. Station

Krasnodolina Park

Grand Star Area

White Birch Park

New Sylvia

1. Grand Palace
2. Private Garden
3. Three Graces Pavilion
4. Triple Lane
5. Voliere
6. Rossi Pavilion
7. Grand Circles
8. Grand Staircase
9. Turkish Gazebo
10. Milk House Pavilion
11. Parade Ground
12. Rose Pavilion
13. Apollo Colonnade
14. Cold Baths
15. Centaur Bridge
16. Temple of Friendship
17. Grand Cascade
18. Cast Iron Bridge
19. Visconti Bridge
20. Rondell of Old Sylvia Park
21. Monument to Parents
22. Amphitheater
23. Ruins Cascade
24. Pil Tower
25. Mausoleum for Paul
26. "End of the World" Marker
27. "Ruins" and Krasnodolina Pavilion
28. Site of former Kurzal
29. Band Shell
30. Amusement Park
31. Playing Field
32. Cast Iron Gates

MAP 18

0   ½ mile

©Charles A. Ward

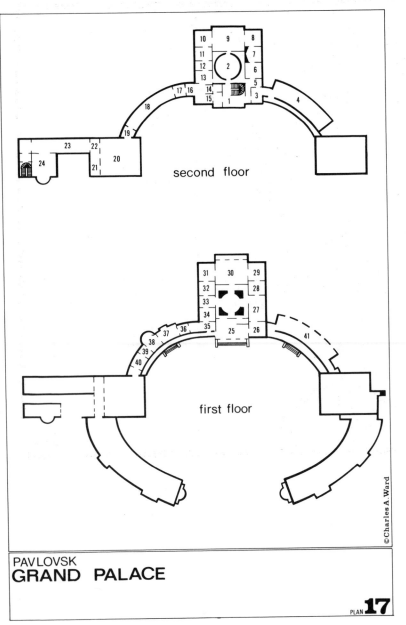

second floor

first floor

©Charles A. Ward

PAVLOVSK
(Map 18)

Pavlovsk, one of Tsar Paul's summer palaces, is located two miles beyond the town of Pushkin (and 17 miles south of Leningrad). The road approach skirts the southern part of the park and passes through the *Cast Iron Gates* (**18**-32), 1826 by Rossi. This estate was begun in 1777 on land given by Catherine to her son, Paul, at the birth of his heir, Alexander. Catherine asked Charles Cameron, a Scottish architect of neoclassical training, to design the palace and grounds. Additional work was done in the 1790's by Brenna. Paul died in 1801, but his widow, Maria Fedorovna, lived at the palace until her death in 1828, and commissioned further remodeling by Voronikhin, Rossi, and Gonzago. Though the palace and grounds were destroyed in 1944, they have been totally restored and present the most complete picture of a Tsarist suburban residence. Pavlovsk is one of the gems of the summer palace complexes, not only for its palace, but also for its park of great beauty laid out along the meandering Slavyanka River.

The **GRAND PALACE (Plan 17)** 1782-1786 by Cameron, was remodeled and enlarged by Brenna in the 1790's. It was he who added the square wings and galleries which almost enclose the entrance court. After a severe fire in 1803 the central part of the palace was redone by Voronikhin. The palace was blown up in 1944, but was partially reopened in 1957, and totally restored by 1970. Fortunately, most of the original furnishings were evacuated before the war. The palace is three stories high in the central section. The formal rooms of the second floor as well as the living rooms of Paul and his wife on the first floor have been restored. The third floor was for servants and storage and is now used for exhibitions, as are the wings added by Brenna. The following description of the rooms, starting on the second floor, mentions only a few of their decorative features. The numbers are keyed to the plan.

17-1. The *Stairway* has wall frescoes by G. Scotti. The *Upper Vestibule*, by Brenna, has military decor, with motifs taken from the Russian defeat of the Turks. The equestrian statue of Hercules is by Kozlovsky, 1799.

17-2. The *Italian Hall*, a two-story central room under the dome, is by Cameron, Brenna, and reworked by Voronikhin, 1803. The walls are in pastel rose and lilac shades which get lighter higher up. Voronikhin added the caryatids, the balustrade of the upper level, and the eagles above the cornice. There are first and second century Roman marble statues in the wall niches, and a late 18th-century chandelier of Russian workmanship. The mahogany doors are by Quarenghi.

17-3. *Toilette Room*, by Brenna. Note the stucco molding and the 2nd-century statue, "Faun and Panther."

17-4. The *Rossi Library*, 1824 by Rossi, now houses temporary exhibits until the cabinetry is totally restored.

17-5. *Paul's Little Study*, with a writing desk by Denizot of Paris, and an excellent Gouthiere chandlier. Other furniture was designed by Voronikhin in 1804.

17-6. *Paul's Library*, 1803 by Voronikhin, with an oval ceiling painting by Scotti. The writing table, mahogany with twelve ivory legs, was designed by Brenna and manufactured in Petersburg. The walls are hung with tapestries depicting scenes from LaFontaine's fables, a gift to Paul from Louis XVI in 1782.

17-7. *Tapestry Room*, named for the tapestries of 1776 illustrating "Don Quixote," a gift from Louis XVI. The tapestries on the side walls are from Belgium. The frieze, molding, and chandelier are by Voronikhin. The mahogany, ivory, and bronze writing table was made in Petersburg, and the chair set, with Lyons silk upholstery, is by Henri Jacob, Paris, 1784.

17-8. The *War Room*, by Brenna, is in white artificial marble with gilt moldings and decorative stucco wall molding on Roman martial themes. The ceiling design is by Voronikhin, and the chandelier by Gouthiere.

17-9. *Greek Hall*, 1780's by Cameron, Brenna, and redone by Voronikhin in 1803. The hall has a colonnade of green artificial marble, plaster casts of statues in niches, and furniture by Voronikhin. The mantles and side tables along the walls are French, as are the draperies of 1782. The large jasper and porphyry vases are by Voronikhin.

17-10. *Peace Hall*, by Brenna, with gilt stucco molding and scenes of pastoral life. Note the carved doors, the chandelier by Gouthiere, and furniture by Voronikhin, including the shallow glass vase on three legs (1811).

17-11. *Maria Fedorovna's Library* displays more tapestries of the "Don Quixote" series, as well as tapestries of the 1770's on the theme of "Portraits of the gods." The statues on the low bookcases are mainly Italian 18th-century copies of ancient originals. The complex floor parquet is made up of twelve types of wood.

17-12. The *Boudoir*, by Brenna, has an opulent interior including marble pilasters on the walls with an arabesque design reproducing Raphael's Vatican loggias. The wall panels have bas-reliefs, oval medallions, and scenes of India, and the ceiling painting, "Times of Day," is by Scotti. The fancy fireplace with porphyry columns is from Rome, the piano from London, 1774, and the chandelier by Voronikhin.

17-13. The *Formal Bedroom* was decorative and was never slept in. The massive bed is by Henri Jacob, Paris, and the Sevres toilette of 64 pieces, 1782, was ordered by Marie Antoinette as a gift for Maria Fedorovna. The elaborate parquet floor and the marble fireplace with malachite pilasters and insets were reconstructed in the 1950's.

17-14. *Maria Fedorovna's Toilette Room*, 1790's by Brenna. The wall panels depict scenes of the Pavlovsk Park, and the molding and relief work is by sculptor I. Prokofiev. The steel vanity table is from the Russian town of Tula, 1788. Opposite the window, on the outside palace wall, is a perspective fresco by Gonzago, rediscovered in 1967.

17-15. *Fraulein Room*, by Brenna, has walls of artificial marble and paintings by Robert, Voile, Van Loo, and Greuze.

17-16. *First Hall-Study*, by Brenna, has stucco molding and reliefs, a marble fireplace, porcelain vases, and bronze statuary.

17-17. *Second Hall-Study*, by Brenna, has walls of pink artificial marble.

17-18. *Picture Gallery*, 1797 by Brenna. The paintings are predominantly Dutch genre pieces, and the central ceiling panel, "Triumph of Apollo," is a copy of a Guido Reni. The hall also exhibits decorative vases, crystal, and other objects.

17-19. *Third Hall-Study*, by Brenna, has a rose-lilac wall treatment and a perspective ceiling painting by Gonzago; fine furniture and decorative vases.

17-20. The *Grand (Throne) Room*, 1798 by Brenna, was originally a dining room. Notable is the perspective ceiling designed by Gonzago. The banquet table has a china service of Petersburg manufacture, 1827, designed by Pimenov. The large porcelain vases in the room are Sevres, 18th century.

17-21. The *Buffet Room* now displays some of the china service.

17-22. The *Orchestra Room* now contains sculptures by Martos and Kozlovsky, early 1800's.

17-23. The *Cavalier Hall*, 1798 by Brenna, was designed as a meeting hall for the Malta Knights, whom Paul protected after Malta was taken by Napoleon. The walls have elaborate stucco molding reliefs on classical themes and a garland motif on the ceiling and lower wall. The hall now displays 2nd- and 3rd-century BC Roman statuary bought in England by Catherine.

17-24. The *Palace Chapel* has an iconostasis decorated with sculpture by Kozlovsky and paintings which are copies of western masters. On display are military standards captured from the French by Suvorov.

The *Cavalier Guards Room* and *Entrance Room*, at the end of the wing, have a display of the efforts involved in the restoration of the palace after its destruction in World War Two.

FIRST FLOOR ROOMS
(Where the royal family actually lived)

17-25. *Vestibule*, 1780's by Cameron, restored in 1803 by Voronikhin. The walls are lined by statues of bronze color representing the twelve months, and above them, zodiac bas-reliefs by Prokofiev. The pastel ceiling by Scotti imitates a cupola, with the four seasons of the year. The chandeliers are late 18th-century Russian.

17-27. The *Ball Room*, by Cameron, was intended for small dances, with rose-pastel coloring and gilded molding. There are four paintings by H. Robert, commissioned by Paul in 1784.

17-28. The *Drawing Room*, by Cameron, contains French tapestries, a gift of Louis XVI to Paul in 1782. The divan and chair set is by Henri Jacob, Paris, 1784.

17-29. The *Billiard Room*, by Cameron, has a restrained wall treatment and 18th-century Italian paintings. The card tables are Russian and the clavichord belonged to Potemkin and was formerly in the Tauride Palace. The billiard table was moved out in the mid-19th century.

17-30. The *Dining Room*, by Cameron, is done with restrained neoclassical decor and stucco molding, but note the elaborate frieze above the capitals of the pilasters. The park is visible through the large windows and scenes from the park are depicted in paintings on the end walls of the room. The table is set with Russian china and English crystal.

17-31. The *Corner Drawing Room*, 1816 by Rossi, was formerly Paul's bedroom. The walls are of lilac color, the doors of birch with gold ornaments. The vases, furniture, and other decor were all designed by Rossi.

17-32. The *New Study*, 1800 by Quarenghi, is in artificial marble with gilt molding. The furniture is German, the writing set on the table is by the French sculptor Houdon, and the walls are decorated with copies of paintings by Raphael in the Vatican.

17-33. The *Common Room Study*, by Brenna, has a ceiling by Scotti ("Apollo and the nine Muses"), and portraits on the walls of members of the Imperial family. The mahogany desk is of German origin, 1780's, and the ivory and amber objects were designed by Rossi.

17-34. The *Old Study* has wall panels depicting Paul's estate at Gatchina. The desk and appointments are of German manufacture, 1780's. To the right of the window is a mosaic of the colosseum in Rome, given to Paul by Pope Pius VI in 1782.

The south wing contains living quarters designed by Quarenghi and Voronikhin. The *Entrance rooms* (**17-35**) have displays of Voronikhin's work and examples of his designs for decorative artifacts.

17-36. The *Kammerdiener Room*, by Brenna, is a round study with sketches on the walls by various artists.

17-37. The *Pilaster Study*, 1800 by Quarenghi. The ceiling design is by Scotti, the bas-reliefs at the top of the walls by Quarenghi, and the furniture by Voronikhin.

17-38. The *Fonarik Study*, 1807 by Voronikhin, has a semi-rotunda extending into the garden, supported by two Ionic columns and two caryatids. The paintings on the walls are by Reni, Dolci, LeBrun, Permiggian, and others.

17-39. The *Toilette Room*, 1800 by Quarenghi, has a frieze and ceiling by Scotti and furniture and toilette set by Voronikhin.

17-40. The *Bedroom*, 1805 by Voronikhin, is done with white imitation marble walls and two jasper fireplaces. Above the divan is a woven portrait of Paul done in Petersburg in 1799.

THE PARKS AND PAVILIONS (Map 18)

The *Private Garden*, (**18-2**), lies along the western side of the palace and is arranged in a formal pattern. At the west end is the *Three Graces Pavilion*, (**18-3**), 1800-1801 by Cameron, a square pavilion with 16 Ionic columns and stucco friezes of Apollo and Minerva on the pediments. In the center is a statue of the graces by Triscorni, 1803, a copy of an original by Canova.

The *Troynaya (Triple) Lane*, (**18-4**), on axis with the entrance to the palace, leads to the southeast. It is planted with four rows of linden trees forming a carriage way and two pedestrian paths. To the south of the Triple Lane are:

The *Voliere*, (**18-5**), 1781-1783 by Cameron, a building with a central section and two pavilions connected to it by Doric colonnades. The colonnades were originally screened in to create an aviary. Now a summer reading room, the building faces on a pond dug in the 19th century, at the end of which stands a statue of Venus (copy of a Canova).

The *Rossi Pavilion*, (**18-6**), beyond the Voliere, was built in 1914 on plans drawn up by Rossi in 1816. It is a semicircular colonnade covered by a half-dome. Inside is a bronze statue of Maria Fedorovna by Beklemishev, 1914.

Between the Voliere and Rossi pavilion is a hedge labyrinth designed by Cameron.

To the north of the Triple lane:

The *Grand Circles*, (**18-7**), 1797 by Brenna, are two round terraces with eight spoke-paths, with statues of "Peace" and "Justice" in their centers and other statues around the perimeter.

The *Grand Stairway*, (**18-8**), by Brenna, consists of 64 steps leading down to the river valley, with sculptures of lions above and below. The stairway is more narrow near the top, to add to the illusion of height. The stairway was being reconstructed in 1976.

The *Turkish Gazebo*, (**18-9**), 1815 by Rossi, is an oblong, open-air sitting area formed by decorative plantings and vases. Beyond it is the *Milk House Pavilion*, (**18-10**), 1782 by Cameron, which was built in an alpine style with thatch roof and stone walls as part of a rustic "farm" near the main palace. It is now a refreshment stand, and with its tar shingle roof awaits complete restoration.

Paul's *Parade Ground* (**18-11**), to the east of the Triple Lane, was rebuilt as a park, 1803-1813 by Gonzago. This is now one of the most picturesque areas of the parks, for Gonzago gave great care to planting trees with their shape and color at different times of the year in mind.

Rossi's *Rose Pavilion*, (**18**-12), 1807-1812, was on the edge of this area. It was totally destroyed during the war, but is scheduled for restoration by the end of the 1970's.

The **WHITE BIRCH PARK**, (Map **18**), by Gonzago, is a large forest area to the east of the Parade Ground.

SLAVYANKA RIVER VALLEY

The *Apollo Colonnade*, (**18**-13), 1782-1783 by Cameron, on the left bank of the Slavyanka River, is a circular paired Doric colonnade with a copy of the Apollo Belvedere in the center. In 1800 Quarenghi moved it to its present site and added a cascade so it would recall Mt. Parnassus and the Castallian spring. The cascade undermined part of the colonnade during a storm in 1817, but it was left with one section missing because of the fashion for "ruins" at the time, and because the statue was then visible from the palace.

The *Cold Baths* (**18**-14), 1799 by Cameron, is a structure in rotunda form used for summer bathing.

The *Centaur Bridge* (**18**-15), has statues added by Voronikhin in 1800.

The *Temple of Friendship*, (**18**-16), 1782 by Cameron, is a rotunda of 16 Doric columns built in honor of Catherine the Great, and extremely well-placed at a bend in the river. It contains a statue of Catherine as Ceres.

The *Grand Cascade* (**18**-17), by Cameron, is a small wall with balustrade on top, from which a stream of water flows toward the Round Pond.

The *Cast-Iron Bridge*, (**18**-18), 1823 by Rossi, has a medallion decor which repeats motifs from the Temple of Friendship.

The *Visconti Bridge* (**18**-19), 1807 by Voronikhin, is a low stone arch with cast iron railings and decorative vases at the ends.

The *Old Sylvia Park* (**18**-20), 1798 by Brenna, is in the shape of a rondell with 12 radiating paths. There is a bronze copy of the Apollo Belvedere in the center and 12 bronze statues at the beginning of each path (9 muses and Venus, Mercury, and Flora; copies of Greek and Roman originals).

The *Monument to Parents* (**18**-21), 1786 by Cameron, is a small square structure in monumental style, with a sculpture by Martos, 1807.

The *Amphitheater* (**18**-22), 1793 by Brenna, is a small semi-circular terrace of seats with a statue of Flora above, on a high bank overlooking the river. On the opposite bank is a grassy "stage" area for performances.

The *Ruins Cascade*, (**18**-23), 1794 by Brenna, is at the border between the Old and New Sylvia Parks and has the form of a bridge with vases and birch log railings, with fragments of columns and statuary in

the water below.

The *Pil Tower* (**18**-24), 1795 by Brenna, is a round structure with conical thatched roof and with wall frescoes by Gonzago. It stands by a bridge across the river to the north of Old Sylvia.

The *Mausoleum for Paul* (**18**-25), 1808-1809 by Thomon, is a four-column structure in the form of a Greek temple, in the New Sylvia Park. The mausoleum contains a statue by Martos.

The *End of the World Marker*, (**18**-26), by Cameron, is a pink marble Ionic column on a square base marking what at one time was the end of the New Sylvia Park. It was moved here from the end of the Triple Lane in 1799.

Across the river at the end of the New Sylvia Park is the end of the Krasnaya dolina Park. There are two pavilions there. The *Ruins*, (**18**-27), consists of two arches, one with a path leading through it. Nearby is the *Krasnodolina Pavilion*, (**18**-27), which is in disrepair.

The **GRAND STAR AREA** is a large forested park making up the western part of the estate. The southern area of the park contained the Railroad station before the war, as well as the "Kurzal" *music pavilion*, (**18**-28), famous for its summer concerts. Johann Strauss often conducted here between 1856-1871. It was totally destroyed in 1944. This area now contains a *band shell*, (**18**-29), *amusement park*, (**18**-30), and several *playing fields*, (**18**-31).

GATCHINA
(Map 10

The palace complex at Gatchina is southwest of Pushkin, 27 miles from Leningrad. The land was acquired in 1765 and given by Catherine to her favorite, G. Orlov, who hired Rinaldi to build a palace. Construction of the limestone palace dragged on from 1766-1781, and Orlov lived there only two years before his death. Catherine bought the estate from Orlov's heirs and gave it to her son, Paul. Engaged in building Pavlovsk, Paul ignored Gatchina until the 1790's when he had Brenna alter the palace. The palace was further altered in the 1840's by P. Kuzmin.

In addition to the main palace, there is the *Priorate Palace*, 1798 by Lvov, in sort of tudor style, built for the Knights of Malta, to whom Paul had given refuge. The grounds of the estate are laid out along a series of small chain-lakes. Numerous stone pavilions, columns and arches in the park are picturesquely placed to take advantage of the vistas and reflections. Gatchina is beyond the 25-mile travel limit from Leningrad, and Intourist does not, as a rule, take tourists there.

NOVGOROD

St. Vlasy Church: Novgorod

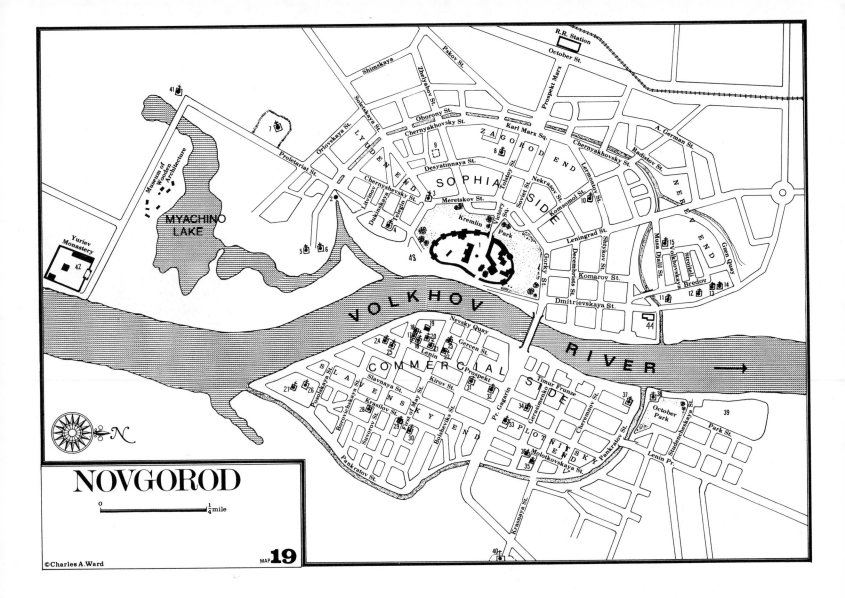

NOVGOROD

0 ___ ¼ mile

© Charles A. Ward

MAP **19**

42

NOVGOROD
(Map 19)

Novgorod, one of Russia's oldest cities, is located on the Volkhov River four miles north of Lake Ilmen and 120 miles southeast of Leningrad. Novgorod developed in the 9th century as a trading center on the "water road" between Scandinavia and Byzantium. The year 862 traditionally marks the arrival of the Norseman Riurik who first organized a "Russian state." The city as a trading center grew and prospered, becoming independent of Kiev in 1014 and independent of the local princes in 1136 with the establishment of a republic based on a popular assembly called the *veche*. The city grew extremely wealthy as a member of the Hanseatic league, and arts flourished, particularly the building of churches and the "Novgorod school" of icon painting. Economic decline came in the 1480's after Ivan III of Moscow subjugated Novgorod and closed its western trading offices. A later attempt to reassert independence was crushed by Ivan the Terrible in 1570.

Novgorod is known now mainly for its old Russian architecture, which survived unscathed into the 20th century. Novgorod was the only major Russian town to avoid capture by the Mongols in the 1230's, and its architecture developed unhindered till the 17th century. The city's loss of importance after 1700 eliminated the likelihood of new construction or city expansion which would disturb the architectural monuments of the past. The city remained intact until the Second World War when it was extensively destroyed. Reconstruction of the churches has restored most to their original external appearance, but irreplaceable frescoes in some churches have been lost beyond recall.

The city is laid out on both sides of the river. On the left bank is the Sophia Side, with a concentration of buildings in the *Citadel* (**19**-1). On the right bank is the Commercial Side, with a concentration of churches in the "Yaroslav Court" area. Several monasteries in the area of the city have also been preserved.

The churches built by the princes in the 11th and 12th centuries were large, six-column, multiple-dome churches of the Kievan type. After the 12th century most churches were smaller, usually four-column, single-dome structures built in the span of one or two years under the patronage of rich merchants or groups of parishioners. The earliest of these small churches usually have three apses in the east wall, a form which, after the 14th century, gave way to a single-apse style.

THE CITADEL (Detinets) - Map 20

The Citadel of Novgorod has existed since 1044, but was enlarged and rebuilt in 1116. It achieved its present appearance in 1484-1490 when Ivan III of Moscow had it rebuilt, concurrent with his reconstruction of the Moscow Kremlin. The citadel area of about 30 acres is

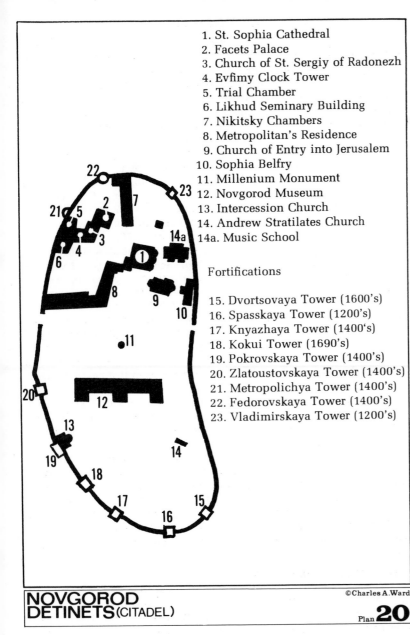

1. St. Sophia Cathedral
2. Facets Palace
3. Church of St. Sergiy of Radonezh
4. Evfimy Clock Tower
5. Trial Chamber
6. Likhud Seminary Building
7. Nikitsky Chambers
8. Metropolitan's Residence
9. Church of Entry into Jerusalem
10. Sophia Belfry
11. Millenium Monument
12. Novgorod Museum
13. Intercession Church
14. Andrew Stratilates Church
14a. Music School

Fortifications

15. Dvortsovaya Tower (1600's)
16. Spasskaya Tower (1200's)
17. Knyazhaya Tower (1400's)
18. Kokui Tower (1690's)
19. Pokrovskaya Tower (1400's)
20. Zlatoustovskaya Tower (1400's)
21. Metropolichya Tower (1400's)
22. Fedorovskaya Tower (1400's)
23. Vladimirskaya Tower (1200's)

NOVGOROD DETINETS (CITADEL)

©Charles A. Ward

Plan **20**

enclosed by a 7/8-mile-long defense wall, a kidney-shaped oval on a north-south axis. The wall is 26-34 feet high and 8-10 feet thick. The southwest section of the wall beginning at the Spasskaya Tower has "swallow-tail" crenellations also found in the Moscow Kremlin.

Nine of the original thirteen towers are extant. The present entrances to the citadel are through two arches on the east-west axis. The archway facing the river was constructed in 1820 on the site of the Prechistenskaya Gate-Tower (from the 1100's) which was demolished in the 1790's. The west arch is on the site of the former Voskresenskaya Gate Tower which was destroyed by fire in 1745. The main road of the town led through these arches and across a bridge, destroyed during World War Two, which connected the Citadel with First of May Street on the Commercial Side. The new bridge downriver was constructed in 1952-1954. Among the remaining towers one can note the six-story *Spasskaya (Savior) Tower* (**20**-16), dating from the 1200's, which was the old entrance tower from the south end of town. The *Kokui Tower* (**20**-18), built in the 1690's on the site of a former tower, is 104 feet tall. Restored in 1962-1963, it now houses a summer exhibition on the restoration of the Novgorod Churches. The *Pokrovskaya (Intercession) Tower* (**20**-19), from the late 1400's, was a cannon tower with lower walls ten feet thick. It now contains the "Detinets" Restaurant, with old Russian decor and national cuisine. The *Zlatoustovskaya (Chrysostom) Tower* (**20**-20), from the 1400's, was reconstructed and enlarged in 1880 to house the Novgorod Museum. It now houses special exhibits.

INSIDE THE CITADEL

The *Sophia Cathedral* (**20**-1) was built in 1045-1050 by Prince Vladimir, son of Yaroslav the Wise. Like the Sophia Cathedral in Kiev, with which it was built to compete, Novgorod's Sophia is a five-aisle church surrounded on three sides by a gallery, which was closed in by the end of the 11th century. The church differs from Kiev's Sophia in its vertical emphasis, created on the interior by closely spaced columns and on the exterior by the monumental style: apses devoid of ornamentation and the south facade (facing the square) with its tall severe pilasters asymmetrically arranged. At the southwest corner is a massive rectangular tower topped by a large dome. This tower, built over the corner of the former gallery, contains a stairway leading to the choir of the church. The doors of the west facade are decorated with medieval bronze bas-relief panels. The doors were made in Magdeburg about 1170 and were brought to Novgorod in 1187 as war booty from Sigtuna, Sweden.

The interior of the church has a vertical emphasis and crowded feel because of the closeness of the columns. The frescoes are mainly 19th-century, though some 12th-century fragments have been preserved. The iconostasis dates from the 16th century, and the chandelier from 1600, a gift to the church from Tsar Boris Godunov. The Chapel of the Nativity of the Virgin, at the southeast corner of the church, has old bronze doors of Byzantine workmanship, and an interesting 16th-century iconostasis.

The *Facets Palace,* (**20**-2) 1433, is the only remaining part of the 15th-century Archbishop's Residence. It is known for its large, central-column, four-vault room on the top floor, an architectural feature which predates by half a century the more famous Facets Palace of the Moscow Kremlin. The palace now contains exhibits of Russian Applied Arts of the 11th-19th centuries, including some former treasures of the Sophia Cathedral. The grave of the poet G. P. Derzhavin is in the garden in front of the building. He was buried in the Khutynsky Monastery near the city after his death in 1816, and his remains were moved here in 1959.

Adjoining the palace on the west is the *Church of St. Sergiy of Radonezh* (**20**-3), 1463, built over an entrance gate of the palace. To the west of it is the *Evfimy Clock Tower* (**20**-4) built in 1443 and rebuilt in 1671. It connects to a building running along the citadel wall. The northern part of this building is the *Trial Chamber* (**20**-5) probably from 1670. The southern wing is the *Likhud Seminary Building* (**20**-6) from the 1400's.

The *Nikitsky Chambers* (**20**-7), from the 17th century, is north of the Sophia Cathedral. It houses the administrative offices and library of the Novgorod Museum.

The former *Metropolitan's Residence* (**20**-8), built in 1770 by architect P. R. Nikitin, is southwest of the Cathedral.

The *Church of the Entry into Jerusalem* (**20**-9), 1759, is sometimes attributed to Rastrelli. It is now used as a lecture hall.

The *Sophia Belfry* (**20**-10), next to the east wall of the citadel, was erected in 1439 and enlarged in the 16th century. It was remodeled in the 17th, 18th, and 19th centuries, and rebuilt after partial destruction during World War Two.

In the center of the citadel is the *Millenium Monument* (**20**-11), designed by M. O. Mikeshin and unveiled in 1862 on the 1,000th anniversary of the founding of the Russian state (dating from the chronicle entry of 862 when the Norseman Riurik arrived in Novgorod).

This 48-foot tall monument consists of a high pedestal decorated with a 3/4 relief bronze frieze of important personages from Russia's past. The pedestal supports an orb 15 feet in diameter surmounted by a kneeling female figure, symbolizing Russia, and an angel holding a cross. Six groups of figures surround the base of the orb. The six groups represent various important rulers in Russia's past:

1. Ruirik is to the south, facing Kiev. He is holding a shield with the letters STO, which in Old Church Slavonic indicate the year 862.
2. On Riurik's right is St. Vladimir Christianizing Russia (in 988), a cross in his upraised hand. A kneeling Slav at his feet is breaking idols, and a woman stands to his left holding a babe to be baptised.
3. On Ruirik's left (to the southeast), facing Moscow, is the Dmitry Donskoy group. Dmitry is depicted, weapons in hand, just after his defeat of the Tatars in 1380.
4. The Ivan III group is to the left of Donskoy. Ivan, in a heavy patterned robe, holds the orb and sceptre in his hands. To his right is a kneeling Tatar, symbol of the final defeat of the Mongols in 1480. To the left is a Livonian knight with a broken sword.
5. To the left of Ivan is the Peter the Great group, facing north toward Petersburg. Peter is wearing a laurel wreath and holds a sceptre in his right hand. He is framed by the wings of an angel standing behind him.
6. To Peter's left is the Mikhail Romanov group. Romanov is flanked to the right by D. M. Pozharsky, standing with sword in hand, and to the left by K. M. Minin, kneeling, holding a sceptre and crown. These two men led the Russian troops which expelled the Poles from Moscow in 1612, after which Romanov was elected Tsar.

On the base of the monument is a bronze bas-relief in four sections with 109 figures important in Russian history. The four sections are "Enlighteners" (31 figures), "Military heroes" (36 figures), "People in Government" (26 figures), and "Writers and Artists" (16 figures). The Nazis disassembled the monument, cutting the tons of bronze sculpture into transportable pieces for removal to Germany. Reassembly of the monument began with the liberation of Novgorod in January, 1944, and the restored monument was unveiled anew on November 5, 1944.

To the south of the monument is the *Novgorod Museum* (**20**-12) in the former city administration building constructed in 1783 and rebuilt, after a fire, in 1817-1823. The museum has a good collection of Novgorod School icons, as well as paintings of the 18th-20th centuries.

Beyond the museum is the *Church of the Intercession* (**20**-13), rebuilt in its present form in the late 1600's with a new octagonal dome, to give the church a pyramidal silhouette. The small chapel of *St. Andrew Stratilates* (**20**-14), built in the early 1700's, is in the southern part of the Citadel.

Between the Zlatoustovskaya Tower and the western arch is the memorial grave of soldiers of the revolution and liberators of Novgorod. The eternal flame was lit in 1965.

SOPHIA SIDE

Over the centuries the city grew up in concentric circles around the citadel. Only the *White Tower* (**19**-2) (Proletariat St. #13), from the 1400's, a circular brick tower 48 feet in diameter, remains of the former defense walls which were demolished in the 1830's. *Victory Square* (formerly Sophia Square) was laid out in the 1830's opposite the west entrance to the citadel. The House of Soviets, on the west side of the square, was built after the war. The building on the south side of the square was constructed in 1851 by Stakenschneider as the Noblemen's Club. It was reconstructed with an additional floor after World War Two.

The Sophia Side was divided into "ends," the Lyudin End to the south of the citadel, the Zagorod End to the west, and the Nerev End to the north.

The **LYUDIN END**, or southern area of the Sophia Side, contains five churches. The nearest to the citadel is the *Church of St. Vlasy* (**19**-3), 1407 (Chernyshevsky Street #2), a small cubical single-dome, single-apse church with trefoil gables reflecting the ceiling vaults of the building. The arches and dome were rebuilt after the war.

The *Church of the Trinity* (**19**-4), 1365, is at Proletariat St. #9. Only the lower part of the walls is original. The upper walls and dome were rebuilt in the 19th century. On the riverbank nearby is the Monument of Victory, an obelisk and equestrian statue commemorating the liberation of Novgorod and the end of the war in 1945.

Beyond the limits of the old city are two churches near the river bank. The *Church of the Convincing of Thomas* (**19**-5), 1463, is a three-apse church purposely constructed in the 13th-century style. The *Church of Ioann Milostivy* (**19**-6), 1422, is a modest one-dome structure.

To the west of these is the *Church of Peter and Paul "on Sinichya Hill"* (**19**-7), 1185-1192, a typical three-apse, single-dome church of the early period. It is in the former city cemetery to the right of the road leading to Yurievo.

A half-mile further along, where the road turns east to the Yuriev Monastery, is the *Church of the Annunciation "in Arkazha,"* (**19**-41), 1179, a three-apse, single-dome church. The upper half was rebuilt in the 16th century. The lower walls of the interior retain some fragments of 12th-century frescoes.

The **ZAGOROD END**, to the west of the citadel, was the home of wealthy boyars. The area had several monasteries, now in ruins (**19**-9), and only the *Church of the Twelve Apostles* (**19**-8), 1454, remains. The proportions of this single-apse, single-dome church make it a typical example of the 15th-century Novgorod style. The sloping roof is a later remodeling of the original trefoil gables.

At the end of Marx Prospekt is the train station, from after the war, designed by Shchusev in a style which harmonizes with the old architecture of the town.

The **NEREV END** of the Sophia Side was north of the citadel. The *Church of Fedor Stratilates "in Shchirkova Street"* (**19**-10) 1292-1294 (Lermontov St. #9) is a three-apse, five-dome church. The upper part of the church was rebuilt in 1682, and the domed belfry was added in the 19th century.

The *Church of Peter and Paul "in Kozhevniki"* (**19**-11), 1406, (Bredov St. #4) is a cubical one-dome church with trefoil gables and pleas-

ing proportions. Badly damaged in World War Two, the church was restored in 1959 and left unstuccoed.

Beyond the Peter-Paul Church was the *Zverin Monastery*, founded in the 12th century. The *Church of Nicholas the White* (**19**-12), 1312-1313, (Bredov St. #14) was rebuilt several times in later centuries and is greatly altered from its original appearance. The *Church of the Intercession* (**19**-13), 1335, (Bredov St. #18) was also rebuilt several times and has acquired heavy proportions. Its appearance was further upset by the construction in the 19th century of a large church just to the west. The *Church of St. Simeon* (**19**-14), 1467, (Bredov St. #16) is a single-apse, single-dome church just to the north of the Intercession Church. It is similar to the Twelve Apostles Church built thirteen years earlier, but has a more bulbous dome. Frescoes of the 15th century survive, but are still largely covered by later paintings.

The *Holy Ghost Monastery*, from the 12th century, was to the west of the Zverin Monastery. The *Trinity Church* (**19**-15), 1557, (Musa Djalil St. #20) is the most interesting building surviving there. It is an unstuccoed two-story church which reflects the Moscow style introduced into Novgorod in the 16th century — the three apses, five domes, ogee arches on the apses, and the small pentagonal-niche decorative band at the top of the apses. A refectory building adjoins the church on the west.

COMMERCIAL SIDE

The architectural monuments of the Commercial Side are centered on an area called "Yaroslav's Court," which was the center of commercial activity in Novgorod's heyday. The Commercial Side was divided into the *Slavensky End* (south of Bolsheviks Street) and *Plotnitsky End* (north of Bolsheviks Street). In 1723 Peter the Great ordered a new "regularized" street pattern for the city, like that in Petersburg. It was then that the grid pattern for the Commercial Side was worked out. Catherine the Great furthered this street reconstruction in 1778. As a result, some of the churches are now in strange locations in the center of blocks, not adjacent to the street. Reconstruction of the city since the war has tried to clear away buildings so the churches can be seen to their best advantage. The main concentration of structures is in Yaroslav's Court, along Lenin St. between Suvorov and First of May streets.

YAROSLAV'S COURT

The *St. Nicholas Cathedral* (**19**-16), 1113-1136, the main structure on the Commercial side, is a six-pier, three-aisle, three-apse church of the Kievan type, built to compete in size and splendor with the Sophia Cathedral across the river. The church originally had five domes, but only the central one remained after later remodeling. The exterior walls are monumental and undecorated. The north and west facades are hidden by additions constructed in the 19th century. Since 1963 the church has housed the "Scientific Atheism" section of the Novgorod Museum, as well as a planetarium in the western wing. The church interior has an interesting iconostasis of the 16th century and some fragments of 12th-century frescoes on the south wall near the iconostasis. There are display cases with icons, church robes, and other exhibits. In the 17th century a hexagonal bell tower with a tent roof was constructed to the west of the cathedral.

To the southwest of the cathedral are the *Church of Prokopy* (**19**-17), 1529, and the *Zheny-Mironositsy (Myrrh-bearing women) Church* (**19**-18), 1508-1511. Both are three-story churches with storerooms on the lower floors. The Prokopy Church reflects the influence of Muscovite architecture in the re-introduction of the triple apse and the use of the ogee arch in the re-center of the facades. The Zheny-mironositsy Church has a lower addition to the north and west, added after a fire in 1541.

The *Trading Court Gate Tower* (**19**-19), 1690's, on the west side of Yaroslav's Court, is a three-story building with two arched passageways and a tent roof over the middle. (This structure is sometimes called the "Veche Tower.")

The *Paraskeva-Pyatnitsa Church* (**19**-20), 1207, is on the north side of the court. It was entirely rebuilt in 1345 after a fire, and again in the 16th century. It is a tall, single-dome church with rectangular apses and with vaulted extensions in the centers of the north, west, and south facades. The church now houses an exhibit of wooden sculpture.

Just northeast of the Paraskeva Church is the *Assumption Church "on the market"* (**19**-21) built by Prince Vsevolod Mstislavich in 1135, but totally reconstructed in 1458.

The *Church of St. George* (**19**-22), 1356, is across First of May Street. It was destroyed by fire in 1605 and totally rebuilt in the 17th and 18th centuries.

Beside it is the *Church of St. John "in Opoki"* (**19**-23), built 1227-1230 by Prince Vsevolod Mstislavich. The church was demolished and entirely rebuilt in 1453, and remodeled again later. It is presently a one-dome structure with the divisions of the facades ending in small pointed gables.

The arcade along the river below Yaroslav's Court was built in the 17th-18th centuries and has been preserved as a frame for the churches of the Court. It was restored in 1950.

Southeast of Yaroslav's Court, across Suvorov Street, is the *Church of St. Michael* (**19**-24), 1300-1302 (Lenin St. #2). It was rebuilt in 1454 and again in 1812 as a three-story structure in neoclassical style. It is connected by a passageway to the *Church of the Annunciation* (**19**-25), 1362, rebuilt in 1466.

The **SLAVENSKY END** was the area south of Bolshevik Street. The southernmost churches there were: *Church of Elijah* (**19**-26), 1198-1202 (Krasilov St. #4), rebuilt in its original style in 1455. It is a single-dome, three-apse church with attached bell tower. The *Church of Peter and Paul "in Slavno"* (**19**-27), 1367, is a single-apse, single-dome church which regained its original trefoil gables when restored during the 1950's.

Further north along Krasilov St., at Suvorov St., is the *Church of the Apostle Philip* (**19**-28), 1383-1384, rebuilt in 1526 as a single-apse, single-dome church. Services are held in this church.

At First of May St. #26 is the *Znamensky Church* (**19**-29), 1682-1688, in the Moscow style, a five-dome church with low galleries on three sides and elaborate window frames. The church was frescoed in 1702 by artists from Kostroma. Note the "Last Judgment" on the west wall.

Across the street is the *Church of the Savior of the Transfiguration "on Ilin St."* (**19**-30), one of the most notable of Novgorod's churches. It has the serene harmony of the Novgorod style developed in the 14th century, with numerous decorative elements on the exterior. On the interior walls are remains of frescoes done by Feofan the Greek in 1378. These reddish monochrome frescoes are in Feofan's energetic, sweeping style and are one of the treasures of Old Russian Art.

The **PLOTNITSKY END** was the area north of Bolshevik Street. The *Church of Kliment* (**19**-31), 1519 (Lenin St. # 36) has the trefoil gables of the Novgorod style. It was restored in 1955. Nearby is the *Church of Dmitry* (**19**-32), 1381-1383 (Lenin St. # 42), totally rebuilt in 1462 as a single-dome, single-apse church with elaborate decorative brick work on the apse, gables, and drum of the cupola. Its bell tower is from the 17th century. The church was restored after extensive damage during the war.

The *Church of Fedor Stratilates "on the brook"* (**19**-33), 1360-1361 (Gagarin St. # 19) is one of the best examples of the 14th-century style. Its original trefoil gables were restored after the war. The octagonal tent-roof belfry is from the 17th century. The interior of the church was frescoed in the 1360's in a reddish monochrome style recalling that of the Savior Church. Fragments of the frescoes remain. The church contains an exhibit of Russian bronze and copper objects.

Northwest of the Fedor Church is the *Church of Nikita the Martyr* (**19**-34), 1557 (Lenin St. # 48a), a six-column church. The original domes and vaults have been replaced and a gallery has been built on three sides. A small one-dome Chapel of St. Nicholas was added to the north facade, and an octagonal belfry to the southeast corner.

Further to the east is the *Church of the Nativity of the Virgin "in Mikhalitsa"* (**19**-35), 1379 (Molotkovskaya St. 18a), a single-apse, single-dome church with decorative window frames from a

17th-century remodeling. It was restored after severe damage during the war. Nearby is the *Church of the Assembly of the Virgin* (19-36), 1557.

Further east beyond the old city rampart on Gagarin St. at the edge of town is the *Church of the Nativity "in the cemetery"*, (19-40), 1381-1382, a squat unadorned church with very interesting frescoes of the 1380's.

The *Church of Boris and Gleb "in Plotniki"* (19-37), 1536, is on the bank of the Volkhov River. The church reflects elements of the Muscovite style: the five domes, ogee-shaped gables at the top of each wall section, and decorative niches on the drums and top of the apse.

Across the former city ramparts is the *Church of John the Divine* (19-38), 1383-1384, a fine example of the simple 14th-century Novgorod style.

The *Antoniev Monastery* (19-39), from the 12th century, was further north along the river. The monastery's *Nativity Cathedral*, from 1117, was extensively rebuilt later, with the addition of a new roof line, oversized onion domes, and galleries added on three sides. Still, one can detect the monumental shape of the original six-column church and its circular tower on the northwest corner. Fragments of frescoes from 1125 are extant, despite the refrescoing of 1837. The church contains a display on the history of the monastery.

The *Refectory Church of the Presentation*, 1533-1536, in the monastery, has a hemispherical vault with no columns and an ogee-arch pattern on the facades, a reflection of the Muscovite style. A refectory adjoins the west side of the church.

SUBURBAN NOVGOROD

The road southwest from the Sophia Side leads past the Petrovskoe Graveyard, on a rise to the right of the road, containing the *Church of Peter and Paul "on Sinichya Hill."* A half mile further along is the *Church of the Annunciation "in Arkazha,"* on the site of the former Arkashki Monastery. At the point the road turns left and crosses Lake Myachino to the *Yuriev Monastery*. In the early 19th century this land belonged to Princess Anna Orlova-Chesmenskaya, daughter of Aleksey Orlov, one of Russia's most powerful men during Catherine the Great's reign. Orlova came under the influence of Photius, the superior of the monastery, who managed to get her to donate her large fortune to the church. It was she who financed the earthen causeway by which the road approaches the Yuriev Monastery. On the left before the monastery is Orlova's two-story summer residence, in a grove of trees. Adjacent to it is an open-air *Museum of Wooden Architecture*, begun in 1964, on an area to be 100 acres, with various wooden structures brought here from villages. In the collection now are typical peasant houses, a windmill, wayside chapel, and several churches, including the tall tentroof *Church of the Assumption of the Virgin*, 1595, from the village of

Kuritsko, a rectilinear *Nikolskaya Church*, 17th century, a 16th-century *Church of the Nativity* from Peredka village, with cantilevered gallery and an octagonal tent tower rising almost 100 feet. In the summer this church has an exhibit of decorative arts of the Novgorod region. The 18th-century peasant house is open with an exhibition of typical furnishings.

The *Yuriev Monastery*, (19-42), from the 12th century, is beyond the museum area on the left bank of the Volkhov near its source in Lake Ilmen. The *Church of St. George*, 1119, was the last of the monumental princely cathedrals built in Novgorod, a three-apse, six-column church with a great feeling of verticality. Its severe monumental facade is broken only by the pilaster strips which are arranged asymmetrically to reflect the inner structure of the church. The three domes (one over the stair tower at the northwest corner) are also asymmetrically arranged. Most of the 12th-century frescoes were ruined during an early 19th-century "restoration." Those in the dome and stairtower were salvaged in 1935-1936. The church also contains the tombs of Alexander Nevsky's mother, of Dmitry Shemyaka (a pretender to the Moscow throne), and others. The gilded iconostasis was sold abroad in 1933.

The monumental and somewhat ungainly entrance bell tower on the monastery wall was designed by Karlo Rossi and built in 1838-1841. (Nicholas I was responsible for the elimination of the middle tier of the tower, which resulted in its awkward appearance.)

The squat *Vozdvizhensky Church*, in the southeast corner of the monastery, stands out with its five blue domes with gold stars. It was built in 1828.

A mile south of the Yuriev Monastery is the *Peryn Hill* and the remains of the *Peryn Monastery*. Only the *Church of the Nativity of the Virgin* remains, a small single-apse, single-dome church with trefoil gables and totally plain walls built in the late 1100's. There are also remains of monks' cells built in 1826 at the request of Photius.

Gorodishche is the name of an area on the right bank of the Volkhov across from the Yuriev Monastery, where the princes established their official residence after the formation of the veche in 1136. No churches survive there. Slightly to the east is the *Church of the Savior "in Nereditsa,"* 1198. It was known for the frescoes of 1199, which were lost when the church was reduced to a pile of rubble in 1943. The structure of the church was restored in 1958, but only tiny fragments of the frescoes have survived.

PUBLIC TRANSPORTATION IN NOVGOROD:

Bus 7 goes from the Railroad Station via Victory Square to the Museum of Wooden Architecture and the Yuriev Monastery.

Bus 4 goes from Victory Square along Gagarin Prospekt of the Commercial Side.

TALLINN
ESTONIA

Great Sea Gates and the "Fat Margaret" tower: Tallinn

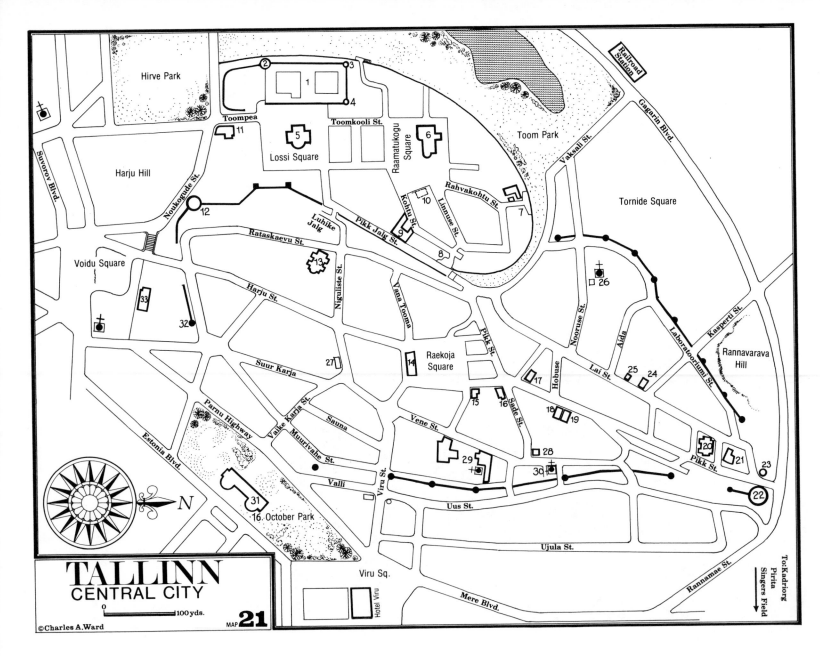

TALLINN
CENTRAL CITY

0 ⊢—————⊣ 100 yds.

MAP **21**

©Charles A. Ward

Hirve Park

Toompea

Toom Park

Railroad Station

Gagarin Blvd.

Suvorov Blvd.

11

Harju Hill

Lossi Square

5

Toomkooli St.

Raamatukogu Square

6

Vaksali St.

Rahvakohtu St.

Tornide Square

Noukogude St.

12

Luhike Jalg

Pikk Jalg St.

Kohtu St.

10

Limuse St.

7

8

9

Voidu Square

Rataskaevu St.

13

Niguliste St.

Vana Tooma

26

Nooruse St.

Laboratooriumi St.

Kasperti St.

Rannavarava Hill

33

32

Harju St.

27

14

Raekoja Square

Pikk St.

Aida

Lai St.

25   24

Rannavarava Hill

Suur Karja

Sauna

Vene St.

17

15

16

Slade St.

Hobuse

18   19

28

20   21   23

Pikk St.

22

Parnu Highway

Valke Karja St.

Muurivahe St.

29

30

16. October Park

31

Valli

Viru St.

Uus St.

Estonia Blvd.

Viru Sq.

Mere Blvd.

Ujula St.

Rannamae St.

To:Kadriorg
Pirita
Singers Field

Hotel Viru

N

50

Key to Map 21

1. Toompea Small Fortress
2. "Tall Herman" Tower
3. Pilsticker Tower
4. Landskrone Tower
5. Church of Alexander Nevsky
6. Dome Church
7. Former Noble's House; City overlook terrace
8. Kohtu Street #12, City overlook terrace
9. Kohtu Street #8, Finance Ministry
10. Former Knighthood House
11. Former Commandant's House
12. Kiek in de Kok Tower, Branch of City Museum
13. St. Nicholas Church
14. Town Hall
15. Apothecary Shop
16. Holy Ghost Church
17. Great Guild Hall - Historical Museum
18. Black Head Brotherhood Hall
19. Former Noble's House
20. St. Olaf's Church
21. "Three Sisters" Medieval Houses
22. "Fat Margaret" Tower
23. Great Sea Gate
24. Medieval House - Museum of Natural Sciences
25. Medieval House
26. Church of the Transfiguration,
    in former St. Michael's Cistercian Abbey
27. "Bishop's House" medieval facade
28. City Museum
29. Former Dominican Monastery
30. St. Nikolai Orthodox Church
31. Opera and Theater Building
32. "Assauve" Tower - Theater and Music Museum
33. "House of Arts" Exhibit Hall

Tallinn, the capital of Soviet Estonia, is located on the Gulf of Finland 200 miles west of Leningrad. The city, which has a population of over 400,000, developed in the 11th century as a commercial center on the trade route from Scandinavia to Byzantium. The first written reference to the city was by the Arab geographer Abu Abdallah Mohammed Idrisi in 1154. In 1219 Tallinn was captured by the Danes, under whom its prosperity grew, especially after joining the Hanseatic league in 1284. Various pressures caused the Danes to sell the city to the Livonian Knights in 1346. The city's prosperous economy declined after Ivan III of Russia closed Novgorod's foreign trading offices in 1494, thereby cutting off Tallinn's eastern markets. The town was won by Sweden in 1561 during the Livonian War, and passed into Russian hands in 1710 during the Northern War. It remained part of the Russian Empire until 1918, when an independent Estonian State was established. In 1940 Estonia was incorporated into the Soviet Union.
[The name Tallinn (from "Taani linn" — "Danish city") became the official name of the city in 1926. Through the centuries Tallinn was known as Reval (in Danish) and Revel (in Russian).]

UPPER TOWN

TOOMPEA is the name given to the upper town, an eighteen-acre rocky hill 140 feet above the rest of the city. The oldest structure there is the *Small Fortress* (21-1), built by the Danes in the 13th century and remodeled by subsequent rulers. The fortress is rectangular in shape and originally had a tower at each corner. It fell into disuse after the Northern War (1700-1721) and was radically remodeled in 1767-1773 by Catherine the Great as the governor-general's headquarters. At that time the southeast tower and most of the east wall were demolished, and were replaced by a three-story administration building in a restrained late baroque style, designed by Johann Schultz. The structure now houses the Supreme Soviet and the Soviet of Ministers of the Estonian SSR.

The *Tall Hermann Tower* (21-2), at the southwest corner of the Small Fortress, dates from the 13th century, with additions in 1500. It is 155 feet tall, 30 feet in diameter, with walls nine feet thick.

The *Pilsticker Tower* (21-3), at the northwest corner, dates from the 13th century, but was extensively remodeled in the 19th century.

The *Landskrone Tower* (21-4), at the northeast corner, is 100 feet tall. These last two towers and the north wall are best viewed from the courtyard of the building at #13 Toomkooli Street.

Opposite the Small Fortress is the Russian Orthodox *Church of Alexander Nevsky* (**21**-5), designed by M. T. Preobrazhensky and built in 1894-1900.

The *Dome Church (Toomkirik)* (**21**-6), the main architectural attraction of the Upper Town, was founded in the 1200's, but acquired its present form after a fire in 1433. The baroque tower and spire were built in 1778-1779 by K. L. Geist. This three-nave Lutheran church is in the severe undecorated style typical of Tallinn Gothic architecture. The hanging pulpit (1686) and carved altar (1694-1696) were done by a local carver, Christian Ackermann. The altar, designed by the Swedish architect N. Tessin, contains a painting of the crucifixion (19th-century, by E. von Gebhardt), framed by Corinthian columns and statues of Peter and Paul. The church also contains numerous sarcophagi of important personages. The walls are partially hung with carved polychrome wood coats-of-arms.

Other notable buildings of the Upper Town include the former *Knighthood House* (**21**-10), built in 1840 in a renaissance style. The building, on Raamatakogu Square between Linnuse and Kohtu Streets, now houses the State Library.

The *home of a former Russian count* (**21**-7), at #3 Rahvakohtu Street, is a three-story building of neoclassical design with rusticated first floor, built 1784-1792 by architect J. C. Mohr.

Rahvakohtu #4, rebuilt after the fire of 1684, is a former noble's house. It is now the Estonian Meteorological Office.

Kohtu Street #8 (**21**-9) is a former home of the nobility, built in 1809-1814 by Engel and Janiken. The six-column portico of this building, which now houses the *Ministry of Finances*, looks out over Pikk Jalg Street. The building at #6 Kohtu is the Praesidium of the Estonian Academy of Sciences.

The former Commandant's House (**21**-11), at the corner of Toompea and Noukogude Streets, is an example of the 18th-century baroque style.

There are *observation terraces* providing an impressive view of the Lower Town at *Kohtu Street #12* (**21**-8). The terrace at Rahvakohtu #3 is also the beginning of the Patkuli Stairway which leads to the park below. This overlook has an excellent view of the harbor and the Gulf of Finland.

Until the 17th century Pikk Jalg Street was the only road leading to the Upper Town. The wall along the east side of the street was built in 1454 because of enmity between the nobles and townspeople. The rectangular gate-tower at the bottom of the street was built in 1380.

Luhike Jalg Street, the oldest foot access to the Upper Town, is the shortest way from Toompea to the main squares of the Lower Town.

LOWER TOWN

The Lower Town is the best preserved part of Old Tallinn. By the 15th century this area of 75 acres had been surrounded by a wall three miles long with 45 fortified towers. At present almost a mile of wall and 26 towers remain. The best preserved section is along Laboratooriumi Street between Vaksali and Lai Streets. Special note may be taken of the *Great Shore Gate* (**21**-23), 1518-1529, at the end of Pikk Street, with its carved coat-of-arms on the northern face, and the adjacent *Fat Margaret Tower* (**21**-22), 1510-1529, a squat defense tower 80 feet in diameter with walls 17 feet thick.

The *Kiek in de Kok ("Look into the kitchen") Tower* (**21**-12), at the south end of the old Town, is 160 feet tall, 58 feet in diameter. This six-story tower, built in 1475, now houses a branch of the City Museum. The basement and ground floors display tapestries, wall rugs, and artistic weavings of contemporary craftsmanship. The upper floors illustrate the history of the Tallinn fortress and the main historical events of 1219, 1560's-1570's, and the early 18th century.

TOWN HALL SQUARE (Raekoja Plats) is the center of the Lower Town. The Gothic *City Hall* (**21**-14), dating from the 14th century, was rebuilt in its present form in 1401-1404, and restored in 1959-1962. The building's original Gothic spire was rebuilt in a baroque style in the 1630's. Inside the open arcade on the street level are two carved stone panels, one representing winged Justice (1629) and the other the coat-of-arms of Tallinn supported by two griffins (1652).

The "Small Hall" on the second floor of the Town Hall contains a narrow fifty-foot carved wooden frieze (1667-1696) along the walls, and eight paintings done in 1667 by Johann Aken in the niches beneath the ceiling vaults.

In the northeast corner of the square is the *Magistrates Apothecary Shop* (**21**-15), in existence since before 1422. The building has been remodeled several times over the years, and in the 1960's was restored to its 17th-century appearance.

The short Saiakaik Lane leads from the Apothecary Shop to the intersection of Pikk and Sade Streets. At Sade Street #2 is the *Holy Ghost Church (Puhavaimu kirik)* (**21**-16). Founded in the 1200's, the church was rebuilt in 1375-1380 as a two-nave church with one central row of columns. The altar, at the end of the north nave, contains a carved triptych by the Lubeck master Berndt Notke, done in 1483. The central scene is a polychrome wood carving of the descent of the Holy Spirit onto the apostles. The side panels represent Saints Victor, Olaf, Anne, and Elizabeth. The fine polychrome carved pulpit was done by the Estonian Berndt Benniker in the late 1500's. The original Gothic spire of the church was replaced in the 1630's by a steeple in a form similar to that of the Town Hall. The only decoration on the exterior of the church is a wall clock carved by Christian Ackermann in 1684.

Across from the church, at Pikk Street #17, is the *Great Guild Hall* (**21**-17), which now houses the Estonian State Historical Museum. The Guild Hall, built in 1410, has an asymmetrical arrangement of three windows and door on the first floor. (The famous lion-head knockers are from 1430.) The mass of the tall gable is somewhat relieved by four narrow vertical niches and the placement of small windows. The large meeting hall inside the building is preserved with its three columns and eight cross-vaults, though the unity of the room is upset by the museum display cases. The museum exhibits early archeological finds; medieval weapons, armory, books; folk costumes, decorative arts, tools; and some political and industrial history of the country.

The building at Pikk Street #19 is a good example of an 18th-century town house in neoclassical style, with rusticated lower floor, cornice, and rich window frames on the second floor.

The building at Pikk Street #18 was remodeled in the "moderne" style in 1908 by I. Rosenbaum.

At Pikk Street #20 is the former Canute Guild Hall, rebuilt in 1863 in the English Gothic style.

The former *house of the Black Head Brotherhood* (**21**-18) is at Pikk Street #26. [The Black Heads, founded in 1399, were unmarried merchants and merchants' sons who, along with guild members, provided defense troops for the lower town. The name derives from their patron saint, St. Mauritius, who was from Egypt by birth and was iconographically represented as a Negro. The Brotherhood existed until 1940.] The facade of the building was remodeled in a renaissance style in 1597. The former Gothic gable was sculpted into volute forms and the windows were rearranged symmetrically, adding to the new horizontal emphasis of the facade. The arched entrance portal is flanked by highly rusticated pilasters supporting a cornice on which rests the coat-of-arms of the Brotherhood. The window frames of the first floor contain sculpture portraits of the Swedish-Polish king Sigismund and his wife, Anne of Austria, while the frieze between the first and second floors has the coats-of-arms of the Hanseatic league towns Bruges, Novgorod, London, and Bergen. The lower half of the gable has two symbolic reliefs representing Justice and Peace, and at the top of the gable is a representation of Christ.

When the Olaf Guild Hall, next door to the right, was taken over by the Black Head Brotherhood, its facade was remodeled, too. The Main Hall of the Olaf Guild, built in 1405-1422, is one of the best preserved gothic halls in the city, with two columns and elaborately articulated ceiling vaults.

At Pikk Street #28 is a *former noble's house* (**21**-19) built in the 1670's in a renaissance style, with a rusticated lower level supporting two-story Ionic pilasters. The strict symmetry of the facade is accentuated by the central pediment and second-story balcony.

At Pikk Street #71 are the so-called *"Three Sisters"* (**21**-21), three adjoining merchant houses of the 15th century. The building on the left has a pointed arch doorway (with a door carved in the 17th century), which was once flanked by large rectangular windows, but now reset with narrow pointed Gothic windows. The building has one of the most decorative gables in Tallinn, with elaborate overlapping niches. [Other typical 15th-century merchants' houses are found at *Lai Street #23* (**21**-25), *#29* (**21**-24), and *Niguliste Street #1* (**21**-27).]

St. Olaf's Church (Oleviste kirik) (**21**-20), #50 Lai Street, between Pikk and Lai Streets, was built in 1425-1470. The large apse, facing Pikk Street, has four columns supporting nine vaulted arches on the inside. The tremendous entrance tower on Lai Street supports the only Gothic spire preserved in Tallinn. The present spire, some 400 feet tall, was restored after a fire in 1820. That same fire destroyed the original interior of the church.

The St. Mary Chapel, or "Bremen Chapel," was built in 1523 to the south of the apse. Between two of the buttresses of the chapel is a carved stone cenotaph, 1513-1516, in memory of a local merchant. The carving consists of eight square reliefs on the subject of Christ's passion, two blocks of four reliefs on either side of an empty central niche. The top four reliefs were carved by Westphalian sculptor Heinrich Bildenscheider, and the bottom four by the Polish master Kliment.

At Nooruse Street #10, off Lai Street, are the remains of the *Cistercian Saint Michael's Convent* (**21**-26) (13th century), an ensemble which has been almost totally rebuilt and adapted to other uses. The main church was rebuilt in 1732 as the Russian Orthodox *Cathedral of the Transfiguration* (further remodeled in 1827-1830). Its main attraction is a baroque iconostasis of 1720 designed by the Moscow architect I. P. Zarudny.

The *St. Nicholas Church (Niguliste kirik)* (**21**-13) at Rataskaevu St. #11, is the only architectural monument of the Lower Town to suffer severe damage during the Second World War. Founded in the 1200's, but given its present form in the 1400's, St. Nicholas's is a three-nave Gothic church with a large apse the width of the building. The Chapel of St. Anthony, with a tall gable, was built to the south of the entrance tower in 1488-1492. There are two chapels flanking the central north portal. The northeast Chapel of A. Klodt was built in 1673 in a baroque style. The northwest Chapel of P. G. Gelstein-Bek was built in 1775 in the neoclassic style. The northern entrance was redone in baroque style in 1674-1677. The church is being restored and will house a museum.

The *Theater and Music Museum* (**21**-32) is in a section of the old fortification wall at Muurivahe Street #12. The third floor display has pianos, organs, and music boxes, some of which are still operating. Folk instruments produced in Estonia in the 18th and 19th centuries include lutes, zithers, flutes and herd horns.

The *City Museum* (**21**-28), at Vene Street #17, is in the former home of a rich merchant. The building has a carved entrance portal and a well-preserved vestibule with an octagonal column supporting the ceiling. The collection is exhibited on four floors of the house, and contains decorative and applied arts of Tallinn's past: furniture, clothing, engravings, as well as a display of Tallinn under Soviet power. The upper two floors exhibit Estonian glass and crystal of the 1960's and 1970's.

At Vene Street #24 is the *St. Nikolai Orthodox Church* (*Nikolai kirik*) (**21**-30), 1822-1827, designed by Luigi Rusca. This neoclassic church has a four-column pediment, broad dome on a high drum, and twin bell towers. The St. Nikolai Church was the first domed structure in Tallinn.

Behind the houses at Vene Street #12-18 is the *site of the former Dominican Monastery* (**21**-29) which was destroyed in 1531. Part of the western facade and portal of the former Catherine Church can be seen from the courtyard of #12 Vene. The courtyard of #18 Vene leads to a restored gallery and courtyard which now house a branch of the City Museum displaying carved stone and architectural ornaments of the 15th-17th centuries.

OUTSKIRTS OF TALLINN

The *Kadriorg Park Ensemble* (outside of Map **21**) is at the eastern edge of the central city. In 1714 Peter the First of Russia acquired land here and constructed a small house. In 1718-1723 he had a palace built, designed by Nicolo Michetti and M. Zemtsov, two architects who were building Peter's summer palace near Petersburg at the same time. The palace was the residence of the president of the Estonian Republic, 1918-1940, and has housed the *Estonian National Art Museum* since 1946.

Between the park and the shore is the "Rusalka" monument, 1902, erected in memory of sailors lost in the sinking of the battleship "Rusalka" in 1893. The figure of an angel holding a cross, on a tall stone base, was sculpted by Amandus Adamson.

The *Pirita Cloister* (or St. Birgit's Monastery), built in 1407-1436, is located four miles to the east of the center of town. The convent was destroyed in 1577 during the Livonian War. Only the walls of this huge church (80 x 184 feet) remain.

A mile beyond Pirita is the Forest Cemetery where simple stone slabs along wooded paths mark the graves of honored Estonians.

The *Singers Field* and Music Shell are in the same eastern area of the city. The tradition of Estonian song festivals goes back to 1869. The first singing festival on this site was held in 1928, and the present amphitheater was built in 1960. The shell-pavilion can hold a chorus of thousands, and the hillside amphitheater facing the shell can accommodate several hundred thousand spectators.

Seven miles west of Tallinn on the coast is the **ROCCA-AL-MARE** open-air Ethnographic Museum (Map **22**) where wooden peasant structures from various sections of the country have been assembled. Interest in open-air ethnological museums developed in Scandinavia in the late 19th century, and exhibits were opened in Sweden in 1891, Norway in 1897, Denmark in 1901, Finland in 1909, and Latvia in 1924. Similar interest grew in Estonia in the 1920's and 1930's, but planning was interrupted by the war and change in the government. In 1957 land was granted at Rocca-al-Mare, and the moving of structures to the area began. The exhibits are divided into four sections — West, North, South Estonia, and the islands. Generally, each exhibit area is a farmstead group with living and service buildings, and fences. By the mid-1970's about half of the projected 100 structures had been moved to the park, along with 7,000 pieces of furniture, clothing, utensils, tools, etc.

The notes that follow describe some of the highlights of the exhibits. The numbers are keyed to the plan.

22-1. *Sassi-Jaani Farmstead*, from western Estonia, late 1700's. This group consists of a House-threshing barn, a Storage barn, and an Animal shed, arranged around a court with a well in the center, and surrounded by a slanted slat fence typical of western Estonia. The House-threshing barn (**22**-1a), moved here in 1959, is 90 feet long and 32 feet deep, with low log walls and a tall thatch roof. The entrance room, living room, and a dirt-floored storeroom, also with a bed, occupy the right-hand half of the building. To the left is the grain threshing and drying room. The living room has a stone floor and a small stove for drying grain and cooking. The family bathed in this room, and slept here in cold weather.

The Barn (**22**-1b), moved here in 1960, has four rooms of equal size for storage of clothes (and summer sleeping), meat, grain, and tools and carts. The Animal shed (**22**-1c) has four rooms reached from a large central room. About 15 people lived on such a farmstead.

22-2. The *Kostriaseme Farmstead*, also from western Estonia, dates from the later 1800's. The ensemble includes a House-threshing barn, a Shed, Barn, and Summer kitchen. The buildings are smaller than those of a century before, and about 10 people would live on such a farmstead. A fence divides the living areas from the animal areas.

The House-threshing barn (**22**-2a), moved here in 1960, consists of six rooms. To the right of the entrance and central room with stove are two storeroom-bedrooms, with wooden floors, large windows, and whitewashed walls. The front room has a loom, bed, table, chairs, etc.

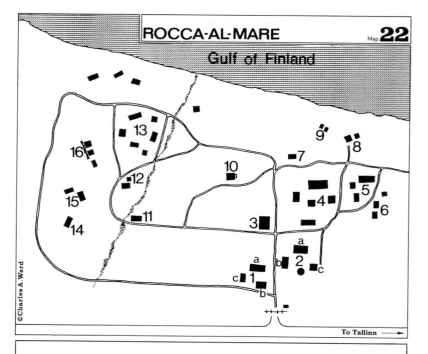

Gulf of Finland

©Charles A. Ward

To Tallinn →

1. Sassi-Jani Farmstead
2. Köstriaseme Farmstead
3. Village Inn, Northern Estonia
4. Pulga Tenant-Farmstead
5. Kutsari Farmstead
6. Northern Estonian Farm, mid 1800's
7. Wind Mill, Western Estonia
8. Fisherman Huts, late 1800's
9. Net Sheds
10. Sutlepa Chapel, 17th Century
11. Water Mill, Northern Estonia
12. Poor Man's Farm, 19th Century
13. Peasant Farmstead, Is. of Saaremaa
14. Poor Man's Farm, Southern Estonia, 1800's
15. Farm from Southeast Estonia, late 1800's
16. Island Windmills
17. Net Sheds, from islands
18. Windmill

The back room was where the master and his wife slept. The central room has a stove for drying grain and cooking. The room was also used as a dining room and for bathing. There was no chimney and the smoke went out the door.

The Barn (**22**-2b), brought here in 1964, has one room and was used for storing clothing and woven materials. The Summer kitchen is a wooden teepee with a stone base. The Shed (**22**-2c) has four rooms for horses, sheep, cows, and pigs.

22-4. The *Pulga Tenant-Farmstead*, from northern Estonia, later 1800's, has a house, barn, shed, smithy, and hay barn. The four-room House-threshing barn (**22**-4a), 1860, was moved here in 1961. The living area is of wood; the threshing area, on the right, has limestone walls. The Barn has two rooms, for storage of clothing as well as grain. The Smithy (early 1700's), a small rectangular building with walls and roof of flat limestone slabs, was brought here in 1964. The four-room Shed housed cows, pigs, sheep, and a grain storeroom. The lower wall is of limestone, and upper wall of wood beams. The Hay barn is a small log cabin with thatched roof.

22-5. The *Kutsari Farmstead*, from northern Estonia, 1891, was moved here in 1960. The House-threshing barn is the most well-built in the park. The drying room was used as a workroom or storeroom at various times of the year. The living rooms are at the right-hand end of the house, with large windows. There is a separate kitchen room with its own stove and with a chimney. The living end of the building is of wood, and the threshing-room end of limestone.

The Barn has four rooms, with grain and clothing storage rooms to the left, and milk and other foodstuffs on the right. The Shed has two rooms for livestock and one for food storage. There is also a Bathhouse, a two-room structure.

22-8-9. Near the shore of the gulf is a small *fisherman's hut* and an outbuilding, from northern areas. Soon an animal shed and smokehouse will be added. Nearby are two small sheds for net storage.

22-11. On an artificial pond in the center of the park is a *Water Mill*, late 1800's, a two-story building of limestone and wood, with an undershot waterwheel.

22-13. The *Peasant Farmstead* from the island of Saaremaa, ca. 1800, has six buildings, a House-threshing barn, Summer kitchen-smithy, Barn, Animal shed, Bathhouse, and Chapel. The chapel, 1780, has the same rectangular shape as the other buildings, and contains several rooms.

KIEV
UKRAINE

Georgievsky Cathedral: Kiev

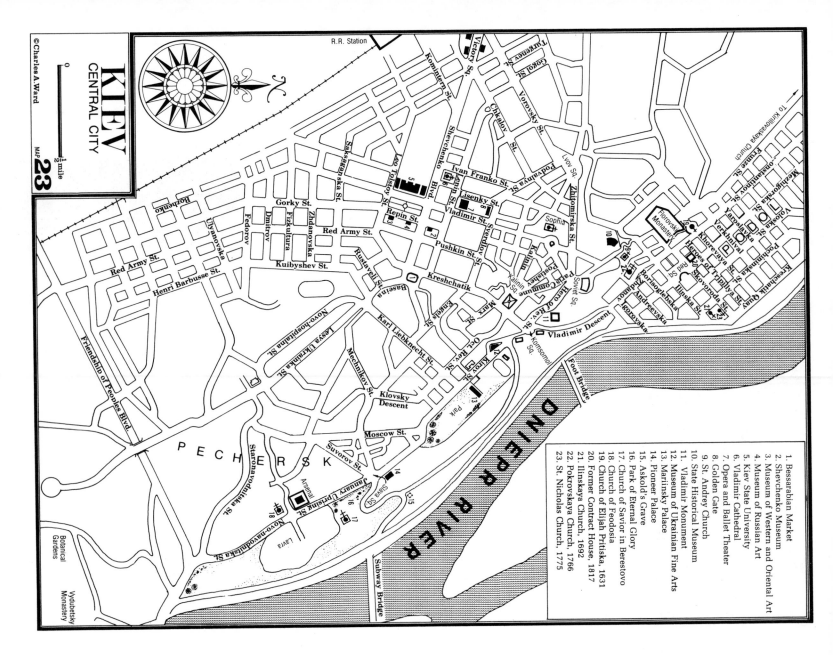

KIEV
CENTRAL CITY

MAP
23

0   ½   mile

R.R. Station

Victory Sq.
Turrenev St.
Gogol St.
Komintern St.
Shevchenko Blvd.
Chkalov St.
Vorovsky St.
Podvyna St.
Lvov Sq.
Zhitomirska St.
To Kirillovskaya Church
France St.
Mezhigorska St.
Konstantinov St.
Voloska St.
Bozhenko
Saksaganska St.
Leo Tolstoy St.
Ivan Franko St.
Lisenky St.
Lenin St.
Vladimir St.
Sverdlov St.
Sophia
Yaroslaviv Val
Verkhniva
Khorevaya
Pochtinska St.
Yaroslavska St.
Gorky St.
Repin St.
Fizkultura
Zhdanovska
Dmitrov
Fedorov
Ulyanovska
Red Army St.
Pushkin St.
Kalinin
Pariz Commune St.
Heroes of Triphily
Heroes of Kiev
Borisoglebska
Ilinska St.
Krasnaya Sq.
Krechatik Quay
Andreevska
Red Army St.
Henri Barbusse St.
Kuibyshev St.
Rustaveli St.
Baseina
Kreshchatik
Engels St.
Marx St.
Hero of Kiev St.
Soviet Sq.
Goroda Sq.
Gorovska
Novo-hospitalna St.
Lesya Ukrainka St.
Karl Liebknecht St.
Oct. Rev. St.
Vladimir Descent
Komsomol Sq.
Mechnikov St.
Kirov St.
Foot Bridge
Klovsky Descent
Park
PECHERSK
Staronavoitska St.
Moscow St.
Suvorov St.
Novo-navoditska St.
January Uprising St.
Arsenal
Slavs St.
DNIEPR RIVER
Friendship of Peoples Blvd.
Botanical Gardens
Vydubetsky Monastery
Lavra
Subway Bridge

1. Bessarabian Market
2. Shevchenko Museum
3. Museum of Western and Oriental Art
4. Museum of Russian Art
5. Kiev State University
6. Vladimir Cathedral
7. Opera and Ballet Theater
8. Golden Gate
9. St. Andrey Church
10. State Historical Museum
11. Vladimir Monument
12. Museum of Ukrainian Fine Arts
13. Mariinsky Palace
14. Pioneer Palace
15. Askold's Grave
16. Park of Eternal Glory
17. Church of Savior in Berestovo
18. Church of Feodosia
19. Church of Elijah Pritiska, 1631
20. Former Contract House, 1817
21. Ilinskaya Church, 1692
22. Pokrovskaya Church, 1766
23. St. Nicholas Church, 1775

KIEV
(Map 23)

Kiev, the capital of the Soviet Ukraine, is located on the Dniepr River 450 miles south-west of Moscow. This city of 2 million is the third largest city in the Soviet Union.

In the 8th century Kiev arose as a trading center on the "water road" between Scandinavia and Byzantium. The city became the capital of ancient Russia in 882 and soon developed into a prosperous town. After prince Vladimir adopted Eastern Orthodoxy as the state religion in 988, cultural ties with Byzantium grew, and the arts, architecture, and learning flourished in Kiev. After the death in 1504 of Vladimir's son Yaroslav, internecine feuds developed and sapped the city's strength. In 1240 the Mongol invasions brought an end to the early period of Kievan history.

Kiev was freed from the Mongols by the Lithuanian prince Gedimin in 1320, and remained in the Polish-Lithuanian state until ceded to Russia in 1686. In the 19th century Kiev began to grow as a provincial administrative center of the Russian Empire, and along with the rest of the Ukraine it was taken into the Soviet Union in 1921. In 1934 the capital of the Soviet Ukraine was moved to Kiev from Kharkov.

Kiev was called the "mother of Russian cities" because of its age, its position of power on the trade routes, and the cultural flourishing that came from its ties with Byantium. Kiev, and particularly its Cave Monastery, became the cradle of Old Russian literature and of one of the early schools of icon painting. The basic types of churches which were later built throughout Russia were first seen here — the large five-aisle St. Sophia, basically a Byzantine type, was later imitated in Novgorod; the six-pier, three-aisle church, first represented by the Assumption Church, 1037, of the Cave Monastery, became the model for large princely churches in Novgorod, Vladimir, and Moscow; the four-pier central plan church so widespread in Russia was first constructed in Kiev. The Trinity Church of the Cave Monastery was an early example of a church built over a gateway, a type often found in monasteries, particularly in Muscovite Russia. All the Kievan churches were rebuilt after the 16th century and none retain their original 12th-century appearance.

By the 11th century Kiev was developing in three sections. The upper city, Staro-Kiev, residence of the princes, was on a hill overlooking the Dniepr. The lower city, Podol, home of merchants and craftsmen, was along the river below the upper town. The third section, Pechersk, was two miles down river in the area of the Cave Monastery. In the 19th century the administrative center of the city developed along the newly created Kreshchatik Street.

The description of the city given below follows the main streets and sites of Kiev.

ALONG KRESHCHATIK STREET

Kreshchatik Street begins at *Komsomol Square*. This square is bounded by the *State Library* (#1 Kirov St.), built in 1911 by E. L. Klave and rebuilt in 1954; the *Philharmonic Society* (#2 Vladimir Descent), built in 1882 by V. M. Nikolaev as the Merchant's Assembly Building; and the *Dniepr Hotel* (#1 Komsomol Square), completed in 1964.

The first street on the left off Kreshchatik is October Revolution Street. Uphill on the right, at #4 October Revolution, is the tall *Moscow Hotel* (1961) which faces Kreshchatik. Across from it, at #1 October Revolution, is the *"October Palace of Culture"*, built in 1838-1842 by V. Beretti as a school for girls of the nobility. It was reconstructed with many changes in 1951-1957.

The second street on the left off Kreshchatik is Karl Marx St., which leads to *Ivan Franko Square* and the *Franko Drama Theater*. At the corner of Marx and Kreshchatik is the *Tchaikovsky Conservatory* (1955-1958). There is a *souvenir-gift store* at Marx Street #9.

On Kreschchatik beyond Marx Street are two large buildings housing the *Arcade shops* and *Children's store*, #13 and #17 Kreshchatik.

On the right-hand side of Kreshchatik, across from the Moscow Hotel, is *Kalinin Square*. The grassy area in the square is where the City Hall stood until 1943. The *Kiev Central Post Office* is on the corner of Kreshchatik.

Two blocks down Kreshchatik, at the corner of Lenin Street, is the *Central Department Store*. There is a *souvenir shop* at Lenin St. #12.

Kreshchatik becomes Red Army Street at Shevchenko Boulevard. On the left at this intersection is the *Bessarabian Market* (23-1) covered farmer's market designed by Bobrusov and Gay and built in 1910.

ALONG SHEVCHENKO BOULEVARD

The boulevard was laid out in 1837 during the expansion of Kiev. The *Shevchenko State Museum* (23-2), established in 1949 in memory of the 19th-century serf-poet and painter Taras Shevchenko, is at #12 Shevchenko Blvd. The museum contains documents on Shevchenko's life, examples of his paintings, and editions of his poetry.

The *Vladimir Cathedral* (23-6), at #20 Shevchenko Blvd., was built in 1862-1896 to commemorate the 900th anniversary of the conversion of Russia to Christianity. The design, in an eclectic pseudo-Byzantine style, was worked on by architects I. Storm, P. Sparro, and A. V. Beretti. The interior decoration was designed by A. Prakhov, an art history professor at Kiev University. Notable are the "Madonna and Child," "Last Judgment" (above the west door), and "Head of Christ" (inside the main dome) by V. Vasnetsov, and icons by Mikhail Nesterov, especially his "Boris and Gleb" and "Olga." The church is 155 ft. long,

90 ft. wide, and 160 ft. to the top of the dome.

Shevchenko Blvd. leads downhill to *Victory Square*, location of the Kiev Circus (1960), the *Hotel "Libid,"* and the *"Ukraina" Department Store.*

On the short Repin Street, which crosses Shevchenko Blvd., are some of the major art museums of Kiev. The *Museum of Russian Art* (**23**-4) #9 Repin St., displays works from the 13th century to the present. Notable icons include "Boris and Gleb" of the Novgorod School and "John the Baptist" by Ushakov. Painters of the 19th century represented include Ivanov, Tropin and Fedotov; Kramskoy, Perov, and Makovsky of the "Peredvizhniki" school; Gue, Repin, Vereshchagin, and Shishkin; landscapes by Levitan, Polenov, and Aivazovsky. There are many paintings by Mikhail Vrubel, including his sketches for proposed murals for the Vladimir Cathedral. Turn-of-the-century art is represented by canvases of Surikov, Vasnetsov, Serov, Nesterov, Korovin, Rorich, Benois, and Kustodiev.

The *Museum of Western and Oriental Art* (**23**-3), is at #15 Repin Street. Its collection includes Greek and Roman art from Black Sea towns. The Italian School is represented by Bellini, Perugino, Giordano, Tiepolo, and others. Netherlands and Flemish Schools: Brueghel the Elder, Hals, Jordaens, Rubens. Spanish School: Velasquez, Zurbaran, Goya. The Oriental section includes works from Egypt, China, Japan, and Central Asia.

ALONG VLADIMIR STREET

Vladimir Street was laid out in 1837 at the same time as Shevchenko Boulevard. Across from the museums on Repin Street is the *Kiev State University* (**23**-5) #60 Vladimir St., designed by V. I. Beretti and completed in 1842. It was destroyed during the Second World War and rebuilt in its original form in 1950. The building is flanked by the *library of the Ukrainian Academy of Sciences* (#62 Vladimir) and by the University Library.

The *Ukrainian Academy of Sciences* (#54 Vladimir St.) is in a building constructed in the 1850's by A. V. Beretti to house the Lavashevoy Pension.

The *Lenin Museum, Kiev Branch* (#57 Vladimir) is in a building constructed in 1911-1913 (architect P. F. Aleshin) to house a Pedagogical Institute.

The *Ukrainian Academy of Sciences Institutes Building* (at #55 Vladimir St.) was built in 1927 by Aleshin in a neoclassical style.

Across Lenin Street at #50 Vladimir is the *Shevchenko State Opera House* (**23**-7), 1898-1901 by V. Schretter. In front of it, to the north, is a *statue* (1965) *of N. Lisenko*, founder of Ukrainian classical music. At the end of the block, on Podvalnya Street, are the remains of the *Golden Gate* (**23**-8) dating from 1037, once the southwest boundary of Old Kiev. The gate suffered only slight damage in the Mongol invasion of 1240 and was used until the mid-1600's. In 1750 its remains were buried by the government as a preservation measure. It was unearthed in 1832 and reinforced in 1837-1838.

SOPHIA CATHEDRAL PRESERVE, #24 Vladimir Street (Map 24)

The *Sophia Cathedral* (**24**-1) was built in the 1030's-1040's by Yaroslav the Wise on the purported site of a military victory of his in 1036. The church, left in ruins and abandoned after the sacking of Kiev by the Mongols in 1240, was rebuilt only after the union of the Ukraine with Russia in the late 17th century. The original lines of the church were greatly altered then, as the number of domes was increased from the original 13 to 19, a second story added to the outside galleries, and architectural detail redone in the Ukrainian baroque style. A model on display inside the church shows a reconstruction of Sophia in its original Byzantine style. Some areas on the outside of the apses have been cleared of later stucco to reveal the original brick wall structure.

The church was originally cross-plan with five aisles. The closed-in arcade galleries make it, in effect, a seven-aisle church. The present dimensions are 180 feet wide, 120 feet deep, and 130 feet to the top of the dome.

The interior of the church is decorated with mosaics and frescoes from the 11th century. The most notable mosaics are the Christ Pantocrator in the main dome, St. Mark on the pendentive of the southwest pier, the three small medallions of Mary, Christ, and John the Baptist above the apse, and the Virgin with uplifted arms in the apse. Beneath her are the apostles at the Eucharist, and below them, ten figures of holy men and archdeacons.

The original frescoes are preserved, but are very faint, having been damaged, painted over, and cleaned. Frescoes in the central part of the church portray various saints, apostles, and Yaroslav's family. The frescoes of the stairways to the choir are interesting for their secular subject matter (princes, judges, hunting scenes, musicians, and so forth).

In the 18th century Metropolitan Rafail Zaborovsky had the church remodeled and had a new baroque iconostasis made (1744-1748) under the artistic direction of architect Schaedel. Schaedel also rebuilt the *Bell Tower* (**24**-2), which was originally constructed in 1697-1707 to replace a wooden one which burned. The exterior of the Bell Tower is done in high-relief stucco figures. The fourth tier and cupola were added in 1853 by architect P. Sparro. The tower is 250 feet tall.

The *Zaborovsky Gate* (**24**-8), noted for its stucco decoration, faces on Streletsky Lane and can be approached only from the outside of the church compound. It was designed by Schaedel and built in 1748. The present level of the sidewalk, 5.5 feet higher than in the 18th century, upsets the proportions of the gate.

The *Refectory* (**24**-3) was built in 1722-1730. In 1822 it was converted into a winter (heated) church, sometimes called the "Warm Sophia."

The *Metropolitan's Residence* (**24**-4) was built in three stages between 1722-1753.

The former *Sophia Seminary* (**24**-5), 1763-1767, a two-story masonry structure, has housed the Central Historical Archives of the Ukrainian SSR since 1921.

Opposite the entrance of the Sophia Preserve is *Bohdan Khmelnitsky Square*. In the center of the square is an *equestrian statue of Khmelnitsky* (**24**-9), a 17th-century Cossack leader, done in the 1870's by M. O. Mikeshin, and unveiled in 1888.

On the embankment overlooking the Dniepr south of Soviet Square is the *Vladimir Monument* (**23**-11), 1853, designed by V. Demut-Malinovsky and K. Thon. The 50-foot tall base in pseudo-Byzantine style supports a 14-foot bronze statue of Vladimir holding a cross (sculpture done by P. Klodt). A bronze bas-relief panel on the pedestal depicts the christening of the Russian people. The monument was restored in 1953.

St. Andrey Church (**23**-9), at the end of Vladimir Street, was designed by Rastrelli and built in 1747-1753. The church is harmonious and refined and is one of the few small-scale works by Rastrelli which have survived. The vertical emphasis of the paired Corinthian pilasters of the exterior is repeated on the iconostasis inside. The icons are of the 18th century. The capitals of the columns and figured details of the exterior were being regilded in 1976.

The *State Historical Museum* (**23**-10) is opposite the Andrey Church, at #2 Vladimir Street.

THE PODOL

The Podol, which extends along the river below the Andrey Church, was the commercial center of Old Kiev. Since it lacked adequate defence, no architecture before the 17th century has survived.

The oldest architectural monument is the *Church of Elijah Pritiska* (**23**-19) (#5 Khorevaya St.), built in 1631. It is a one-dome cross-plan church with a severe, monumental exterior.

Red Square is the center of the Podol. At the east end of the square and extending along G. Skovoroda Street are the walls of the former *Bogoyavlensky Monastery*. The wall facing the square has plaques to the 18th-century Russian scientist and writer, Lomonosov, and the Ukrainian thinker, Skovoroda. The monastery was the home of the Kiev

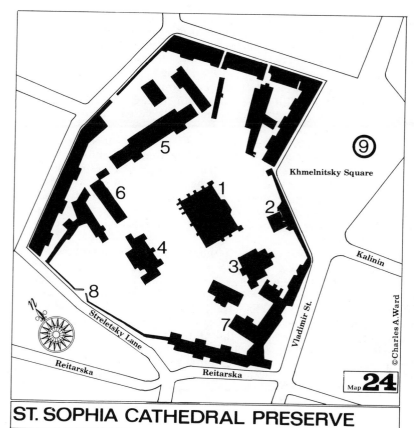

ST. SOPHIA CATHEDRAL PRESERVE

Map **24**

©Charles A. Ward

1. Sophia Cathedral
2. Bell Tower
3. Refectory Church ("Warm Sophia")
4. Metropolitan's Residence
5. Former Seminary
6. Monk's Building
7. Consistory
8. Zaborovsky Gates
9. Monument to Bohdan Khmelnitsky

Brother's Academy in the 18th and 19th centuries. The west side of the square has the decrepit buildings of the *former Gostiny Ryad shopping area*. The north side of the square is formed by the former *Contract House*, (23-20), 1815-1817 by V. Geste, a two-story neoclassic building with rusticated lower floor and Doric porticoes.

The *Ilinskaya Church* (23-21) (#2 Pochaininska Street), is a simple three-section church built by a merchant in 1692. Outside the church there is an interesting 18th-century gate with paired columns, open pediment, and iron railings.

The *Voznesensky Cathedral* of the *Florovsky Monastery*, #5 Georgy Liver Street, was built in a severe monumental style in 1732. The original interior has not survived and the present paintings are of poor artistic value. Just to the west is the *Refectory Church*, 18th century, with an interesting apse and cupola which are difficult to see when the leaves are on the trees. There is also a *Rotunda Church* of 1824. It and the Bell Tower near the entrance to the monastery were designed by A. Melensky.

The main architect working in the Podol in the 18th century was Ivan Grigorovich-Barsky. His *Pokrovskaya Church of 1766*, (23-22), (#5 Zelinska Street, just below Andrey Church) shows him at his best. The church reveals a forceful exterior treatment with marked vertical emphasis. The apse and side chapels are topped by an elevated "wing" roof line, an interesting baroque effect which reflects the same device used by Rastrelli on the apse of the Andrey Church above.

The *St. Nicholas Church*, (23-23), (#12 Skovoroda Street) was built by Grigorovich-Barsky in 1775. It is unlike most Ukrainian churches in that, though cross-plan, it has a very short transcept which ends in shallow rectangular chapels. Its tall external silhouette is accented by paired Corinthian pilasters, deep-set windows, and formidable cupola.

On July 8, 1811, a fire destroyed all wooden structures in the Podol. Even masonry churches suffered interior damage. After the fire a new street plan by V. Geste was adopted, resulting in the present grid pattern fitting around the stone buildings which survived the fire. The Contract House was the first major building after the fire.

PECHERSK

Pechersk ("Caves") got its name from the Cave Monastery located on the bank of the Dniepr 1.5 miles south of Kreshchatik. *Kirov Street* is the main road running south to Pechersk.

#1 Kirov, at Komsomol Square, is the *State Library*, 1911 by Klave, rebuilt in 1954.

#3 Kirov St. is the *"Dynamo" Stadium* and sports complex.

#6 Kirov St. is the *Museum of Ukrainian Fine Arts* (23-12), 1900 by Boitsov and Gorodetsky, built as a museum of Antiquities and Art. The present collection of Ukrainian fine arts opened in 1936 and contains works of artists from the 15th century through the Soviet period.

#12 Kirov St. is the *Council of Ministers Building*, 1935-1938 by Fomin and Abrosimov.

#5 Kirov St. is the *Building of the Supreme Soviet*, 1936-1938 by Zabolotny (across from the Ministers Building).

Also at #5 Kirov St., behind the Soviet, is the *Mariinsky Palace* (23-13), 1750-1755 by Rastrelli. The upper floor burned in 1819 and was rebuilt only in 1870. The palace was destroyed in the war and restored in 1945-1949.

Opposite the palace is *Soviet Park* (between Kirov St. and the river), which contains several monuments to heroes of the revolution and the Second World War. The 15-foot grey granite statue to General Nikolai Vatutin (who died in 1944 liberating Kiev) was done by sculptor Vuchetich in 1947.

Kirov Street is continued by January Uprising Street, which leads to Slava Square. On the left at Slava Square is the *Pioneers Palace* (23-14), (various architects, 1965), and across the Dniepr Descent is the *Park of Eternal Glory* (23-16), with an obelisk and eternal flame marking the tomb of the unknown soldier.

Between the Pioneers Palace and the river is *Askold's Tomb* (23-15) a stone rotunda built in 1810, and reconstructed in 1935, on the purported site of the grave of one of the founders of Kiev.

CAVE MONASTERY (KIEVO-PECHERSKA LAVRA), #21 January Uprising St., (Map 25)

The monastery, founded in the eleventh century, is divided into the Upper Lavra, and two groups of caves, or catacombs, further down the river bank. The monastery was the most important center of Old Russian culture. It was here that the Primary Chronicle was written by the monk Nestor, who is buried in the Near Caves. The monastery later housed the first printing press in the Ukraine. In 1926 the Monastery was made into a national monument.

The monastery is entered from January Uprising Street through a passageway beneath the *Trinity Church over-the-gates* (25-2). Built in 1108, this church was remodeled in the Ukrainian baroque style in 1722-1728. It was at this time that the frescoes on the exterior walls were added. The church contains an elaborate carved, gilded iconostasis of the 18th century.

The monastery received much of its present appearance between 1690-1702 with the building of the defense walls, the All-Saints Church, the Nicholas Hospital Church, monks cells, and the churches in the cave areas. The *Monks Cells* (25-3 and 4) on each side of the entrance roadway were done in 1720-1721 and were restored in 1945-1947.

The *St. Nicholas Hospital Church* (**25**-5), 1702, a small church with simple exterior in the same style as the nearby monks' cells, is distinguished by its blue dome with gold stars. It was restored after World War Two.

The *All Saints Church* (**25**-7), over the "Economic" Gates, 1696-1698, is one of the best examples of Ukrainian baroque architecture in Kiev. It should be viewed from both inside and outside the monastery. An open arcade gallery leads to the stairway to the church above. Its frescoes were done in 1906.

On April 22, 1718, in a terrible fire, all wooden structures in the Lavra were destroyed, along with the library, iconostases in some churches, and other flammable church treasures. The monastery was reconstructed in 1720-1729.

The *Bell Tower* (**25**-8), was built in 1731-1744 by Schaedel, to replace wooden belfries burned in the fire. It is 300 feet tall, and is built in three tiers marked by differing groupings of columns and other architectural detail. It was restored in 1961.

Opposite the belfry are the *ruins of the Assumption Cathedral* (**25**-6), built in 1073, the largest and most important church in the monastery. It was blown up by the Nazis in 1941. Just to the south of the ruins is the *Refectory Church* (**25**-12), 1893-1895 by V. Nikolaev in an eclectic style. The two-story church is topped by a hemispherical dome 70 feet in diameter, and five small gilt domes. The church was frescoed in the 20th century to designs by Shchusev, and still contains a carved marble iconostasis. To the west of the church is the Refectory hall.

To the west of the Refectory is the former Metropolitan's Residence, now a *Museum of Ukrainian Decorative Folk Art* (**25**-11). The Refectory itself has an exhibition of "Christianity and Atheism in the Ukraine." The former Typography Building on the east side of the central square houses a *Museum of Books and Printing in the Ukraine* (**25**-10). The *Kovnir Corpus* (**25**-9), which adjoins the Typography building from the north, houses a Museum of Valuables and Church Treasures.

The *Near Caves* (**25**-13), or Caves of St. Anthony, are a series of excavations along a main passage 730 feet long. They contain the remains of 73 monks. Some of the bodies were preserved without decomposition because of the chemical properties of the soil and the uniform temperature in the caves. Other graves contain only skeletons or partial skeletons. The above-ground ensemble of the Near Caves includes the *Church of the Raising of the Cross* (**25**-15), 1700, in a style similar to the Ilinskaya Church in the Podol, a one-story *Refectory* (**25**-14), adjoining, and a two-story cell block of the 19th century, with a four-column portico entrance. This cell building serves as the entrance to the caves.

The *Far Caves*, or *Caves of St. Theodosius*, (**25**-16), are reached by a covered walkway from the square in front of the Cells of the Near Caves. The building opposite the end of the walkway to the Lower Caves is the

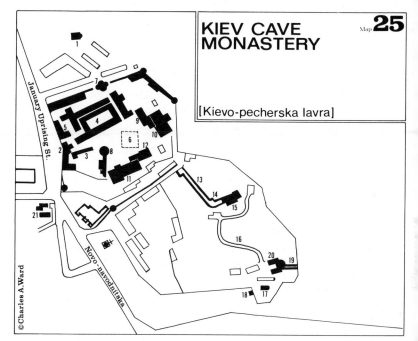

KIEV CAVE MONASTERY

Map **25**

[Kievo-pecherska lavra]

©Charles A. Ward

1. Church of the Savior in Berestovo
2. Trinity Church "over the gates" (Entrance to Monastery)
3. Monks cells, Exhibit of metal artifacts
4. Monks cells
5. St. Nicholas Hospital Church
6. Ruins of Assumption Cathedral
7. All-saints Church over "Economic Gates"
8. Bell Tower
9. Kovnir Corpus, Museum of Valuables and Church Treasures
10. Typography Bldg., Museum of Books and Printing
11. Metropolitan's Residence; Museum of Folk Arts
12. Refectory and Church, Exhibit of Christianity and Atheism in the Ukraine
13. Passage to (near) Caves of St. Anthony
14. Refectory (entrance to near caves)
15. Church of the Raising of the Cross
16. Passage to (far) Caves of St. Theodosius
17. Church of Nativity of the Virgin
18. Bell Tower of Far Caves
19. Church of Joachim and Anna
20. Church of Anna (entrance to far caves)
21. Church of Theodosius

Church of the Nativity of the Virgin, (**25**-17), 1696, a three-dome, three-section church which was later remodeled with the addition of corner towers each topped by a gilded dome. The seven domes of the church rise in a pyramidal form and provide a continually changing harmony as the observer walks around the church. In front of the church is an arcade designed by Schaedel in 1745. Just to the west is the *Bell Tower*, (**25**-18), 1754-1761, designed by Grigorovich-Barsky. Downhill, at the eastern end of the area, is the *Church of Joachim and Anna* (**25**-19) from the 1500's, but greatly altered over the centuries. To the north is the one-dome *Church of the Conception of Anna* (**25**-20), 1679, reconstructed in 1810-1819. This church serves as the entrance to the lower caves.

Just south of the Upper Lavra, at #25 January Uprising Street, is the *Resurrection Church*. Across the street is the *Feodosia Church* (**23**-18), a good example of late 17th-century Ukrainian architecture.

A short walk to the north of the "Economic" Gates of the monastery is the stone *Church of the Savior of Berestovo* (**23**-17), built in the early 1100's by prince Vladimir Monomakh. Prince Yury Dolgoruky, the founder of Moscow, was buried there in 1158. His black granite tomb is in the north section of the church. The church was largely destroyed by the Mongols and was rebuilt in the 1640's as a small cross-plan church with no columns. The attached belfry of 1813 was designed by Melensky.

A mile south of the Cave Monastery are the extensive *Botanical Gardens*. On the grounds of the Gardens are the remains of the *Vidubetsky Monastery*, which was founded in 1070. The oldest structure is the St. Michael Church, 1070-1088, originally a large eight-column church. Most of it washed into the Dniepr during a flood in the 16th century, and the part that remained was made into a small but tall chapel in 1767-1769.

The *Georgievsky Cathedral*, 1696-1701, is a notable example of the Ukrainian baroque style, a cross-plan church with five tightly grouped cupolas. The nearby refectory has an ornate carved entrance portal. The squat Bell Tower of the monastery is from 1727-1733. There are several graves on the grounds, including that of K. D. Ushinsky, a 19th-century Russian educator. The Botanical Gardens can be reached by taking trolleybus 14 from Baseina St. behind the Bessarabian Market.

In the northern part of town at Frunze St. #103, is the *Kirillovskaya Church*, built 1146-1171 by prince Vsevolod Olgovich. Originally a six-column church with one cupola, it was destroyed by the Mongols. It was rebuilt in the 17th and 18th centuries and made into a five-dome church, in part to designs by Grigorovich-Barsky. The church was made into a museum in 1929 and underwent extensive restoration in 1949-1952 and 1965-1967. The church was frescoed at various times.

About 800 square yards of the original 12th-century frescoes survive. In the 1880's the church was restored by Professor Prakhov and the artist Vrubel. His fresco, the "Descent of the Holy Ghost" is entirely preserved on the vaults of the choir (steps in the north wall to the left of the main entrance). Vrubel also did the four icons of the iconostasis: St. Afanasy, the Virgin, Christ, and St. Cyril. The church can be reached by taking trolleybus 18 from Kalinin Square.

SHOPPING IN KIEV:

Department Stores: #2 Lenin Street (corner of Kreshchatik)
"Ukraina" at Victory Square

Gifts and Folk Art: Lenin Street #12, #16, #18, #27
Karl Marx Street #9
Lesya Ukrainka Street #24 (foreign currency only)

Public Transit:

Trolleybus 20 runs along Kreshchatik and to the Cave Monastery.

Trolleybus 8 runs from Victory Square along Shevchenko Blvd., then down Lenin Street and along Kreshchatik.

Trolleybus 12 runs along Vladimir Street.

Trolleybus 14 runs from Baseina Street (behind the Bessarabian market) to the Botanical Gardens.

Trolleybus 18 runs from Kalinin Square to Frunze Street (for the Kirillovskaya Church).

MOSCOW
AND PALACE ESTATES
NEAR THE CITY
KOLOMENSKOE
KUSKOVO
OSTANKINO
ARCHANGELSKOE

St. Basil's Cathedral: Moscow

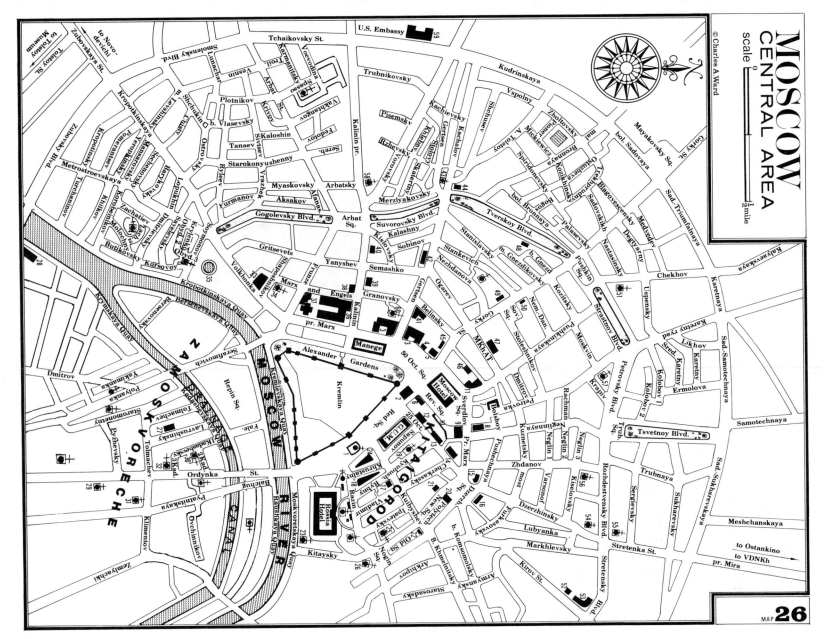

MOSCOW
CENTRAL AREA

© Charles A. Ward

scale

0
½ mile
1 mile

U.S. Embassy

Tchaikovsky St.

Trubnikovsky

Kudrinskaya

Smolensky Blvd.

Vspolny

Mayakovsky Sq.

Plotnikov

Pisemsky

Kachievsky

Sichtchev

Zholtovsky

bol. Sadovaya

b. Vlasevsky

Rzhevsky

Gertsen

Kachalov

Mickiewicz

Sad. Triumfalnaya

Tanaev

Kaloshin

Spiridonevsky

Medvedev

Starokonyushenny

Merzlyakovsky

bol Bronnaya

Palasevsky

Degtyarny

Myaskovsky

Arbatsky

Suvorovsky Blvd.

Tverskoy Blvd.

Sad. Sadovskih

Nastasinsky

Aksakov

Gogolevsky Blvd.

Arbat Sq.

Kalashny

Stanislavsky

Pushkin Sq.

Chekhov

Gritsevets

Sobinov

Stankevich

m. Gnezdikovsky

Uspensky

Karetnaya

Yanyshev

Semashko

Ogarev

Gorky

Nem.-Dan.

Karetny ryad

Likhov

Volkhonka

Frunze

Granovsky

Belinsky

MKhAT

Stoleshnikov

Krapiv.

Kolobov

Kropotkinskaya Quay

pr. Marx

Kalinin

Manege

50 Oct. Sq.

Moscow Hotel

Bolshoi

Petrovka

Rachman

Tsvetnoy Blvd.

Samotechnaya

Alexander Gardens

Kremlin

Sverdlov Sq.

Pr. Marx

Pushechnaya

Neglin

Trub. Sq.

Dmitrov

Repin Sq.

Red Sq.

C.U.M.

Kuybyshev

Cherkassky

Zhdanov

Varsonof.

Kiselevsky

Trubnaya

Sergievsky

Ordynka St.

Khrushaly

Razin

Dzerzh. Sq.

Rozhdestvensky Blvd.

Pyatnitskaya

Rossia Hotel

b. Komsomolsky

Lubyanka

Stretenka St.

Ovchinnikov

Markhlevsky

Klimentov

Kitaysky

Arkhipov

B. Khmelnitsky

Kirov St.

Starosadsky

Stretensky Blvd.

Meshchanskaya

to Ostankino
to VDNKh
pr. Mira

MAP 26

Key to Map 26

1. Basil's Cathedral
2. Historical Museum
3. Old University Buildings
4. Intourist Headquarters
5. National Hotel
6. Lenin Museum
7. Bolshoy Theater
8. Maly Theater
9. Metropol Hotel
10. Kitaigorod wall
11. House of Unions
12. Zaikonospassky Monastery site
13. Old Printing House
14. Slavyansky Bazaar
15. Detsky Mir (Children's Store)
16. Ministry of Internal Affairs
17. Former Stock Exchange
18. Former Gostiny Dvor
19. Cathedral of Bogoyavlensky
    Monastery
20. Polytechnical Museum
21. Museum of History
    and Reconstruction of Moscow
22. Monument to Grenadiers
23. Church of St. Anne
24. Former "Middle Trading Rows"
25. Church of Trinity in Nikitniki
26. All Saints Church
27. Tretyakov Gallery
28. New Tretyakov Gallery
29. Church of St. Nikola
30. Church of the Resurrection

31. Church of Kliment
32. Church of All Sorrows
33. Museum of Fine Arts
34. Church of Antipy
35. "Moscow" Swimming Pool
36. Lenin Library
37. Pashkov Palace
38. Shchusev Museum of Architecture
39. Voentorg Department Store
40. House of Friendship
41. Zoological Museum
42. Moscow Conservatory of Music
43. Church of the Ascension
44. Gorky Museum
45. "Intourist" Hotel
46. Glinka Museum of Music
47. Moscow Art Theater
48. New Moscow Art Theater
49. City Soviet
50. Eliseev Food Store
51. Church of the Nativity
    "in Putniki"
52. Former Perlov Tea Store
53. Former Art School
54. Cathedral of former Sretensky
    Monastery, 1679
55. Museum of Soviet Navy, in
    former Uspenie Church
56. Rozhdestvensky Monastery
57. Petrovsky Monastery
58. Church of Simon Stylites
59. United States Embassy
60. Znamenie Church "in Sheremetev's Yard"

MOSCOW

(Map 26)

Moscow was first mentioned in the chronicles in 1147, the date considered to be its founding. Moscow was then an insignificant outpost in the southern region of the Vladimir-Suzdal princedom of Northeast Russia. In the 12th century the Vladimir-Suzdal princedom was developing trade contacts and trying to rival Kiev, which since the 9th century had been the capital and cultural center of the Russian state. In 1238 Russia fell under Mongol domination and in the ensuing century lost western lands to Lithuania and Poland.

It was the Muscovite princes who began to unify Russia into a single state against the Mongols. They used their position as the tribute collectors for the Mongols to build a power base. In 1333, the Khan recognized Prince Ivan Kalita of Moscow as Russia's formost ruler. In this position Moscow gained wealth and political influence, and developed a centralized state by gradually absorbing the nearby towns of the former Vladimir-Suzdal princedom. In 1380, as a result of a military campaign, Moscow Prince Dmitry Donskoy was able to reduce the amount of tribute paid to the Mongols. Under Ivan III, in 1480, the Russians finally freed themselves of the Tartars, whose strength had been weakened by factionalism. At the same time Ivan III completed the subjugation of important rival Russian cities like Tver and Novgorod. Ivan's son, Vasily III, regained Smolensk and western areas from the Poles in 1514. Ivan the Terrible opened up trade with England via Archangelsk in the north in 1553, and defeated the Volga Tartars at Kazan in 1552, and at Astrakhan in 1554. Though the Crimean Tartars raided Moscow in 1571, the threat of Tartar domination was over.

The first years of the 17th century are known as the Time of Troubles. Boris Godunov, regent for Ivan the Terrible's incompetent son Fedor, took the throne in 1598 on Fedor's death. Several impostors appeared claiming the throne, and chaos ensued. The Poles, taking advantage of the confusion, invaded in 1610 and occupied Moscow. In 1613 after the defeat of the Polish invaders, Michael Romanov was elected Tsar, and an orderly succession of rulers was re-established. Moscow flourished in the 17th century, but in 1712 Peter the Great moved the capital to Petersburg and Moscow became the second city for 200 years.

In 1918 Moscow again became the capital and has been growing steadily since. In 1935 a general plan for the reconstruction of the city was adopted. Several times revised, the plan is still being implemented. Because of constant construction, demolition, and re-building in Moscow, some of the buildings and museums mentioned in this book may have disappeared or been transformed, and others are slated for eventual moving or demolition.

The center of Moscow since its founding has been the Kremlin, a citadel which by the 15th century was Russia's strongest fortress. To its east was Red Square, and beyond it, "Kitaigorod," the former commercial center of the city. The city expanded along radial roads leading from the Kremlin, and within concentric fortification walls, now replaced by the two rings roads of central Moscow. The city was largely destroyed in the fire of 1812 during the Napoleonic invasion, and few architectural monuments outside the Kremlin are older than the 18th century. The description of the major sights that follows begins with the Kremlin.

THE CENTRAL AREA

The. **KREMLIN (Map 27)**, former Moscow citadel, is situated on hills 130 feet above the Moscow River. Its walls enclose an area of 69 acres and form a rough triangle a mile and a quarter in circumference. The Kremlin originally housed the residence of the Grand Prince as well as the church patriarch, so was both the political and religious center of the town. It now contains palaces and official buildings of the Soviet Government, historic churches from the 15th century, conference halls, museums, and theaters.

The first small oak and earthen rampart on this site was built in 1156 by Yury Dolgoruky. By the time of Dmitry Donskoy (1367) it had achieved its present size and was surrounded by a white stone wall. The present brick wall was built between 1485-1508 for Ivan III by Marco Ruffo and Pietro Antonio Solario, Italian builders from Milan. The 21 towers of the Kremlin have been damaged and reconstructed several times over the centuries. The present wall varies from 11-22 feet thick and 16-64 feet tall. The walls were originally surrounded by water, the Moscow River to the south, a moat along the edge of Red Square, and the Neglinka River to the northwest. The river was enclosed in 1819, and covered by the Alexander Garden built along the northwest wall. The bridge from the street to the Trinity Tower is a reminder of the old river bed.

The three entrance towers of the Kremlin are the *Spassky Tower and Gate* (from Red Square) (**27**-1), the *Trinity Tower and Gate* (from Kalinin Street) (**27**-4), and the *Borovitsky Tower and Gate* (at the southwest corner) (**27**-5). The 220-foot tall Spassky Tower, overlooking Red Square, was built in 1491 by Solario and Ruffo. The upper part and the carillon were added by Englishman Christopher Galloway in 1625. The present clock is from 1851. The Spassky Gate is for official use only. The main squares, cathedrals, and museums inside the Kremlin are open to tourists and are reached through the Borovitsky Gate at the southwest

MOSCOW KREMLIN

Map 27

Red Sq.

©Charles A. Ward

1. Spassky Tower and Gate
2. Nikolsky Tower
3. Sobakin Tower
4. Trinity Tower and Gate
5. Borovitsky Tower and Gate
6. Water Tower
7. Armory Museum
8. Great Kremlin Palace
9. Assumption Cathedral
10. Rizpolozhensky Church
11. Annunciation Cathedral
12. Archangel Cathedral
13. Facets Palace
14. Patriarch's Palace, Church of Twelve Apostles

15. Ivan the Great Bell Tower
16. Belfry
17. Tsar-Bell
18. Tsar-Cannon
19. Praesidium of Supreme Soviet
20. Council of Ministers
21. Arsenal
22. Palace of Congresses
23. Historical Museum
24. Lenin's Tomb
25. G.U.M. Department Store
26. Basil's Cathedral
27. Statue of Minin and Pozharsky
28. Lobnoe mesto
29. Manege - Central Exhibition Hall

corner of the Kremlin. Evening performances in the Palace of Congresses are reached through the Trinity Gate. The Kremlin towers were originally flat-topped, and were given their decorative tent-roofs and spires only in the 17th century. The *Nikolsky Tower* (**27**-2) on Red Square was damaged in 1812 and was rebuilt in a pseudo-Gothic style by Bove in 1816.

The *ARMORY MUSEUM* (**27**-7), built in 1849-1851 by Thon and located just to the left inside the Borovitsky Gate, is Russia's greatest collection of applied arts, arms, and carriages. Housed after 1547 in the Kremlin Armory, the collection originated in the 14th century as heredity possessions of the Muscovite princes, and was expanded by centuries of diplomatic gifts. The richness and detail of the collection are impossible to absorb in the hour and a half viewing time allowed. The following list includes the highlights of each display case:

UPPER FLOOR

HALL I. ARMOR AND WEAPONS
Case 1: 13th-17th century: Chain mail vests of Prince Shuisky, mid-1500's, and of Boris Godunov, late 1500's; helmet of Yaroslav Vsevolodich (Alexander Nevsky's father), mid-1100's; sabers, boar spears, battle axes. **Case 2:** Decorative arquebuses from Kremlin workshops, 16th-17th centuries. **Case 3:** Ceremonial gear: jewel-studded sabers; Mikhail Romanov's dress helmet, 1621, and bow & arrow case, 1628. **Case 4:** Diplomatic and trade gifts: Bow case and saber, 1656, a gift of Constantinople merchants to Aleksey Mikhailovich; three pound gold mace, 1658, gift of Persian shah. **Case 5:** Early 18th-century rifles and swords: booty from the Northern War (1700-1721), three Swedish drums; Swedish mace; bust of Peter I by Rastrelli, 1743. **Case 6:** Western armor, 15th-17th century: German horse armor; suits of armor from Poland, Germany, France.

Hall II. RUSSIAN GOLD AND SILVER WORK, 12th-19th CENTURY
Case 7: Mixed weapons, 17th-19th century: Tula rifles, dress swords; Turkish rifles; Central Asian sabers. Saber of 1829 with scenes of the fall of Varna engraved on the blade. **Case 8:** Pistols, rifles, sabers from Europe, 16th-17th century. **Case 9:** Early Russian Gold and Silver, 12th-15th century: Old Ryazan treasures, 12th-13th century, ceremonial insignia collars in filigree and cloisonne enamel; head dress ornaments, jewelry, earrings; Yury Dolgoruky's silver chalice, 12th century,

from Vladimir-Suzdal; frame for the icon of Vladimir Mother-of-God, 13th century, in stamped gold, from Vladimir-Suzdal; the "Morozov" Gospel cover, 1400's, from Moscow, with relief figures, precious stone incrustation, and filigree work; Gospel cover of 1499. **Case 10:** Muscovite works, 1600-1650: Golden censer in shape of a chapel, 1616; Golden Gospel cover, 1632. **Case 11:** Dishes and plates, 17th century: various shapes; note especially the three gold duck-shaped dippers (kovshch) which belonged to Aleksey Mikhailovich and weigh four pounds apiece. **Case 12:** Seventeenth-century engraved work and niello (a black alloy filling for engraved areas on gold or silver): vessels by Constantinople craftsmen, 1660's; plates belonging to Khitrovo and Golitsyn; Gospel cover for Chudov Monastery, 1668. **Case 13:** Early 17th-century works: gold loving cup with floral design, 1653; "Morozova" Chalice, 1664, of gold with enamel, diamonds, rubies, sapphires, and emeralds, a gift to the Chudov Monastery; Gospel cover of 1678, with enamel and metal chasing: bejeweled gold frame for Vladimir Mother-of-God icon, 1657. **Case 14:** Ivan the Terrible's reign, later 16th century: folding triptych icon case of silver, gold, and jewels; gold and niello censer; round gold and niello dish, 1561; icon covers of 1554 and 1571. **Case 15:** Byzantine art, 5th-15th century: icons, cameos carved on semi-precious minerals; cloisonne enamel; gold filigree. **Case 16:** Items from Novgorod and Pskov: jasper and gold chalice with filigree and jewels, 1329; silver filigree Gospel cover, 1500's: enamel work; drinking vessels. **Case 17:** Enameled items from Solvychegodsk, late 1600's: bowls, boxes, plates, silverware. **Case 18:** Items of 17th century from Yaroslavl and Kostroma: Chalice of 1697; censors, kovshchi. **Case 53:** Moscow trade pieces, late 1600's: carved ivory loving cup; plates, personal and trade items.

HALL III. POST-PETRINE WORK

In 1711 the Kremlin silversmiths were moved to Petersburg, and their work came to reflect rococo and neoclassic styles and subjects. **Case 20:** Gold and diamond snuff box with Elizabeth Petrovna's portrait, by Pozier; silver rococo soup tureen; silver platters by Ratkov, 1780's; Gospel covers. **Case 21:** Eighteenth-century "panagia," miniature enameled portraits. **Case 22:** Crafts from Veliki Ustyug and Tobolsk: gold and niello works, snuffboxes, other small items; niello tea service from Tobolsk, 1775. **Case 23:** Goldsmiths of 19th century: Silver statuettes by Sazikov, 1830's; enamels by Ovchinnikov Company, mid-1800's, niello works by Khlebnikov firm, late 1800's. **Case 24:** Works by Faberge Company. (Gustav Faberge, of French Huguenot

extraction, was born in Estonia. He studied jewelry making in St. Petersburg, and set up his firm there in 1842. His son Karl, who ran the shop from 1870, developed it into a company with 500 employees. The firm's European fame came especially after it won a prize at the Paris exposition in 1900, and opened a showroom in London in 1903.) Superior craftsmanship and virtuoso technique mark the products of the Faberge firm. See especially the "Easter Eggs" by his craftsman, Perkhin: "In memory of Azov," 1891, a gold and platinum model of a ship, to scale accuracy, in a sheet of aquamarine for the sea, placed in a heliotrope egg adorned with baroque gold applique; a clock in the form of a large egg topped by a bouquet of imitation lilies of milk-white onyx, 1899; a gold wind-up model of the Trans-Siberian express, accurate to compartment signs, kept in a large silver egg engraved with a map of the Railroad system. Note too the model of the imperial yacht, "Standart," 1909 by Wiegstrom, in a rock crystal egg supported by lapis lazuli dolphins. **Case 25:** Works of later 1700's: classical style samovar; cups; Gospel covers of 1790's; chalices; an oval gold platter of 1788.

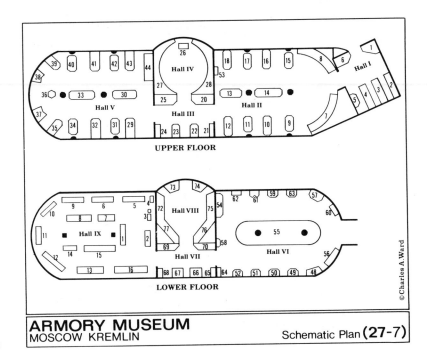

ARMORY MUSEUM
MOSCOW KREMLIN

Schematic Plan (27-7)

©Charles A.Ward

HALL IV. PRECIOUS FABRICS, CHURCH VESTMENTS, 14th-18th CENTURY

Case 26: Patriarch Nikon's vestment of 1655, gold embroidered cloth and pearls. **Case 27:** Vestments of Byzantine fabric, 1300's; Persian silk surplices, 1600's; Turkish satin vestments, early 1600's; the Puchezh shroud, 1441. **Case 28:** French, Italian, Spanish, Russian fabrics, 17th-19th century: Patriarch Nikon's vestment of double looped Venetian samite silk, 1654, with pearls, precious stones, and medallions; the embroidered robe Catherine gave to Metropolitan Platon, ornamented with 150,000 seed pearls arranged in large diamond shapes.

HALL V. WESTERN SILVER WORK, 15th-19th CENTURY

Cases 29 & 31: Dutch silver from 1600's; various dishes, jugs, cups, plates, candelabra, generally with restrained ornamentation. **Case 30:** English silver, 16th-17th century: goblets, dishes, salt-cellars, pitchers; note particularly the two wine flagons in the form of leopards rampant, ca. 1600. **Case 32:** Polish Diplomatic gifts (mostly made in Germany): goblets and pitchers made in Danzig and Augsburg; note especially the eagle with spread wings holding an orb and scepter in its claws, mid-1600's from Augsburg. **Case 33:** Swedish gifts, 17th century: silver lion rampant and two large oval basins from Augsburg, mid-1600's; silver goblet cornucopia and a table fountain, 1670's, from Hamburg; some cups, candlesticks, and other items from Stockholm. **Case 34:** Danish gifts: bowls, dishes, goblets and other items, mostly made in Hamburg. **Case 35:** Works of German silversmiths (Augsburg, Hamburg, Nuremberg): note expecially the elaborate goblets from Hamburg, some designed by Durer and Holbein; goblets in shapes of animals, trees; works by Wenzel Jamnitzer family of Nuremberg; works of other famous craftsmen. **Case 36:** Pitchers; goblets from ostrich eggs, coconut shells, nautilus-shaped shells and mother-of-pearl; rock crystal carving, ivory and horn carving. **Cases 37 & 38:** Works of Augsburg silversmiths, 16th century: drinking vessels, double goblets in many imaginative shapes. **Case 39:** Works of Hamburg craftsmen, 17th century: massive goblets, gloves, candlesticks, censers. **Case 40:** German goblets commissioned by Russians: gifts to the tsar from boyar Morozov, Prince Golitsyn, and others. **Case 41:** French silver, 18th century: various pitchers, dishes, snuff boxes, services. **Case 42:** French silver: tureens, plates, and other pieces from the "Orlov" silver service ordered by Catherine from France. It had some 3,000 pieces and weighed over two tons. Catherine gave it as a present to Count Orlov. **Case 43:** French empire china service by Odiot, 1825. **Case 44:** Sevres china service, ordered by Napoleon as a gift to Alexander I after the treaty of Tilsit in 1807. **Case 45:** Turkish Diplomatic gifts: jasper bowl with rubies and emeralds, early 1600's; enameled gold pitcher, with jewels; crystal objects.

LOWER FLOOR

HALL VI. IMPERIAL REGALIA

Case 48: Ivan the Terrible's throne, 16th century, of western origin; wood with carved ivory panels. **Case 49:** Persian throne, ca. 1600, in stamped gold with rubies, turquoise, and pearl studding, a gift to Boris Godunov from Shah Abbas I, in 1602. **Case 50:** Mikhail Romanov's throne, early 1600's, remade from an older Persian throne; gold and precious stones. **Case 51:** The "Diamond Throne," a gift in mid-1600's to Aleksey Mikhailovich from Armenian-Persian merchants; carved gold and silver openwork and inlay, encrusted with more than 800 diamonds. **Case 52:** Double silver throne, 1682, designed for child-heirs Ivan and Peter; there is a hidden seat behind from which their older sister Sofia would whisper answers to the questions asked by ambassadors at official audiences. **Case 54:** Secular dress of the 16th and 17th century: Peter the Great's boots and cane; fur coats, caftans. **Case 55:** Formal gowns of the 18th and 19th century: Coronation gown (crimson with silver embroidery), and a light-blue dress of Catherine I, 1720's; Anna Ioannovna's gold brocade coronation dress with gold embroidery; sleeveless silver brocade coronation dress of Elizabeth Petrovna, 1742, with a 17-foot silver lace mantle-train; Catherine the Great's silver brocade wedding dress, 1745, and her coronation gown, 1762, embroidered with gold doubleheaded eagles; tsar's coronation mantles of gold brocade edged with ermine, from 1883 (Alexander III), and 1896 (Nicolas II). **Case 56:** Persian carpet, early 1600's. **Case 57:** Late 19th-century Japanese work: life-sized carved ivory eagle (2,000 carved ivory feathers attached to a wooden form); four-panel silk screen. **Case 58:** Crowns, orbs, scepters: the "Cap of Monomakh," ca. 1300, of gold, pearls, jewels, and sable, of oriental origin; the gold "Cap of Kazan," made in 1553 for Ivan the Terrible, with niello gold plates, jewels, and fur trim; Mikhail Fedorovich's crown, orb, and scepter, 1628, in gold, enamel, and precious stones; orb and scepter of Aleksey Mikhailovich, of Turkic origin, with symmetrical abstract pattern of precious stones; Western-style silver crown of Anna Ioannovna, with 2,500 diamonds and a giant tourmaline on top. **Case 60:** Orders, medals, and decorations: Order of St. Andrew, St. Catherine, St. George, and others, 18th and 19th century. **Cases 61 & 63:** Eighteenth and 19th-century fans, snuffboxes, canes, buttons, watches, and some clothing of fashionable circles. **Case 62:** Garments, headgear, earrings, and kerchiefs of the 17th and 18th centuries. **Case 64:** "Posokh," or staffs of state for ceremonial occasions, from the reign of Aleksey Mikhailovich and others.

HALLS VII & VIII. CEREMONIAL HARNESSES

Case 65: Sledge cloth of Persian velvet with pearl ornaments, Russian work of the 17th century. **Case 66:** Saddle blankets and saddles from China, 1678. **Case 67:** Polish and German saddles, 1600's. **Case 68:** Sledge cloth of Italian fabric. **Case 69:** Persian dress harness of late 1500's; Persian gold saddle, 1590, with rubies and emeralds; Persian gold saddle with pearls, turquoise, emeralds, and rubies, 1635, a gift to Mikhail Fedorovich; Persian yellow saddle "cloth," or feather blanket, made of parrot skins, early 1600's. **Case 70:** Russian dress harnesses of 16th and 17th centuries; saddles belonging to Ivan the Terrible and Boris Godunov. **Case 71/72:** Various Turkish and Central Asian saddles and harnesses of 17th and 18th centuries. **Cases 73 & 74:** Turkish dress saddle and bridle of 1775, in gold, silver, diamonds, and Turkish saddle of 1793, gold and gems, gifts to Catherine the Great after Russian victories in wars with Turkey. **Case 75/76:** Russian harnesses and saddles of the 18th century.

HALL IX. CARRIAGES

This collection presents excellent examples of carriagemaking art of the 17th and 18th centuries. The models on display begin with primitive springless coaches with no window glass, no coachman's seat, and no provision for turning the front wheels. Successive displays follow the evolution of carriages to comfortable, well-sprung models. **(1):** An English carriage, ca. 1600, a gift to Boris Godunov from either Elizabeth I or James I; it has curtained windows, Persian velvet interior, and exterior carvings which depict battles between Turks and Christians, and other scenes. **(2):** A Polish carriage of early 1600's, with mica windows, an exterior pattern formed with copper nails, and red velvet interior. **(3):** A child's summer cart and sleigh, ca. 1675, which belonged to Peter the Great as a child. **(4):** A maple "Porte-chaise" from Western Europe, later 1700's. **(5):** An oak two-seat carriage made in Petersburg in 1739 for Anna Ioannovna, a carved baroque carriage with plate glass windows and painted scenes. **(6):** A French carriage of oak, 1721, thought to have been made for the Duke of Holstein, who married Peter's daughter, Anna. **(7):** An oak and birch sleigh build in Petersburg

in 1742. This long enclosed sleigh, with many windows, was used by Elizabeth Petrovna to go to Moscow for her coronation. **(8):** An oak carriage built in Berlin, mid-1700's. **(9/10):** Two Viennese carriages built in 1740 for Anna Ioannovna; one has magnificent gilded carved figures and detail work. **(11):** An English two-seat phaeton, of maple, 1770, a gift to Count Orlov from Catherine the Great; it is most elaborately carved and gilded, an example of consummate craftsmanship. **(12):** A French traveling coach, of ash, built in 1765 for Catherine the Great; the sides have large paintings by Francois Boucher. **(13):** A state coach of maple, built in 1769 for Catherine by English carriage maker John Buckendale, a most graceful carriage with paintings from the school of Watteau. **(14):** A Russian garden carriage, 1739, for Anna Ioannovna, with wide wheels to preserve the garden paths. **(15):** A ponderous French carriage, 1757, made in Paris by Bournihall. It is elaborately carved in baroque style with painted scenes by Boucher, a gift to Elizabeth Petrovna from Count Razumovsky. **(16):** An intricately carved baroque carriage made in Berlin by Hoppenhaupt, 1746, of beech wood, a gift of Frederick II to Elizabeth Petrovna. It was used by royalty on ceremonial occasions until the 20th century.

The **Diamond Fund** of the Armory, a precious gem collection housed in the same building, requires a separate admission ticket. The collection is shown only a few times a week. It contains an astounding "Tsar's treasure" of diamonds, jewelry, and other valuables: Catherine the Great's crown, with over 5,000 diamonds; the Orlov and Shah diamonds; a 136-carat emerald, a 260-carat Ceylon sapphire; Soviet diamonds from Siberia, collectively equaling 30,000 carats; huge gold nuggets from Siberia, miscellaneous Tsar's jewelry, and so forth.

Up hill from the Armory is the *Great Kremlin Palace* **(27-8)**, 1839-1849 by Thon and others, built for Nicholas I. It is used by the Supreme Soviet and is closed to tourists.

Just east of the palace is Cathedrals Square. If you face this square with your back to the river, the Assumption Cathedral will be straight ahead, the Annunciation Cathedral to your left, and the Archangel Cathedral to the right.

The *Assumption Cathedral* **(27-9)**, 1475-1479 by Rudolpho ("Aristotle") Fioravanti of Bologna, is the largest church in the Kremlin, a five-dome, six-column structure 82 x 125 feet. The design of the cathedral is based on traditional Russian architectural style of the Vladimir-Suzdal princedom, with curved zakomara gables at the tops of the walls, and the column "belt" at mid wall. However, Fioravanti's mastery of renaissance harmony and proportion can be seen in the division of the walls into equal sections, and the equal height of the zakomara gables. This rational division can be seen in the airy interior, where the slender round columns of the church are placed equidistant from the walls and from each other.

This church was the coronation cathedral of the tsars and the burial place of church patriarchs. The church was frescoed around 1500 and again in 1642. Restoration has gone on at various times in the 20th century and patches of frescoes from both periods are preserved in different areas. Icons include the Virgin of Vladimir (the original is in the Tretyakov Gallery), as well as St. George of the Novgorod School, a 14th-century "Trinity," "Apostle Paul" and other outstanding large icons, including Saints Peter and Paul, attributed to Feofan the Greek. The church contains Ivan the Terrible's carved wood coronation throne, 1551, by the south portal, called "Monomakh's Throne" because Kievan prince Vladimir Monomakh is depicted in the carvings. In the southeast corner is a small shrine of bronze grillwork housing the remains of patriarch Germogen, who perished in the Polish invasion of 1612. The cathedral was used as a stables by Napoleon, and icons were used as firewood. It is estimated that 635 pounds of gold and five tons of silver were carried off at that time.

The *Rizpolozhensky Church* (**27**-10), 1485-1486, built by masons from Pskov, is to the left of the Assumption Cathedral. A simple, single-dome, white church, it served as the "house church" of the Russian patriarchs. The gallery inside the church now houses a Museum of Polychrome wood carving, three-dimensional icons, and statues of saints. The church preserves frescoes of 1643, and has icons

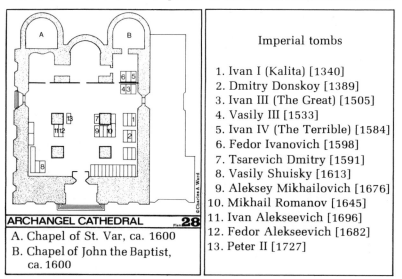

ARCHANGEL CATHEDRAL **28**

A. Chapel of St. Var, ca. 1600
B. Chapel of John the Baptist, ca. 1600

Imperial tombs

1. Ivan I (Kalita) [1340]
2. Dmitry Donskoy [1389]
3. Ivan III (The Great) [1505]
4. Vasily III [1533]
5. Ivan IV (The Terrible) [1584]
6. Fedor Ivanovich [1598]
7. Tsarevich Dmitry [1591]
8. Vasily Shuisky [1613]
9. Aleksey Mikhailovich [1676]
10. Mikhail Romanov [1645]
11. Ivan Alekseevich [1696]
12. Fedor Alekseevich [1682]
13. Peter II [1727]

and an iconostasis by N. Istomin, 1627.

The *Annunciation Cathedral* (**27**-11), 1484-1489, by builders from Pskov, was remodeled with the addition of the enclosed gallery and additional domes by Ivan the Terrible in the middle 1500's. The present church is a rebuilding of an earlier church on this site from 1398. The church has nine gold domes (regilt in 1963) and a floor of jasper stone taken from the cathedral in Rostov. The small dimensions of the church give it a marked vertical emphasis inside. The iconostasis has portraits of saints by Feofan the Greek and Andrey Rublev (1405). The south portal from the gallery into the church is original from the 15th century, and forms an ogee arch with three sets of receding columns. The elaborately carved north portal, from the mid-16th century, reveals the influence of the renaissance, and in particular of the west portal of the Archangel Cathedral.

The *Archangel Cathedral* (**27**-12 and Plan **28**), 1505-1509, by Alevisio Novi of Milan, is a large six-column, five dome church. The exterior walls are divided into five unequal sections because Alevisio built a special chamber at the west end, with a balcony, for women of the royal family. The exterior is a catalogue of Northern Italian decorative detail of the early renaissance. The building is divided into two "floors" by two rows of decorative Corinthian pilasters separated by an entablature, a device which destroys the monolithic wall appearance characteristic of Old Russian churches. The external columns, the raising of the church on a basement level, the use of blind arcading on the lower half of the walls, and the scallop-shell insets in the zakomara gables at the top of the wall sections all found imitators in later Russian architecture. Note the elaborate carving on the archway of the west portal.

The interior of the church was frescoed in 1557, and the icons date from 1680. The icon of the Archangel Michael is attributed to Andrey Rublev. The interior of the church is dark, in part because of the large square columns, and is crowded because it was the burial spot for Russian rulers from Ivan Kalita (1341) to Aleksey Mikhailovich (1675). All the tombs were given identical bronze coffin covers in 1903, except for the carved coffin (1630) of Tsarevich Dmitry, on the north side of the southeast column.

The *Facets Palace* (**27**-13), on the west side of the square, built in 1487-1491 by Ruffo and Solario, gets its name from the diamond-point rustication of its wall. The figured window frames were added in the 17th century. The palace is not open to tourists.

The *Church of the Twelve Apostles* and the *Patriarch's Palace* (**27**-14), 1655-1656, rebuilt after a fire in the 1680's, are located behind the Assumption Cathedral. The structures were built for patriarch Nikon, who led a drive for conservative, five-dome, plain-walled churches, and opposed the decorative style best exemplified by the Basil Cathedral in Red Square. The church has a carved, gilt wooden iconostasis in the baroque style, ca. 1700, taken from the cathedral of the former Monastery of the Ascension in the Kremlin. The church now houses a Museum of Applied Arts of the 17th century.

Ivan the Great Bell Tower (**27**-15), 1505-1508 by Marco Bono, is a 265-foot tall octagonal structure next to the Archangel Cathedral. The top tier and gold dome were added by Tsar Boris Godunov in 1600.

The *Belfry* (**27**-16), 1532-1543 by Italian builder Petroch the Younger, is the rectangular building next to the Bell Tower. It contains bells and a chapel. The stone stairway to the chapel from the square was added in 1552. "Filaret's Addition," 1624, is the square tower with the tent roof to the north of the belfry. It was restored after partial destruction in 1812.

The *Tsar Bell* (**27**-17), cast in 1733-1735, is located behind the Archangel Cathedral. The bell is 20 feet tall, 21 feet in diameter, 2 feet thick at the base, and weighs about 460,000 pounds. It is decorated with a bas-relief of various saints and of Tsar Aleksey Mikhailovich and his wife. During a fire in the casting pit a piece broke off the bell in 1737. The bell remained in the ground in the casting pit until 1836 when it was raised by Montferrand and put on its present granite base.

The *Tsar-Cannon* (**27**-18), cast in 1586, weighs 40 tons and has a barrel 17.5 feet long and 3 feet in diameter. The cannon was never fired; the cast-iron cannon balls in front are purely decorative and were added in the 19th century.

The *Praesidium of the Supreme Soviet* building (**27**-19), 1932 by Rerberg, is just to the west of the Spassky Gate-Tower. Behind it is the *Council of Ministers Building* (**27**-20), 1776-1786 by Kazakov, the former senate building in Moscow. It is a triangular structure designed to fit into an odd space in the Kremlin. The building's low green dome is visible from Red Square. The building is closed to tourists.

The *Arsenal* (**27**-21), from 1702, finished in 1786 by Gerard, was destroyed in 1812 and rebuilt by Bove in the present form, 1816-1823. In front of it are 875 cannon, 830 captured during the Napoleonic wars. The remainder are 16th and 17th-century Russian and foreign cannon.

The *Palace of Congresses* (**27**-22), 1959-1961, was built for the 22nd Party Congress in 1961. The exterior is of marble, aluminum, and glass. The interior hall seats 6,000, and is often used by the Bolshoy and other troupes for ballets and similar performances. The main hall is fitted with a complex acoustic system with time-delay relays, so that the amplified sound reaches all seats at the same time.

RED SQUARE

The square (Map **26**) is bounded on the west by the Kremlin, to the north by the Historical Museum, to the east by G.U.M. Department Store, and to the south by Basil's Cathedral. The square is 400 yards long and 140 yards wide.

The *Historical Museum* (**27**-23), 1875-1883 by Sherwood, is in pseudo-Byzantine style, an eclectic style of the late 19th-century which attempted to duplicate early Russian architecture. The museum is on the site of a former two-story structure in which Lomonosov established Moscow University in 1755. The Museum was reorganized in 1921 and contains 3 million items. The 300,000 items on exhibit follow the Marxist-Leninist teachings on history.

Rooms 1-4: Prehistoric archeological finds in the territory of the Soviet Union. **Rooms 5-6:** archeological finds, 1000 BC to 400 AD. **Rooms 7-12:** Old Russian princedoms. **Rooms 13-19:** Rise of Moscow and centralized government, 1350-1700. **Rooms 20-21:** The founding of Petersburg. **Rooms 22-27:** last half of the 18th century. **Rooms 28-32:** first half of 19th century. **Room 33:** Crimean War. **Room 34:** liberal intellegentsia. **Room 35:** Development of Capitalism and Agriculture, last half of 19th century. **Rooms 36-37:** Proletarian movements, 1905-1917, and the Russian Revolution.

Lenin's Mausoleum (**27**-24), 1929-1930 by Shchusev, is made of red granite and black porphyry. Lenin's embalmed body is displayed in a glass case inside. The honor guard in front is changed every hour on the hour. Behind the mausoleum are graves of most of the leading revolutionaries: Sverdlov, Dzerzhinsky, Frunze, Kalinin, Stalin, Zhdanov, Voroshilov. Memorial tombs in the Kremlin Wall include writer Maxim Gorky, bolshevik Kirov, cosmonaut Yury Gagarin, American journalist John Reed, and others.

G.U.M. (Government Department Store) (**27**-25), 1888-1894 by Pomerantsev. The building is 830 feet long, 290 feet deep, and consists of three long glass-roofed passages containing 130 departments. The building was reconstructed in the 1920's and again in 1953.

Basil's Cathedral (**27**-26) (officially, the Church of the Intercession), 1554-1561, was built for Ivan the Terrible to commemorate his conquest of Kazan in 1552. The church was damaged by the Poles in 1611 and by Napoleon in 1812. The building consists of a tall central church surrounded by eight chapels. The church was designed for its external appearance. Original frescoes remain, but the interior is a labyrinth of twisting narrow corridors connecting the small chapels. The entrance is from the lower level, which contains an exhibit on the history of the building. The domes with their various patterns, and the painted patterns on the exterior, were added in the 1680's.

The *Statue to Minin and Pozharsky* (**27**-27), 1818 by Martos, is in front of the cathedral. Minin, a Novgorod merchant, and Pozharsky, a Russian nobleman, led the army which expelled occupying Polish troops from Moscow in 1612.

Lobnoe Mesto (**27**-28) a round low platform for public announcements and occasional executions, was built in 1534, rebuilt by Kazakov in the 1780's, and restored in 1964.

Beyond the Historical Museum is the *Square of the 50th Anniver-*

..ary of the October Revolution (Manege Square until 1967). The square was created in the 1930's by clearing an area of small houses and shops. The first name of the square was from the Manege, or riding ring, now the _Central Exhibition Hall_ (27-29) which forms the west end of the square. The Manege, built in 1817-1825 by engineer Betancourt and architect Bove, is 557 feet long and 148 feet wide, and has no central supports, an engineering marvel of its day. [In 1867 Hector Berlioz conducted a concert in the Manege with a 700-member orchestra and chorus, to an audience of 12,000 people.] The building was used as a Kremlin garage after the revolution, then restored in 1958 as an exhibition hall.

The north side of the square is traversed by Prospekt Marx. The buildings on either side of Gercen Street are the old _Moscow University Buildings_ (26-3). Further east is the _Headquarters of Intourist_ (26-4), #16 Pr. Marx, and the _National Hotel_ (26-5), corner of Gorky Street.

The east end of the square is formed by the Hotel "Moscow," 1932-1935. Facing it, on the south side of the square, is the _Lenin Museum_ (26-6), in the former City Assembly Building (Duma) built 1890-1892 by Chichagov.

Sverdlov Square is to the east beyond the Hotel "Moscow." On its northern edge is the _Bolshoy Theater_ (26-7), built 1821-1824 by Bove and Mikhailov. Burnt down in 1853, it was rebuilt in its present form by Kavos. Facing the theater, in the park in the center of the square, is a granite bust of Marx, 1961, by Kerbel.

To the east of the Bolshoy is the _Maly Theater_ (26-8), 1821 by Bove, redone 1838-1840 by Thon. The theater was associated with the works of the 19th-century playwright N. Ostrovsky, whose statue, 1928 by Andreev, is before the entrance. The theater also saw touring artists: Franz Liszt played there in 1843, and Clara Schumann in 1844.

The east end of Sverdlov Square is formed by the _Metropol Hotel_ (26-9), 1899-1903 by Valkot, Erikson, et.al. On the front is a ceramic frieze designed by M. Vrubel. This hotel has the offices of Pan Am, American Express, and several foreign banks. The main restaurant on the first floor is an example of turn-of-the-century elegance. Behind the hotel and along the south side of the square is the _Kitaigorod fortification wall_ (26-10), restored in 1961.

The building at the northeast corner of Sverdlov Square, at the beginning of Pushkin Street, is the _House of Unions_ (26-11). Built in 1784 by Kazakov, it became the Noblemen's Club in Moscow. Its famous Columned Hall was the largest ballroom in Moscow, as well as a concert hall. Events there were attended by writers like Pushkin, Lermontov, Turgenev, Tolstoy, and Chekhov. The building was restored after the fire in 1812, and was expanded with a third story in 1903. Both Lenin and Stalin lay in state in the Columned Hall after their deaths.

KITAIGOROD, and adjacent squares

Kitaigorod, the trading area east of the Kremlin, was enclosed by a wall in 1535-1538 by Petroch the Younger. When the city spread in the 19th century this area gradually shifted to wholesale trade, and in the 20th century it has come to house government ministries and administrative offices. The wall was largely demolished in 1935 as part of the general plan for the reconstruction of Moscow, but parts of it can be seen along Sverdlov Square behind the Metropol Hotel, and along Kitaisky proezd, the street beyond the new _Rossia Hotel_. The main streets of Kitaigorod run east-west. In 1700 the area had 72 trading rows, each named by what was traded there. Rybny (fish) and Krustalny (crystal) Streets still reflect that tradition.

25th October Street begins at the Historical Museum. The courtyard of the building at #7 contains the remains of the _Zaikonospassky Monastery_ (26-12) established in 1600 by Boris Godunov. In this monastery, in 1687, the Slavyano-Greko-Latinskaya Academy was established, Russia's first institution of higher education. (It functioned until 1814.) The Historico-Archival Institute at #15 is on the site of the _Old Printing House_ (26-13), 1553-1563. A building in the old style, authentically reconstructed in 1879, is in the courtyard and gives a good impression of the 17th-century style. The main building at #15 was constructed in 1814. The Printing House was established by Ivan the Terrible, and the Acts of the Apostles, 1564, is often considered Russia's first printed book.

At #17 is the _Slavyansky Bazaar Restaurant_ (26-14), which opened in 1966 on the site of a former hotel and restaurant of the same name, where many 19th-century cultural figures stayed and dined. It is remembered particularly for the meeting in 1897 between theater director Stanislavsky and playwright Nemirovich-Danchenko, which resulted in plans for opening the famous Moscow Art Theater. The building at #17 also houses the Moscow Children's Musical Theater.

Dzerzhinsky Square is at the end of 25th of October Street. The building at Prospekt Marx #2 is _Detsky Mir_ (26-15), Moscow's largest store for children's goods. The building on the far side of the square, between Dzerzhinsky Street and Kirov Street, is the _Committee of State Security_ (26-16), more commonly known as the Lubyanka Prison, headquarters of the secret police. The building belonged to the Rossia Insurance Company before the revolution. The taller wing on the right, from 1947, was designed by Shchusev as part of a remodeling of the building. In the center of the square is Vuchetich's statue (1955) of Dzerzhinsky, who was the first head of the Cheka and of the Soviet's internal security forces.

Kuibyshev Street was the central trading street of Kitaigorod. Its present appearance dates from the late 19th century. The building at #6, with a colonnade, is the _former stock exchange_ (26-17), 1875 by

Kaminsky. It is now the All-Union Chamber of Commerce. Between Rybny and Khrustalny Streets is the *former Gostiny dvor* (**26**-18), 1790-1805, a commercial building by Quarenghi and others. The buildings at #9 and #10 house the Ministry of Finance.

Kuibyshev proezd, between Kuibyshev Street and 25th of October Street, contains the *Cathedral of the Bogoyavlensky Monastery* (**26**-19),

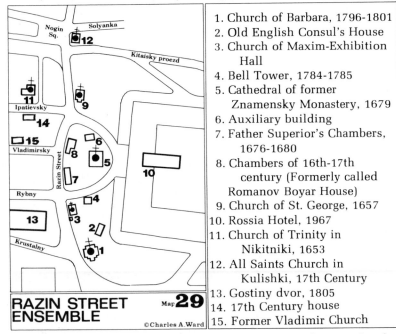

1. Church of Barbara, 1796-1801
2. Old English Consul's House
3. Church of Maxim-Exhibition Hall
4. Bell Tower, 1784-1785
5. Cathedral of former Znamensky Monastery, 1679
6. Auxiliary building
7. Father Superior's Chambers, 1676-1680
8. Chambers of 16th-17th century (Formerly called Romanov Boyar House)
9. Church of St. George, 1657
10. Rossia Hotel, 1967
11. Church of Trinity in Nikitniki, 1653
12. All Saints Church in Kulishki, 17th Century
13. Gostiny dvor, 1805
14. 17th Century house
15. Former Vladimir Church

RAZIN STREET ENSEMBLE Map **29**
©Charles A. Ward

1693-1696, an example of the "Moscow Baroque" architectural style.

New Square and *Old Square* at the end of Kuibyshev Street, were enlarged in 1935 by the demolition of the Kitaigorod wall. At #¾ New Square is the *Polytechnical Museum* (**26**-20), 1877-1907 by various architects. It has extensive exhibits on the history of technology in Russia and of Soviet technical achievements in science and industry. New Square #12, the *Museum of the History and Reconstruction of Moscow* (**26**-21), is in the former Church of John the Divine, 1825. The museum exhibits plans for the long-range development and reconstruction of Moscow.

At the beginning of Old Square is a small, chapel-like *monument*, 1887 by Sherwood, to the Grenadiers killed in the battle of Plevna in the Russo-Turkish War, 1877-1878 (**26**-22).

Razin Street was the border between the central part of Kitaigorod and "zaryadye", an area which housed service and minor artisans. This

whole area was cleared in the 1950's for a 37-story administrative building in the "Stalin Gothic" style, but plans were changed in the later 1950's and the 12-story *Rossia Hotel* was built, completed in 1967. At the corner of Kitaisky proezd and the Moscow River, beyond the hotel, is the *Church of St. Anna* (**26**-23), 1478-1485, rebuilt after a fire of 1547, with the addition of side chapels. This is one of the few remaining 15th-century churches in Moscow.

The building at the beginning of Razin Street, opposite Basil's Cathedral, is the *former "Middle Trading Rows"* (**26**-24), 1912 by Klein, a commercial building in an eclectic style. Along the east side of Razin Street are a series of churches and old buildings which were spared when the area was reconstructed.

RAZIN STREET ENSEMBLE (Map 29):

The *Church of Barbara* (**29**-1), 1796 by Kazakov, in neoclassical style. Below it is the *English Consul's House* (**29**-2), ca. 1600, "discovered" and restored in 1956. Foreign emissaries usually stayed there while visiting Moscow in the 17th century. It now has an exhibition of archeological findings from the zaryadye area.

The *Church of Maxim Ispovednik* (**29**-3), 1699, is at the ramp leading to the Rossia Hotel's west wing. The church houses an exhibit on nature and the environment. Its belfry, on the street, is from the 19th century. Between the church and the hotel is the *bell tower* (**29**-4) of the Znamensky Monastery, 1784-1789.

Inside the circle of the Rossia's entrance ramp is the five-domed brick *Cathedral of the Znamensky Monastery* (**29**-5), 1679-1684. Along the street is the *Father Superior's Chambers* (**29**-7), 1676-1680, and the *16th-17th Century Museum Chambers* (**29**-8), often called the House of the Romanov Boyars. The chambers were reconstructed in 1859 by architect F. Richter in the old Russian style. The building now houses an exhibition of furnishings of the 17th century. The two vaulted basement rooms display tools, trunks, and utensils; the four rooms of the upper level display furniture, clothing, and belongings of a well-to-do member of the upper class of the 1600's, before the wholesale influence of western manners on the Russian upper classes. Further down the street is the *Church of St. George*, 1657 (**29**-9).

Near the end of Razin Street is Ipatievsky Lane. House #12 is a restored 17th-century building, reputed to have been the residence for a time of Simon Ushakov, a 17th-century icon painter. To the right is the *Church of the Trinity in Nikitinsky* (**29**-11), also called the Church of Our Lady of Georgia, 1628-1653, an "encyclopedia" of 17th-century architectural ornamental detail, and one of Moscow's more interesting churches. Frescoes inside are by Ushakov. The church is open as a museum.

Nogin Square is at the end of Razin Street. It was from this area of town that Dmitry Donskoy left to fight the Tartars in 1380. He constructed the *All Saints Church "na Kulishkakh"* at that time (**29**-12 and **26**-26). The present church dates from the 16th-17th centuries (on the south side of the square).

BEYOND THE CENTRAL SQUARES

The area south of the Kremlin across the river is called **ZAMOSKVORECHE**. It is the location of the *Tretyakov Gallery of Russian Art* (**26**-27), at #10 Lavrushinsky Lane, about a one-half mile walk from the Rossia Hotel. The building and art collection were given to the city of Moscow by the Tretyakov brothers in 1892. (The facade in Old Russian Style was done in 1909 by B. Vasnetsov.) Among the famous exhibits in this overcrowded museum are the icons, including Rublev's "Trinity," and "Savior," the original icon of the "Holy Virgin of Vladimir," works of the Novgorod School, and mosaics from the former Mikhailovsky Cathedral in Kiev. There is likewise a broad selection of 19th-century artists: Levitan, Repin, Surikov, Vrubel, the famous portrait of Tolstoy by Kramskoy, of Dostoevsky by Perov, and many others. A *new museum* (**26**-28) nearing completion on the Krymskaya Quay will have four times the display space of the present gallery.

Notable churches in this section of Zamoskvoreche include the *Church of St. Nikola "v Pyzhakh,"* (**26**-29), 1657-1670, at #27a Ordynka St.; the *Resurrection Church* (**26**-30) on 2nd Kadashevsky Lane, 1677, and the *Church of St. Kliment* (**26**-31), on Klimentovsky Lane at Pyatnitskaya St., 1762-1770.

Southwest of the Kremlin, Prospekt Marx becomes Volkhonka Street. Volkhonka #12 is the **"PUSHKIN" MUSEUM OF FINE ARTS** (**26**-33 and **Plan 30**). The collection of the museum began in 1857 at Moscow University. The present building, 1898-1912 by Klein, was constructed to display the university's collection of plaster casts of Greek and Roman sculpture, and an Egyptian collection. After the Russian Revolution the Museum became Moscow's main gallery of Western art, and was expanded with some of the best works from the Tretyakov Gallery and Rumyantsev Museum, as well as from the nationalized private collections of Yusupov, Shchukin, Morozov, and Shuvalov families.

Unlike the Hermitage in Leningrad, the Museum of Fine Arts is small enough to be "done" in part of a day, and its excellent collection should not be missed by art lovers. The collection is very strong on French Impressionists, and has good representative works of most major schools of western art since the renaissance. The plaster casts bring to the collection masterpieces of earlier eras.

The works on display are occasionally rearranged, or away on loan. Some of the highlights of the collection are:

First Floor (Plan 30)
Room 4: Italian Art, 13th-15th century. Botticelli's "Annuncia-tion," Perugino's "Madonna and Child," Veronese's "Minerva," Bronzino's "Holy Family," Caesaro da Sesto, Sebastiano del Piombo, F. Bassano, Parmigianino.

Room 6: Dutch & German Art, 15th-16th Century. P. Breughel, Lucas Crannach the elder, Jan Gossart.

Room 15: Italian Courtyard, a copy of the 14-century "Bargello Court" of the Palazzo de Podestu in Florence. It contains copies of Italian renaissance sculpture.

Room 13: French Art, 17th-18th Century. Poussin, Claude Lorraine (5), Watteau, Boucher (5), LeNain, Chardin, Fragonard (3) David (3), Houdon.

Room 12: Italian Art, 17th-18th century. Guido Reni, Bernini, Strozzi, Salvator Rosa, Crespi, Tiepolo, Canaletto.

Room 11: Italian and Spanish Art, 17th Century. El Greco, Robera, Morales, Zurbaran, Murillo.

Room 10: Dutch Art, 17th century. Pieter de Hooch, Terborcht, van Ostaade, Jakob Ruysdael, Rembrandt's "Chasing Money changers from the Temple," "Thomas's Doubts" (1630's), "Portrait of an old woman" (1630's), "Portrait of the artist's brother" (1650's), Portrait of his brother's wife" (1650's), Ahasuerus, Hamam, and Esther" (1660's).

Room 8: Flemish Art, 17th century. Rubens, "Bachanalia," "Portrait of a Lady," and others; several Van Dykes, Jordaens, Snyders, Teniers the younger.

Second Floor
Rooms 17-21: French Art, late 19th, early 20th century. Corot (14), Daubigny (10), Manet (2), Monet (11), Pissaro (3), Sisley (3), Renoir (5), Cezanne (14), Van Gogh (4), Gauguin (14), Toulouse-Lautrec (2), Degas, Utrillo, Bonnard, Vlaminck, Derain, Matisse, Picasso, Rouault, Rodin, and others.

Room 23: French and English Art, early 19th century. Ingres, Delacroix, Gericault, Gros; Reynolds, Romney, Raeburn, Dawe, Morland.

Room 26: Copies of Medieval Art. Mosaics from San Vitale and St. Apollinaire Nuovo in Ravenna; from San Marco's in Venice. Copies of part of the door of St. Michael's Church in Hildesheim (11th-century), and of other German and Dutch Church doors. Copies of statues from Gothic cathedrals, particularly from Amiens. There are also objects of carved ivory, Byzantine icons of the 11th century, and early Italian icons.

Room 28: Italian Sculpture of the 15th century. Copies of Donatello's "St. George" and "Annunciation," of L. della Robbia, and other sculptors; copy of Giberti's doors of the Bapistry in Florence, and of other Italian church door panels, and sarcophagi.

Room 29: Copies of Michelangelo's works: Moses, Dying Slave, Medici Tomb group, etc.

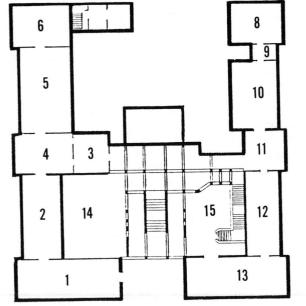

First Floor

1. Ancient Egyptian Art.
2. Assyrian & Babylonian
3. Byzantine Art, 1st-8th Cent.
4. Italian Art, 13th-15th Cent.
5. Italian Art, 15th-16th Cent.
6. Dutch & German Art, 15th-16th
14. Greek Courtyard
15. Italian Courtyard
13. French Art, 17th-18th Cent.
12. Italian Art, 17th-18th Cent.
11. Italian & Spanish Art, 17th Cent.
10. Dutch Art, 17th Cent.
9. Dutch & Flemish, 17th Cent.
8. Flemish Art, 17th Cent.

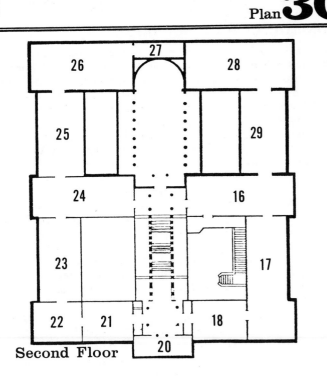

Second Floor

16. Greek Plaster casts, 5th Cent. BC
17. French Art, early 20th Century
18. French Art, late 19th Cent.
20. 20th Century European & American Art
21. French Art, 2nd half, 19th Cent.
22. European Art, 2nd half 19th Cent.
23. French & English Art, 1st half 19th Cent.
24. Plaster casts, 4th-1st Cent. BC
25. Roman Plaster Casts
26. European Middle ages, plaster casts
27. Small works, Renaissance sculpture & casts
28. It. Renaissance plaster casts
29. Plaster casts of Michelangelo's works

Volkhonka Street is continued by Kropotkinskaya Street, which becomes Zubovskaya Street after crossing Zubovsky Blvd. Leo Tolstoy Street is the second on the left after crossing the boulevard. There, at #21 Leo Tolstoy Street, is the *Tolstoy Home-Museum* (outside of **Map 26**) the house where Tolstoy spent the winter months, 1882-1901. The rooms have been preserved and restored as they were when Tolstoy lived there. (The "Tolstoy Museum," at Kropotkinskaya St. #11, has manuscripts and works about Tolstoy, but is not a place where he ever lived.)

Zubovskaya Street becomes Bol. Pirogovskaya Street, which leads on toward Lenin Stadium and to the **NOVO-DEVICHI CONVENT (Map 31).** The Novo-devichi ("New Maiden") Convent was founded in 1524 by Vasily III to commemorate his capture of Smolensk in 1514. The Convent continued to be associated with the royal family and for several centuries played a role in important historical events. It was here that Boris Godunov arranged his election as Tsar in 1598. The Convent achieved its present appearance in 1682-1689 during the regency of Peter the Great's half-sister, Sophia. She died here and is buried in the cathedral. In 1812 Napoleon used the convent as a provisions depot. His soldiers mined the buildings and lit time-delay fuses as they retreated, but nuns extinguished the fuses in time and saved the convent from destruction.

The brick walls of the convent, over 3000 feet in length and up to 35 feet high, received their present form in the 1680's during Sophia's regency. The defense towers were rebuilt at that time with "crowns," open-topped vertical extensions with narrow window embrasures elaborately framed in white limestone. The convent has twelve towers, round ones at the corners and square ones along the walls.

The convent is entered from the north through passageways beneath the 100-foot tall *Church of the Transfiguration* (**31**-1), 1687-1688. The church's brick exterior is marked by carved limestone window frames and scallop zakomara gables at the top of the walls. The church interior has a carved seven-tier iconostasis. In the corner of the small refectory attached to the church is a colored tile stove of the 17th century. The building adjacent to the west is the *Lopukhina Chambers* (**31**-2) 1687-1688, which has wall and window treatment similar to that of the Transfiguration Church. Irina Lopukhina, Peter the Great's first wife, lived here from 1727 till her death in 1731.

The entrance walkway leads past a cell building of the 17th century, rebuilt in the 19th, and past the small *Prokhorov Chapel* (**31**-3), to the Cathedral. The *Smolensky Cathedral* (**31**-4), 1524-1525, a six-column, three-apse church with five large domes, shows the influence of the Kremlin cathedrals, having the overall shape and smooth wall surfaces of the Assumption Cathedral, the tall basement level and gallery of the Annunciation Cathedral, and an interior similar to that of

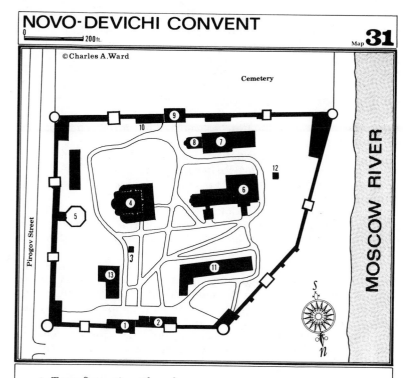

NOVO-DEVICHI CONVENT

©Charles A.Ward

Cemetery

Pirogov Street

MOSCOW RIVER

Map **31**

1. Transfiguration Church
2. Lopukhina Chambers
3. Prokhorov Chapel
4. Smolensky Cathedral
5. Belfry
6. Refectory
7. Old Refectory (Irina Godunova's Chambers)
8. Amvrosievskaya Church
9. Intercession Church
10. Mariinsky Chambers
11. Nuns cell building
12. Volkhonsky Mausoleum, early 1800's
13. Nuns cell building

the Archangel Cathedral. The basement was used for burial of women of noble families, including daughters of Ivan the Terrible and Aleksey Mikhailovich.

The view of the interior of the church from the west entrance door is dominated by the magnificent iconostasis and the giant fresco of the Virgin of Smolensk on the wall behind it. The convent and church were built in honor of a military victory and in general the frescoes were designed to glorify Vasily III and the Muscovite princedom. The frescoes on the columns depict Russian princes and patron warrior saints of earlier Russian city-states. In the 1590's Boris Godunov had some of the walls refrescoed to include numerous depictions of Saints Boris and Irina. The wall and ceiling frescoes were redone in 1666 and repainted in oils in 1757.

The magnificent iconostasis of carved gilded wood, 1683-1686, was commissioned by Sophia. Rising 67 feet in five tiers, it is marked by 84 columns carved as entwined grape vines, framing the icons. There are nine icons on the bottom, or Veneration, row. To the left of the central door is the Smolensk Mother of God, in a jewel-encrusted frame. Third to the left, a gift of Ivan the Terrible, is John the Baptist as an angel of the desert, holding a chalice. Next to it are Saints Boris and Gleb, a gift of Boris Godunov.

To the right of the central door is Christ on a golden throne, with small kneeling figures of John the Baptist and Apostle Peter at his feet. The icon, painted by Simon Ushakov in the 1680's, was a gift of Peter and his half-brother John. Next to it is a depiction of St. Aleksey and Mary, whose face bears a close resemblence to Sophia.

The Cathedral houses a museum of church treasures and religious decorative arts. The displays are in the altar area behind the iconostasis and in the Sophia Chapel in the south gallery of the church. While the most valuable treasures were removed to the Kremlin Armory Museum, there are still outstanding gold and silver chalices, censers, dishes, jewel-embedded crosses and personal icons, cameos, gospel covers, and embroidered vestments and coffin shrouds of astounding virtuosity.

The main floor of the cathedral houses several tombs. Sophia is in the southwest corner. Her sisters Ekaterina and Evdokia are on the east and west sides of the south portal. Evdokia Fedorovna, Peter the Great's first wife, is on the south side of the southwest column.

Directly east of the cathedral is the Bell Tower (31-5), 1690, a six-tier, 240-foot tall octagonal brick structure with white limestone detail work. The decorative details of each tier are different. Half of the tiers have open bell arches, the other half have niches surrounded by elaborate frames. The corners of the octagons are marked by pillars, and the top edge of each tier has a balustrade.

West of the cathedral is the Refectory (31-6), 1685-1687. The large refectory hall, 85 x 48 feet without internal support, is now used for church services. The east end of the building is the Uspenskaya Church, rebuilt after a severe fire in 1796.

South of the refectory is the Old Refectory (31-7), also known as Irina Godunova's Chambers, named for Boris Godunov's sister, widow of Tsar Fedor, who lived here from 1598. The east end of the building is the Amvrosievskaya Church (31-8), from the late 1500's.

On the south wall of the convent is the Intercession Church (31-9), 1683-1688, topped by three domes in a row. Next to it are the Mariinsky Chambers (31-10), from the 1600's, named for Tsar Aleksey Mikhailovich's daughter Maria, who lived there in the 1690's.

One of the largest buildings in the convent is the cell block (31-11) between the refectory and the Lopukhina Chambers. It is 280 feet long and 48 feet wide, and was constructed in the 1680's.

Many famous people were buried in the convent grounds. The historian S.M. Soloviev and philosopher-poet Vladimir Soloviev are along the path from the entrance to the cathedral, just to the west of the Prokhorov Chapel. Early 19th-century poet Denis Davidov is just to the east of the northern entrance stairs to the cathedral gallery. The grounds here also contain the graves of 19th-century novelists Lazhechnikov, Zagoskin, and Pisemsky. Beyond the south wall of the convent is the New Cemetery, with a separate entrance further down the street. Among the famous people buried there are writers Gogol, Chekhov, Mayakovsky, and Stanislavsky; composers Scriabin and Prokofiev; painters Levitan, Serov and Nesterov; film directors Eizenstein and Pudovkin, and political leaders including Khrushchev, with a grave sculpture by Ernst Neizvestny.

Kalinin Prospekt is the main radial road to the west of the Kremlin, beginning at the Trinity Tower. At #3 is the Lenin Library (26-36) 1939, which occupies the whole block to the south. The neoclassical building on Prospekt Marx, to the south, is the "Pashkov Palace" (26-37), 1784-1786 by Bazhenov. It housed the Rumyantsev Museum from the mid-1800's, the collection out of which the Lenin Library grew. Kalinin Pr. #5 is the Shchusev Museum of Russian Architecture (26-38), since 1957, in a building constructed in 1773 by Kazakov for F. Talyzin. By tradition this house has been considered the home of Pierre Bezukhov in Tolstoy's War and Peace.

Across the street at #10 is Voentorg (26-39), the "army-navy" department store, one of Moscow's largest. Further along at #16 is the Moscow House of Friendship (26-40), in a former home of A. Morozov, built in 1894 in a Moorish style influenced by a building Morozov saw while traveling in Portugal.

This section of Kalinin Prospekt between Prospekt Marx and Arbat Square is scheduled for widening by demolishing the buildings on the south side. The Museum of Architecture will be moved back, in line with the Lenin Library. The "high-rise" section of Kalinin between Arbat Square and Tchaikovsky Street, completed in the mid-1960's, is a successful experiment in city planning and a pleasant shopping area.

Gertsen Street is the next radial road to the north of Kalinin. At its beginning at Prospekt Marx are the *old buildings of Moscow University* (**26-3**). No. 6 Gertsen Street is the *Zoological Museum of Moscow University* (**26-41**). Further along, at #13, is the *Moscow Conservatory of Music* (**26-42**). Before it is a statue of Tchaikovsky, 1954, designed by Vera Mukhina. At the fork with Kachalov Street is the *Church of the Ascension*, 1830 (**26-43**), where the poet Pushkin was married in 1831. Opposite it, at #6 Kachalov Street, is a fantastic art nouveau house by Shekhtel, 1902-1906, built for the merchant Ryabushinsky. It now houses the *Maxim Gorky House-Museum* (**26-44**) in honor of the writer who lived there from 1931 until his death in 1936.

Gorky Street, the main radial road to the northwest, is considered Moscow's most important shopping street. At the beginning of the street is the *National Hotel* (**26-5**) and the 27-story tower of the *Hotel "Intourist"* (**26-45**). Across the street is Georgievsky Lane, beginning at a large archway. At #4 Georgievsky is the *Glinka Music Museum* (**26-46**), in the restored 17th-century home of Boyar Troekurov. The next side street off Gorky is Moscow Art Theater Street (MKhAT), named for the *theater at #3* (**26-47**) which achieved its present form when remodeled by Shekhtel in 1902. A *new building of the Art Theater* opened in 1973 at Tverskoy Blvd. #22 (**26-48**).

A block further up Gorky Street is Soviet Square, with an equestrian statue of Prince Yury Dolgoruky, considered the founder of Moscow. Across the street, at #13 Gorky, is the *City Soviet Building* (**26-49**). At Gorky St. #14 note the turn-of-the-century *food store* (**26-50**), formerly owned by the Eliseev brothers. It is the companion to a similar building on Nevsky Prospekt in Leningrad.

Three blocks beyond Soviet Square is Pushkin Square, with a statue of the poet unveiled in 1881. Chekhov Street begins at the northeast corner of the square. At Chekhov St. #4 is the elaborate *Church of the Nativity "in Putniki,"* 1649-1652 (**26-51**), a superb example of the 17th-century decorative style of Russian church architecture.

Kirov Street, the main radial road to the northeast beginning at Dzerzhinsky Square, has a number of interesting buildings. *Kirov Street #19*, 1894 by Klein (**26-52**), was designed with a Chinese-style facade for the tea merchant Perlov. Kirov St. #21, the Physical Engineering Institute, 1780's by Bazhenov, was the *Moscow Art School* (**26-53**) from 1844-1914. Leonid Pasternak taught at the school from 1894, and his son, Boris Pasternak, grew up there. (They lived in an apartment in the school.) At #39 Kirov St. is the Central Statistical Bureau, in a building designed by LeCorbusier, built 1929-1936 under the supervision of Soviet architect Kolli.

SITES FARTHER FROM THE CENTER OF MOSCOW

The *Exhibition of Achievements of the National Economy* (VDNKh) (outside of **Map 26**), is a sort of permanent fair grounds in the northern part of the city, on Prospekt Mira. Originally an agricultural exhibition area, it has been expanded to include all aspects of Soviet economy. Note particularly the "Kosmos" display, with rockets, satellites, and space vehicles; "Atomnaya Energiya", with displays of peaceful uses of atomic energy; the Consumer Goods Pavilion (Promyshlennost tovarov narodnogo potrebleniya) in a new glass building, with a large exhibit of a variety of consumer goods. Technical exhibits include "Fizika," "Biologiya," "Khimiya" (chemistry), "Metallurgiya," and "Elektrofikatsiya," with displays of power plants, turbines, etc. There are agricultural exhibits on all types of animal and plant cultivation in the Soviet Union.

Many dachas, villas, and country estates were built around Moscow. Four ensembles stand out in particular and have been preserved as museums. Kolomenskoe, summer residence of the tsars near Moscow, has the most magnificent location on a bluff over the Moscow River, and has several churches and other examples of Old Russian architecture. Kuskovo, the State Ceramics Museum, was an estate of the Sheremetev family and is Russia's best-preserved 18th-century estate with formal park. Ostankino, another Sheremetev estate, contains a remarkable 17th-century church and a palace which has the most opulent interior decoration in the Moscow area. Archangelskoe, a former estate of the Yusupov family, contains the best collection of paintings and scultpure of the suburban palaces.

KOLOMENSKOE, (Map 32), a summer residence of the tsars, is located on the high bank of the Moscow River ten miles southeast of the center of town. The estate belonged to the Grand Princes from the 14th century, but achieved its greatest expansion in the 16th and 17th centuries. The Kolomenskoe Metro Station is in the general area of the estate.

The entrance from the "Back Gates" leads to the *Kazanskaya Church* (Map **32**) 1649-1650, a five-dome, three-apse church on a high basement level reached by a staircase to a closed-in gallery. The interior was redone in the 19th century and is of no artistic interest. Services are still held in the church.

To the right are several wooden structures which were brought there in the 1930's. *Peter's House* (Map **32**), was built for Peter the Great in Archangelsk in 1702. It is a one-story log house of oblong shape and contains a table, chairs, bench, model ship, and other furnishings of the 17th century. Beyond it is the square *Tower of The Bratsk Prison*, (Map

32), 1652, moved here in 1959 at the time of the building of the Bratsk hydroelectric dam in Siberia.

The *Gate-Tower of the Nikolo-Karelsky Monastery*, (Map **32**), 1692, is a low log building with a tent roof over the entrance passageway. It was moved here in 1932. There is also a 17th-century *Mead Brewing Hut*, (Map **32**), of the Moscow region. These wooden buildings roughly outline the *area occupied by the famous wooden palace* (Map **32**), of 1668, built for Aleksey Mikhailovich. The palace fell into disuse and disrepair in the 18th century and was dismantled in 1768.

Beyond this area is the *Front Gate* (Map **32**), 1672-1673, a low rectangular masonry structure with two passage archways of unequal size. This part of the building serves as a base for a smaller gallery which contained the mechanism for running the clock located in the square tower above. It is topped by an octagonal tent-roof belfry. The Front Gate is flanked by 17th-century chambers which housed the chancellory and other offices. These rooms now serve to display the museum exhibits. The Chancellory room is restored with natural oak ceiling and has a long table with red tablecloth, inkwells, and documents. The furniture consists of oak chairs and benches.

The *Museum* (Map **32**), houses a collection of decorative and applied arts and crafts of the 17th century. Metal work includes candelabra of various shapes, decorative edging, a wide variety of forged window and door lattices, weather vanes, locks and keys. There are decorative tiles from 17th-century stoves, polychrome and carved wood, as used in ceiling and wall decor of the palace, as well as a series of carved and painted iconostasis doors of impressive variety and accomplishment. There are also carved architectural details from 17th-century wooden houses of various regions. The museum collection contains a scale model of the former wooden palace, one of the most interesting examples of Old Russian secular architecture.

Between the Front Gate and the river are the main architectural monuments of the estate. The dominant building of the ensemble is the remarkable *Ascension Church* (Map **32**), 1530-1532, a 200-foot tall masonry structure with a cubical base and tall tent roof. The cubical part is raised on a high "basement" level and is reached by a gallery and three stairways. The corners of the church are marked by brick pilasters which support the kokoshnik gables forming the transition to the roof. In addition to its sheer impressiveness, the church is important historically for signalling the break with the traditional low rectilinear church and paving the way for tent-roof churches like the Basil Cathedral on Red Square, and numerous 17th-century churches.

Next to the church is the *Georgievsky Bell Tower* (Map **32**), 16th-century, a two-level cylindrical structure with fine detail work on the outer wall. The blind arcading of the base and the cornices above were probably influenced by Alevisio's Archangel Cathedral in the

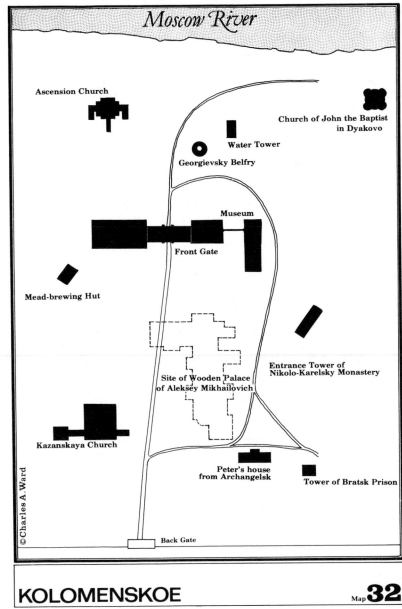

©Charles A. Ward

KOLOMENSKOE Map **32**

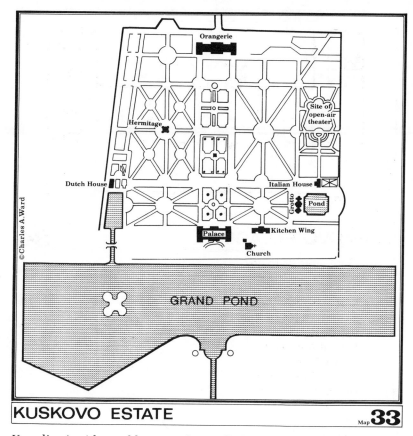

Orangerie

Site of open-air theater

Hermitage

Dutch House

Italian House

Grotto

Pond

Palace

Kitchen Wing

Church

GRAND POND

©Charles A. Ward

KUSKOVO ESTATE

Map **33**

KUSKOVO (Plan 33)

The Kuskovo Estate, now the State Ceramics Museum, was acquired by the Sheremetev family in the 1500's. In 1715 it became the property of Boris Petrovich Sheremetev, one of the associates of Peter the Great. Boris's son, Peter Borisovich Sheremetev (1715-1788) inherited the estate after his father's death. In 1743 Peter Borisovich married Varvara Alekseevna Cherkasskaya, the daughter and only child of A. M. Cherkassky, who had been head of the Construction Ministry in Petersburg and was one of the wealthiest men in Russia. The joining of the two families gave Sheremetev almost unlimited funds. He worked on the estate from the 1740's till the 1770's. The estate gained importance after 1748 when Tsarina Elizabeth had Rastrelli build a palace for her favorite, Razumovsky, in the neighboring village of Perovo. Since royalty would be visiting nearby, Sheremetev went ahead with construction of a palace for entertaining. Despite some damage at the hands of Marshal Ney's retainers in 1812, the estate preserved most of its original furnishings and was not remodeled in the 19th century. A museum was established there in 1918, and since 1932 Kuskovo has housed the State Ceramics Museum, with an excellent collection of Russian and foreign china.

The *Church*, (Plan **33**), 1737-1739, is the oldest building on the estate, a single-dome neoclassic structure with four-column Doric porticoes on three sides. The detached belfry topped with a slender spire is from 1792.

Beyond the church is the *Kitchen Wing*, (Plan **33**), 1755-1756, a focus of one of the longitudinal paths of the park.

The *Palace*, (Plan **33** and **34**), 1769-1775, by Karl Blank, a Moscow architect, replaced an earlier palace of almost the same size. The palace is picturesquely located on the bank of a large pond. On axis with the entrance of the palace, across the pond, is a canal marked by two columns. The canal leads into the distance and becomes a path, at the end of which is the tent roof Church of the village of Veshnyaka, 1646. The Palace is of wood, with wood siding on the exterior. The 210-foot exterior is finished in a restrained neoclassical style with Ionic wall pilasters and a projecting portico on the pond side. The rooms of the western half of the palace are described in brief below. (Plan **34**).

34-1. *Vestibule*, a square room with rounded corners, with tall fluted Corinthian pilasters of pink artificial marble on grey-green marble walls.

34-2. The *Entrance Drawing Room* has Flemish tapestries with park scenes and a woven portrait of Catherine II, designed by Rotari, to the right of the corner fireplace.

34-3. The *Second Drawing Room* also has tapestries, a decorative central fireplace with French irons, and a tile stove in the northeast corner that is as tall as the ceiling. Furnishings include Flemish oak chairs of

Kremlin. A wide entablature and row of kokoshnik gables separates the squat base from the taller, more slender upper section, which has open arches for the bells.

Behind the belfry is the 130-foot tall *Water Tower*, (Map **32**), 1600's, on the edge of a brook flowing into the river. The mechanism has not survived and the exact method by which the water was raised is unknown.

Beyond the ravine is the *Church of John the Baptist in Dyakovo* (Map **32**), mid-1500's, built by Ivan the Terrible on his ascension to the throne. The church consists of a central section with tall tent roof surrounded by four smaller chapels, and is considered a precursor of the Basil Cathedral on Red Square. Each of the five chapels has its own entrance. The church was rebuilt with changes over the centuries, and restoration to its original appearance was completed in 1964.

the 1600's, two English armchairs by the fireplace, from the early 1700's, and a long music table with an inlaid top depicting a panorama of the estate in 1770. There is a marble bust of P. B. Sheremetev by Shubin.

34-4. The *Raspberry Drawing Room*, in the corner, is named for its silk wall coverings. The room seems to focus on the ceiling-height tile stove in the corner. Note, too, the three-color geometric parquet and the baroque style crystal chandelier.

34-5. The *Formal Bedroom* continues the parquet of the corner room, but adds a painted ceiling. The bed is in an alcove.

34-6. The *Office-Study* is in oak, recalling Peter the Great's interior style.

34-7. The *Private Dressing Room*, with a patterned chintz wall covering, has a smoked cyrstal chandelier.

34-8. The *Divan Room* has three ceiling paintings and *trompe d'oeil* still lifes by Teplov, 1730's.

34-9. The *Library* displays scientific instruments rather than books.

34-10. The *Bedroom* is in white and blue-green with a fireplace on the west wall, and beside it an 18th-century English grandfather clock.

34-11. The *Picture Gallery* has French, Italian, Flemish, and Dutch canvasses chosen for size and color harmony. There is an optical illusion parquet and a nice stove of white and blue tiles with a garland and vase decorative pattern.

34-12. The *Mirror Hall* (or *White Hall*, or *Dance Hall*) is the largest and most formal interior of the palace. It has white and gold decor with mirrors, crystal chandeliers, a round-pattern parquet, and garland wall frieze. The ceiling painting is by LaGrenaille.

The 70-acre *Formal Park* (Plan **33**) was laid out in mid-century and is Russia's best preserved park in the French (Versailles) manner. The central parterre leads from the palace to the *Orangerie* (Plan **33**) at the far end of the park. In the center of the formal lawns are a marble obelisk, 1787, an Italian sculpture "Scamander," early 1700's, and the Minerva Column, 1776. The Orangerie, 1761-1765, has a two-story central pavilion once used for concerts and dances, flanked by the glassed galleries which lead to end pavilions.

The *Italian House* (Plan **33**), 1754-1755, is a fine small two-story palace with Doric pilasters and elaborate formal window frames. The building contains paintings, sculpture, and furniture as well as a display on the open-air summer theater of the estate, which was located north of the Italian House. Inside, a graceful curving stairway leads to the main hall on the upper floor.

The *Grotto* (Plan **33**), 1755-1761, just to the west of the Italian House, was designed by F. Argunov, a serf architect of Sheremetev's. It is the only 18th-century Russian grotto building to be preserved in its

©Charles A. Ward

KUSKOVO·PALACE

Plan **34**

Southern suite of rooms:

1. Vestibule
2. Entrance Drawing Room
3. Second Drawing Room
4. Raspberry Drawing Room
5. Formal Bedroom
6. Office-Study
7. Private Dressing Room
8. Divan Room
9. "Library"
10. Bedroom
11. Picture Gallery
12. Mirror Hall

original condition. The oblong squat building with heavily rusticated walls supports a large hemispherical dome. Intricate wrought-iron gates lead to the vault-like interior. The grotto is reflected by a small pond next to which it is so picturesquely situated.

The *Dutch House* (Plan **33**), 1749, is a small two-story masonry building with stucco walls painted to resemble brick. It is at the edge of a small pond which flows into the main pond, and is at the west end of the first transverse path of the park. The close interior is finished in Delft tiles and displays Netherlands paintings and furniture as well as porcelain from Holland, China, and Japan.

The *Hermitage* (Plan **33**), 1765-1767 by Blank, in the center of eight paths in the western part of the park, is a rectangular building con-

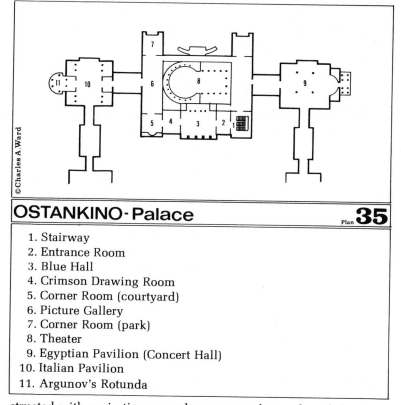

©Charles A. Ward

OSTANKINO - Palace
Plan **35**

1. Stairway
2. Entrance Room
3. Blue Hall
4. Crimson Drawing Room
5. Corner Room (courtyard)
6. Picture Gallery
7. Corner Room (park)
8. Theater
9. Egyptian Pavilion (Concert Hall)
10. Italian Pavilion
11. Argunov's Rotunda

structed with projecting curved corners so that each path leads to a facade. The two-story building has monumental walls with Corinthian pilasters and a wide entablature and cornice. Like the Hermitages in Petrodvorets and Pushkin near Leningrad, this one was equipped with a table which lowered through the floor to be reset.

OSTANKINO (Plan 35)

The Ostankino Estate Museum is just to the west of the Exhibit of Economic Achievements in northern Moscow. (A 1,700-foot tall stressed concrete TV tower is in front of the palace.) The estate belonged to the Cherkassky princes in the 1600's, and it was under them that the Church of the Trinity was built. In 1743 the last Cherkassky's daughter married P.B. Sheremetev (1715-1788), who then received the estate. In the 18th century Ostankino was known for its orchards, for Sheremetev devoted his energies to his estate at Kuskovo. In the 1790's Ostankino went to his son, N.P. Sheremetev, an extremely well-educated man,

European traveler, and patron of the arts. He had planned an arts palace on Sheremetev property in Moscow, but it was never realized. In 1790 he began work on a theater at Ostankino. The plan was revised and enlarged during the decade and was worked on by Camporesi, peasant architects Mironov and Argunov, and by Quarenghi. The final version was complete in 1797, and is surprisingly harmonious considering the many hands that worked on it. The living rooms were in wings to the front of the palace. The rooms around the theater are decorative and display the artistic abilities of Sheremetev's serf decorators and craftsmen.

Five central doors of the ground floor lead into the vestibule, a silver-grey room with a perspective ceiling by Scotti. To the right is a *staircase* (**35**-1) leading to the formal rooms of the upper floor. The *Entrance Room* (**35**-2) has tapestries, low-hanging chandeliers of various designs, and a rich cornice and ceiling treatment. This room leads to the *Blue Hall* (**35**-3), the most opulent of the interiors, with an abundance of draperies, crystal, marble, and inlay. The blue tonality is provided by drapes, wall coverings, upholstery, and painted details, like the bases of the Egyptian-style statues supporting the cornices over the doors. The rosette of the fancy ceiling, painted by Ferrari, is reflected in the parquet of birch and walnut. At the rear of the room is a loggia of four Ionic columns and pilasters of artificial marble, flanked at the ends by niches with statues of Venus and Apollo. The recess of the loggia contains 18th-century furniture and oval medallions of Peter I and Catherine II by Wedgwood. Illumination is provided by several chandeliers and highly ornamental torcheres.

The *Crimson Drawing Room* (**35**-4) gets its name from the red velvet wall covering. The room displays N. Argunov's portrait of Paul I in a rich gilt frame. The room has an elaborate wall frieze, cornice, and ceiling, slender chandeliers, and a quadrant parquet.

The *Corner Room* (**35**-5) is notable for its molded stucco ceiling and crystal chandelier. The *Garden Corner Room* (**35**-7) is similar, but with a fine central-medallion parquet.

The *Picture Gallery* (**35**-6) also serves as the chief foyer of the theater. It has plain blue wallpaper as a background for the paintings, and three huge crystal chandeliers for lighting. Among the furniture pieces along the walls are four malachite-topped tables with elaborate carved bases, designed by Starov.

The *Theater* (**35**-8) is the heart of the palace, a hall 120 feet long and 58 feet wide. The movable floor was so arranged that the stage and parterre seating could be lowered to one level, for use as a dance hall. That is how it is displayed now. The 16 white columns at the stage end are hollow and on tracks, and were moved back against the walls when the stage was raised. The main chandelier was also raised to provide clear sight lines for spectators in the loges. The entrance end has an

18-column horseshoe-shaped gallery. The fluted Corinthian columns are wood, painted like marble, and support a highly figured entablature beneath a low domed ceiling with a geometric and garland design.

Sheremetev had an excellent acting company, an orchestra and chorus, and a huge collection of over 5,000 costumes. The stage decor was designed by the leading artists of the time, including Gonzago. The Dramatic Troupe was active 1797-1801.

On the ground level low galleries lead to side pavilion wings, from which other galleries lead to the former living areas of the palace.

The *Egyptian Pavilion* (35-9) is reached through a low vaulted gallery with octagonal parquet, Ionic pilasters, and relief insets above the windows. The Egyptian Pavilion, by Camporesi, resembles a Roman atrium and is supported by four fluted Corinthian columns of blue artificial marble. The walls are plain except for a frieze of griffins at the top. The decorative features are the vaulted ceiling beneath the sky light and the parquet floor. The room was a concert hall and on the east has a recess for the orchestra and balcony for the chorus.

The *Italian Pavilion* (35-10) is in the western wing. The walls of the gallery leading to it are lined by sculptures. Notable are the "Cocks" by Canova and bronzes by Falconet and Gordeev. The ceiling treatment is more elaborate than that in the eastern gallery. The highly figured entablature of the doorframe leading into the pavilion is surmounted by two sphinxes.

The Italian Pavilion has a greenish-gold tonality and ranks with the Blue Hall as the most opulent in the palace. The fine parquet by Argunov is of rosewood, ebony, walnut, and birch, and in part reflects the ceiling pattern. The room serves as a gallery for about 30 classical and 18th-century marble sculptures.

To the west of the hall, through a set of doors, is a *Rotunda* (35-11) of Ionic order by Argunov. The ceiling dome is decorated with three types of rosettes and the parquet is of eleven types of wood with lead and mother-of-pearl inlay. The furniture dates from the 1850's.

The Park of the estate was not kept up and all the pavilions have disappeared, though in the early 1970's it was decided to restore the park buildings. Some sculptured urns and a "Three Graces" sculpture near the palace are by Germoni. The garden facade of the palace is by Quarenghi and Argunov. The further reaches of the grounds are now part of the Dzerzhinsky Culture and Rest Park of the city of Moscow. In front of the palace is a small lake with boating in the summer.

Between the palace and the lake is the *Trinity Church*, 1678-1692 by Potekhin, an excellent example of the Muscovite decorative architectural style of the late 17th century, with ceramic tile inlay, molded brick, and elaborate door and window frames of a variety of styles. The bell tower was added in 1832, but was remodeled with a tent roof in 1878 by Sultanov. The intricately carved and gilded iconostasis, 44 feet tall, was completed in 1691.

Across the pond from the palace is the *Ostankino Television Broadcast tower*, a 1740-foot tall stressed concrete structure completed in the later 1960's. The cylindrical tower rests on an open conical base forming nine "legs" encompassing a circle 195 feet in diameter. At about 1,000 feet up is the "Seventh Heaven" restaurant, consisting of three revolving tiers. Above it is an observation platform.

ARCHANGELSKOE

Archangelskoe, 18 miles northeast of Moscow, was a suburban estate of the Yusupov family. In the late 17th century the land belonged to Prince Cherkassky, but it became the property of D.M. Golitsyn in 1731. He laid out a formal park and built a palace, but it was abandoned after his death in 1736. His grandson, N.A. Golitsyn, had a palace designed by French architect Chevalier de Guerne. The palace construction went slowly in the 1790's and was not yet complete at Golitsyn's death in 1810, when the estate was purchased by Nikolay Borisovich Yusupov.

N.B. Yusupov was one of the richest nobles in Russia and one of the most active in the arts. Interested in art, he had collected paintings and sculpture in the capitals of Europe. His collection of over 500 paintings was one of the best private collections in Europe. He began training talented serfs in decorative arts around 1800, sending some to study with Scotti in Petersburg, and established an art school in Archangelskoe which operated for 30 years. He operated a silk-weaving factory from 1804, as well as a ceramics factory, 1818-1831, some products of which are in the Kuskovo Museum. Yusupov was from 1790 the director of the Imperial Theaters, and he had his own artistic troupe, as well as theaters in his Moscow palace and at Archangelskoe. Many of his stage sets were designed by Gonzago, the leading decorator in Russia at the time. Yusupov also had an outstanding library of 18,000 volumes.

The palace was damaged in the war of 1812, but was restored by Yusupov's serf architect, V. Strizhakov. A fire destroyed the interior in 1819, and it was again restored during the 1820's. Yusupov died in 1831 and the estate stayed in the family till 1917, though most of the art was moved to the Yusupov home in Leningrad. Archangelskoe was nationalized after the Revolution and made into a museum. The best art works were put into national art museums, and eight thousand of the books were sent to libraries in Moscow, but the palace still displays many fine works of art, and has 16,000 books in various rooms. The ensemble at Archangelskoe includes the Church of Archangel Michael, from the 1600's, restored in 1955, the Theater, 1817-1818, and the formal terrace and lawn beyond the palace, with a vista of the Moscow River.

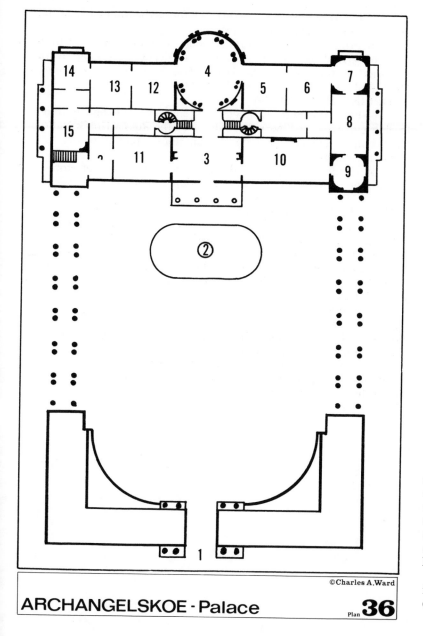

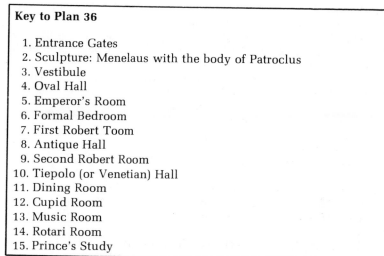

ARCHANGELSKOE - Palace

Plan **36**

The Palace (Plan **36**) is approached through monumental *wrought-iron gates* (**36**-1) between service wings which form the end of a courtyard outlined by a double colonnade. The two-story yellow stucco palace has a four-column Ionic portico and a 34-foot tall flat-topped rotunda belvedere on the roof at the center of the building. A planted area immediately before the portico contains the sculpture group *"Menelaus with the body of Patroclus"* (**36**-2). The walls of the palace are severely neoclassic, but have a white cornice separating the floors, and extremely tall windows on the lower floor. The following brief description of the rooms mentions the main features of the decor.

The *Vestibule* (**36**-3) has Corinthian pilasters at each end framing niches with fireplaces which act as the base for sculpture groups. The wall panels and ceiling are painted in imitation of bas-relief.

The *Oval Hall* (**36**-4) is the central room of the palace, formed by a semi-rotunda extending from the garden facade. The room was used for concerts, dances, and receptions. The entablature, balustrades and dome are supported by eight pairs of Corinthian columns of yellow artificial marble. Mirrors are the main wall decoration, though there are allegorical panels depicting "Music," "Painting," and "Sculpture" above the doors. The top of the dome has a painting of "Cupid and Psyche" by Nicholas Courteille.

The *Emperor's Room* (**36**-5) has portraits of Russian tsars and royal families. The furniture is painted white, with gilt details. The room also contains various pieces of sculpture.

The *Formal Bedroom* (**36**-6) has a blue and gold bed with canopy of blue Lyons silk with silver embroidery in an alcove behind four Corinthian columns of white artificial marble.

The *First Robert Room* (**36**-7), in the corner, has four paintings by French artist Hubert Robert (1733-1808), classical busts around the walls, and a statue in the center under the chandelier.

The *Antique Hall* (**36**-8) is a gallery with Roman marble statuary discovered in excavations in Pompeii in the 18th century. The walls have some 19th-century French paintings on classical themes, and the flat ceiling is painted to appear vaulted.

The *Second Robert Room* (**36**-9) has six canvasses by Robert and two by Canaletto.

The *Tiepolo Hall* (**36**-10) is named for two of Tiepolo's large works, "The Meeting of Antony and Cleopatra" and "Cleopatra's Feast." The hall also contains several paintings of Italian, French, and German masters. There are busts and furniture around the walls and an anonymous 18th-century sculpture, "Sleeping Venus," in the center of the room.

The *Dining Room* (**36**-11) was redone in an eclectic style in the 19th century with oriental porcelain, neoclassic chandeliers, and pseudo-Egyptian wall details. The walls are hung with various portraits and paintings.

The *Cupid Room* (**36**-12) is hung with paintings, including LeBrun's "Iphigenia's Sacrifice," Boucher's "Startled Nymph" and two sea-scapes by Claude Vernet. The furniture in the room is upholstered with fabric from Yusupov's factory.

The walls of the *Music Room* (**36**-13), a reception room for the princess's guests, are covered with paintings, including "Portrait of a Lady" by Van Dyke and canvasses by Monier, Dawe, Canaletto, and Vernet. Furnishings include an early 19th-century piano, a French writing table, and miscellaneous pieces of white birch furniture.

The *Rotari Room*, 1837 (**36**-14), in a former bedroom, has portraits by Rotari and baroque style furniture.

The *Prince's Study* (**36**-15) has book cases and family portraits.

The second floor of the palace has plain decor and low ceilings, and contains furniture and more bookcases. The room over the vestibule has an exhibit on the construction of the estate.

SHOPPING IN MOSCOW

The best value and best selection of souvenirs is to be found in the foreign currency, or "Beriozka," shops in the Rossia Hotel, National Hotel, and elsewhere (particularly the store across from the Novodevichi Convent).

For window shopping and browsing through Soviet stores for items in general, begin with the main department stores:

G.U.M., Red Square

TS. U.M., #2 Petrovka Street

Voentorg, #10 Kalinin Prospekt ("Army-Navy" department store)

Detsky Mir - #2 Prospekt Marx (everything for children)

The main shopping streets near the center are Gorky Street, Stoleshnikov Lane (sidestreet off Gorky at Soviet Square), Kalinin Prospekt (the "high-rise" section), and Arbat Street (parallel Kalinin from Arbat Square).

Shopping by item:

Antiques - Second Hand: Arbat 19

Books: Gorky 6,15; Stoleshnikov 16, Dom knigi on Kalinin Prospekt, Kirov 6, Kuznetsky most 18, Pr. Marx 1

Phonograph records: Kalinin 40; Arbat 6, Kirov 17

Sheet music: Neglinnaya 14; Gorky 15; Gertsen 13

Slides and filmstrips: Gorky 32

Maps: Kuznetsky most 9

Arts and crafts by Soviet artists: Kutuzovsky prospekt 17

CITIES AND TOWNS NORTH AND NORTHEAST OF MOSCOW

ZAGORSK
PERESLAVL-ZALESSKY
ROSTOV
YAROSLAVL
VLADIMIR
SUZDAL

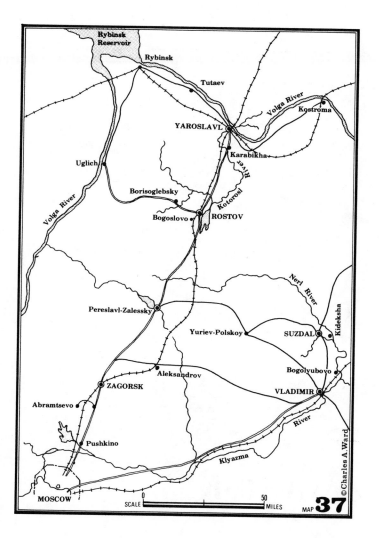

Rybinsk Reservoir

Rybinsk

Tutaev

Volga River

Kostroma

YAROSLAVL

Karabikha

Uglich

River

Borisoglebsky

Kotorosl

Volga River

Bogoslovo · ROSTOV

Nerl River

Pereslavl-Zalessky

Kideksha

Yuriev-Polskoy · SUZDAL

Bogolyubovo

Aleksandrov

ZAGORSK

VLADIMIR

Abramtsevo

River

Pushkino

Klyazma

MOSCOW

SCALE 0 — 50 MILES

MAP **37**

©Charles A. Ward

1. Vvedenie Church, 1547
2. Pyatnitskaya Church, 1547
3. Pyatnitsky Well, ca. 1700
4. Red Gate Tower, ca. 1600
5. John the Baptist Church, 1699
6. Assumption Cathedral, 1585
7. Godunov Mausoleum
8. Well-Chapel, 1684
9. Dukhovskaya Church, 1476
10. Trinity Church, 1423
11. Nikon's Chapel, 1553
12. Metropolitan's Residence, 1778
13. Refectory and Church of Sergiy, 1692
14. Mikheevskaya Church, 1734
15. Imperial Chambers, 1690's
16. Museum
17. Zosima and Savvaty Church, 1638
18. Smolenskaya Church, 1748
19. Belfry, 1770
20. Obelisk, 1792
21. Cells
22. Classroom building, 1884
23. Bathhouse, 1847
24. Hospital, 1835
25. Library, 1877
26. Kazanskaya Church, 1752
27. Elijah Church, 18th century
28. Civil building, 19th century
29. Stables, 1790
30. Former monastery Hostel, 1861
31. Foreign Currency Souvenir Store

ZAGORSK
Troitse-Sergieva Lavra

Proletariat St.

to Moscow

Vokzalnaya St.

Pervomaisky St.

Parking Lot

Marx St.

to Yaroslavl

ZAGORSK

scale 0 ▭▭▭ 200 ft.

© Charles A. Ward

MAP **38**

ZAGORSK
(Map 38)

Zagorsk (Sergiev until 1930) is a small manufacturing city of 100,000 located 44 miles northeast of Moscow. The town developed around the *Trinity Monastery of St. Sergiy (Troitse-Sergieva Lavra)*, Russia's foremost monastery and the residence of the Patriarch of the Russian Orthodox Church. The monastery was founded in the 1340's by the monk Sergiy of Radonezh, who politically was allied with the Moscow princes and worked for the unification of Russian lands under their rule. Ties between the monastery and the state were always close. Dmitry Donskoy stopped here for Sergiy's blessing when he went to battle the Mongols in 1380, and it was at the monastery that heirs of the Moscow princes were baptised. As a bulwark of defense in the "Time of Troubles," the monastery withstood a 16-month siege by Polish interventionists, 1608-1610. Enjoying the generous patronage of the Moscow princes, the monastery became the leading religious cultural center of Russia.

When approached from Moscow, the monastery can be seen ahead on a hillside, its many domes rising behind the massive defense walls. Two churches sit next to the road at the foot of the monastery wall. The *Vvedenie Church*, 1547 (**38**-1) is a tall brick, cubical church with one dome rising above a high sloping roof. The apses facing the road are divided into tall narrow sections by vertical brick courses. Thirty feet away is the *Pyatnitskaya Church*, (**38**-2), also 1547, a refectory church with walls accented by large figured window frames and a cornice near the top of the wall. Across the road is the *Pyatnitsky Well*, (**38**-3), ca. 1700, housed in an octagonal structure of three receding tiers, with heavy frames on the windows of the lower level.

The main entrance into the monastery is from the east through the single-dome *Red Gate Tower* (**38**-4) ca. 1600, and beyond it, through the frescoed arch under the *Church of John the Baptist* (**38**-5), 1693-1699. The church, best seen from the center of the monastery, is a tall two-story structure with five gold domes, and is similar in appearance and age to the entrance church of the Novo-devichi Convent in Moscow.

Directly ahead of the entrance is the *Assumption Cathedral* (**38**-6), 1559-1585, begun at Ivan the Terrible's behest. Construction was delayed by a fire in 1564 and by Ivan's later disaffection. The cathedral is slightly larger (98 x 138 feet) than its namesake, the Assumption Cathedral of the Moscow Kremlin. It has five apses, hidden except in winter by trees, and five massive drums and domes. The large and high interior preserves frescoes and an iconostasis from 1684. Outside the church to the north of the west portal is the *mausoleum of Tsar Boris Godunov*, (**38**-7), and some members of his family.

Dukhovskaya Church: Zagorsk

Next to the southwest corner of the cathedral is a *Well-Chapel*, (38-8), ca. 1684, a three-tier structure with square base and octagonal upper sections, all highly decorated with the curlicues of the "Moscow baroque" style. South of this chapel is the *Dukhovskaya Church*, 1476 (38-9), by Pskov masters, a cubical brick church with marked vertical emphasis created in part by the large, six-arch belfry under the cupola, wall pilasters ending in ogee zakomaras, and large ogee portals on two sides.

Due west is the oldest building in the monastery, the *Trinity Church*, 1422-1423 (38-10), a four-column, three-apse church erected over the grave of Sergiy. The exterior has been restored to its original appearance, with walls divided into thirds, rising to ogee zakomaras. Horizontal emphasis is given by a finely carved decorative band with a cross and interweaving vine pattern. The frescoes by Rublev have not survived in their original form, but an iconostasis with icons of the early 15th century by Rublev's school still adorns the church. Rublev's famous "Trinity," now in the Tretyakov Gallery, was painted for this church. On the southeast side of the church is *Nikon's Chapel*, 1548-1553 (38-11), built over the tomb of Nikon, Sergiy's successor. Facing this church to the south is the *Metropolitan's residence*, (38-12), 16th century, rebuilt in 1778 in the neoclassic style.

The main structure of the south side of the monastery is the *Refectory and Church of Sergiy*, 1686-1692 (38-13), a huge building in the Moscow baroque style, and one of the most remarkable structures of the late 17th century in Russia. The refectory building, totally surrounded by a terrace, is 275 feet long and is raised on a high basement which contained the bakery, kitchen, and pantries. The walls are painted in a diamond-point rustication pattern and are divided by giant-order Corinthian columns which support an entablature of decorative scallop zakomaras. The wall columns bracket windows with frames consisting of carved baroque columns and highly figured pediments. The refectory hall itself, 49 x 112 feet, is covered by a barrel vault. At the time of its construction this was the largest room in Russia spanned by a single arch. At the east end of the building is the Church of Sergiy, divided from the refectory hall by a screen added in the 19th century. Beyond the screen is one of Russia's most elaborate baroque iconostases, from the late 1600's.

In the 1690's the *Imperial Chambers*, (38-15) were built in the northern part of the monastery in a position symmetrical to the Refectory. The chambers were remodeled over the centuries, but still retain diamond-point painted rustication. The windows of the upper floor have frames of carved baroque columns, while those of the lower level are in a more restrained neoclassical form.

The Vestry-Treasury building along the west wall of the monastery now houses the *Monastery Museum*, (38-16), with a rich collection of icons, paintings, embroidered works (vestments, shrouds), applied arts (chalices, Gospel covers, censers), illuminated manuscripts, furniture, and carved, polychrome wood work.

To the north of the Museum is the *Church of Zosima and Savvaty* and the Hospital Wing (38-17). The church, 1635-1638, is a columnless, cubical church with ogee zakomaras, a large semi-circular apse, and a tall octagonal tent roof. The apse repeats the narrow decorative columns of molded brick found on the Dukhovskaya and Vvedenie Churches.

Opposite the Zosima and Savvaty Church is the *Smolenskaya Church*, 1745-1748 (38-18), a circular church 41 feet in diameter, in the western baroque style. Four semi-circular niches rising the full height of the church create four "facades," an emphasis which is reinforced by arched pediments and the entrance stairs below. The capitals of the pilasters and frames of the upper windows were never completed.

The monastery *Belfry* (38-19), opposite the Museum, was built 1740-1770 to replace a smaller, earlier tower which was east of the Dukhovskaya Church. The new neoclassical tower, 285 feet tall, was designed by Michurin and completed by Ukhtomsky. It has a large rusticated square base above which rise four slender tiers accentuated by two sets of paired Corinthian columns on each facade. South of the tower is a small *obelisk and terrace*, 1792 (38-20), built as a marker to celebrate the completion of the monastery.

PERESLAVL-ZALESSKY
(Map 39)

Pereslavl-Zalessky is an old Russian town 85 miles northeast of Moscow on the banks of Lake Pleshcheevo. The town was founded by Prince Yury Dolgoruky in 1152 as a portage point on the trade route from the Klyazma River to the Volga. It was named for the town of Pereyaslavl near Kiev, and was called Zalessky ("beyond the forest") to differentiate it from its namesake. Though protected in the 12th century by an excellent earthen rampart, still quite impressive, Pereslavl-Zalessky was overrun by the Mongols in 1238. The town became part of the Moscow princedom in 1302. Relative stagnation of the Mongol years was replaced by active construction in the 16th century under the patronage of Vasily III and Ivan the Terrible. In 1680 Lake Pleshcheevo was the site of Peter the Great's first sailing lessons. Of the flotilla of boats he had built, only one has survived, now kept at the Botik Estate two miles from town on the southern shore of the lake.

If you approach Pereslavl-Zalessky by road from Moscow, you will notice, on the left hand side of the road four miles from town, a small brick structure, the Holy Cross Chapel, erected in 1557 by Ivan the Terrible to mark the place where his son, Fedor, was born. At the edge of town on a hill to the left is the *Goritsky Monastery* (39-1), one of a half-dozen monasteries which survive in this area. Though founded in the 14th century, the monastery's greatest flourishing was in the 17th and 18th centuries. Most notable are the two sets of decorative brick gates on the south and east sides of the southeast corner of the monastery wall. The Holy Gate on the south with its large passage archway is of figured brick arranged in many patterns — ribs, columns, reliefs, niches. Above the gateway is the St. Nikola Church, with smooth walls broken by elaborate window frames. At the corner of the monastery wall to the right of the gate is a chamber with decorative ribbing, niches, and window frames adorning its walls. The entrance gate on the east wall is just as elaborate as the formal entrance to the south. The east gate seems to be supported on four squat columns and has molded figures of horses in niches. Both gates and the chamber probably date from the late 1600's.

The Assumption Cathedral of the monastery dates from the 1750's. Its exterior follows the traditional five-dome style, but the interior reflects decorative details of the western baroque style — stucco molding of volutes, acanthus leaves, cherubs and angels, and miscellaneous neoclassical arthitectural detail. The iconstasis of 1759 also reflects the western baroque. Just to the west of the church is a vacant lot where originally a building to house a triumphal stairway to the choir of the church had been planned. The building to the west of this is the All-Saints Church and refectory, late 1600's, which now house the administrative offices of the monastery. The monastery also contains the local Pereslavl-Zalessky Museum, with some interesting icons and religious decorative arts, and a gallery with paintings by Dmitry Kardovsky, a native of this area.

To the right of the road into town is the *Fedorovsky Monastery* (**39**-2), from the mid-1500's. The main building is the Church of Fedor Stratilites, 1557, built by Ivan the Terrible after the birth of his son, Fedor. Remodeling of the church over the centuries has changed its original roof line and added new galleries.

Further along the main road is the *Danilov Monastery* (**39**-3), founded in 1508 by a monk Daniil, who was a friend of Vasily III and who christened his son, Ivan the Terrible, in 1530. In 1532 the Trinity Cathedral of the monastery was built, probably with Vasily III's money. This single-dome church has been remodeled over the years, with new roof line and windows, but it preserves the original wall cornice and peculiar 12-sided apses. The church preserves interesting frescoes of 1662 in the drums and domes and in some areas of the walls.

The monastery contains the All-Saints Chapel, 1687, a one-dome, columnless church with exterior decor which harmonizes with the cathedral. The cathedral's Belfry, 1689, is a massive structure with a square base supporting an octagonal tent roof topped by a rather small dome. The Refectory by the church has wall patterns of molded brick.

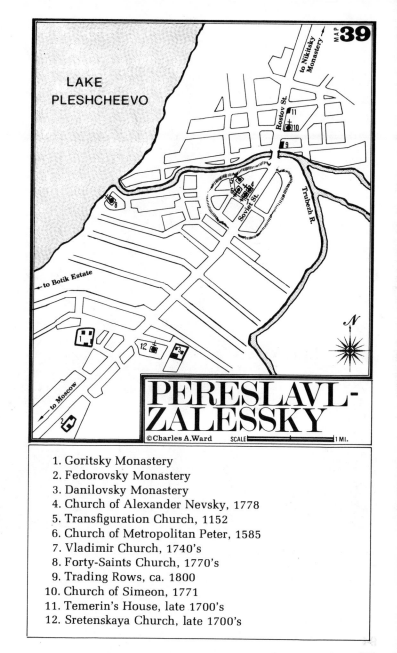

1. Goritsky Monastery
2. Fedorovsky Monastery
3. Danilovsky Monastery
4. Church of Alexander Nevsky, 1778
5. Transfiguration Church, 1152
6. Church of Metropolitan Peter, 1585
7. Vladimir Church, 1740's
8. Forty-Saints Church, 1770's
9. Trading Rows, ca. 1800
10. Church of Simeon, 1771
11. Temerin's House, late 1700's
12. Sretenskaya Church, late 1700's

Church of Transfiguration:
Pereslavl-Zalessky

The two-story Cell Building has plainer walls, but highly figured window frames.

Pereslavl-Zalessky is most famous for the *Church of the Transfiguration*, 1152-1157 (**39**-5), the oldest church in northeastern Russia. It is a simple cubical, single-dome white limestone church with walls divided into thirds by pilaster strips. The interior decoration has not survived.

Not far away is the *Church of Metropolitan Peter*, 1585 (**39**-6), a two-story central plan cubical church with a tall octagonal tent roof. The original interior has not survived. A new two-tier belfry of neoclassical line was added to the south side in the 1800's.

In the 1740's the *Vladimir Church* (**39**-7) with its five distinctive onion domes was built in the center of town to take over the functions of the Transfiguration Church. Somewhat later in the 1770's the *Forty-Saints Church* (**39**-8) was built on the shore of the lake where the Trubezh River flows in. It has a high-pitched pyramidal roof with central drum and dome, four small subsidiary domes on small triangular pediments, flamboyant window frames, and a refectory and neoclassic belfry from the 19th century.

There are several notable buildings on the main street rising up hill from the center of town. Just beyond the river is the *Gostiny dvor shopping rows* (**39**-9) of the early 1800's, and next to them a hotel and restaurant (Rostov St. #7). In the next two blocks are the *Church of Simeon*, 1771 (**39**-10), somewhat in the western baroque style, and an old private home, *Temerin's House* (**39**-11) from the later 1700's.

To the north of town on the road to Rostov is the *Nikitsky Monastery* (outside of Map **39**) founded in the 12th century, but revitalized during Ivan the Terrible's reign in 1561-1564 when a new five-dome Cathedral was built. In the late 1960's restoration work was begun on the cathedral, to reconstruct the original roof line and windows which had been changed over the centuries. The monastery also preserves a five-dome Refectory Church of the Annunciation, with attached octagonal tent roof Belfry of the 1660's. The monastery's fortification walls are impressive in their size and monumentality and have fine corner towers.

By the main road there is a small three-tier octagonal Chapel, 1702, built in memory of Prince Michael of Chernigov.

ROSTOV
(Map 40)

Rostov Veliki ("Rostov the Great") is a town of 38,000 people 125 miles northeast of Moscow on the road to Yaroslavl. One of Russia's most ancient settlements, Rostov was mentioned in the first chronicle entry of 862. The town and environs were gradually settled by Slavs and Christianized in the 10th and 11th centuries, and were ruled by Yaroslav the Wise of Kiev (990's) and later by his grandson Vladimir Monomakh (1090's). In the mid-12th century Rostov became one of the main cities of northeast Russia, part of Prince Andrey Bogolyubsky's Rostovo-Suzdal princedom with its capital in Vladimir.

The city's wealth and position, which had begun to dissipate in the early 13th century, was totally lost at the arrival of the Mongols in 1238. The process of absorption by Moscow began in the mid-14th century by Ivan Kalita. Rostov formally became part of the Moscow Princedom in 1474 under Ivan III.

Always important as a religious center, Rostov became the seat of a metropolitan, the highest church rank, in 1589. While Rostov preserves two monasteries, miscellaneous churches, and the old city cathedral, the flourishing of Rostov's architecture is associated with the magnificent architectural ensemble of the Metropolitan's Kremlin, built in the 17th century under the direction of Iona Sysoevich (1607-1690; metropolitan from 1652), one of the leading churchmen in Russia at the time. After the founding of St. Petersburg, Rostov declined in importance. The town received a new street plan in 1779 during Catherine's reign, but no new large-scale structures were built. In the 19th century the metropolitan's Kremlin, having fallen into disrepair, was almost demolished, and only after 1875 were concentrated efforts at restoration made. A hurricane in 1953 did great damage, knocking off nearly all the church domes, but since then the buildings of the ensemble have been totally restored.

The *Metropolitan's Kremlin* (**40**-1 and Plan **41**) is located on the edge of Lake Nero and consists of a large walled area containing five churches and other buildings. A peculiar feature of the ensemble is the elevation of the buildings. In the 17th century all the structures were connected on the second floor level by walkways and terraces. The Kremlin had two main entrances, from the north and west, through gateways beneath churches. The main tourist entrance today is through an archway made in the east wall of the Kremlin in the 19th century. The main feature of the east wall of the Kremlin is the massive square *Water Tower* (**41**-11), a former passage tower with two unequal openings. It is topped by a tall tent roof crowned with a lookout platform. The tower got its name because it was from here that servants went to the lake for water.

ROSTOV

SCALE 0 ——— ½ MI

©Charles A. Ward   MAP **40**

1. Metropolitan's Kremlin, 1660-1690
2. Church of the Savior "on the market", 1690
3. Nativity Church, ca. 1700
4. City park
5. Church of Isadore the Blessed, 1566
6. Tolgskaya Church, 1761
7. Church of Nikola, 1813
8. Former Customs House, 1813
9. Emelyanov's House, 1770's
10. Serebrennikov's House, 1800's
11. Former Boys High School
12. Yakovlev Monastery
13. Spassky Cathedral, 1603
14. Church of St. John "on the Ishnya", 1689
15. Kozma and Demyan Church, 1775
16. Avraamievsky Monastery

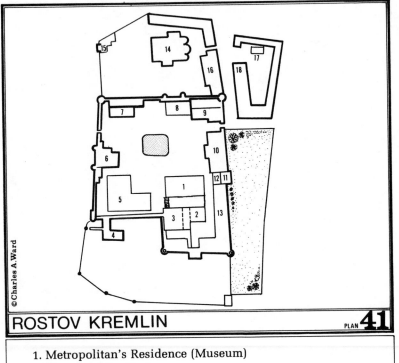

ROSTOV KREMLIN

PLAN **41**

1. Metropolitan's Residence (Museum)
2. Church of the Savior
3. White Chambers
4. St. George Church
5. Red Chambers (Youth Hostel)
6. St. John the Divine Church
7. Odygytria Church
8. Resurrection Church
9. Former monk cells
10. Former servants building
11. Water Tower
12. Hierarch's Chambers
13. Service building
14. Assumption Cathedral
15. Holy Gate
16. Belfry
17. Savior Church on the market
18. Trading rows

The entrance arch leads to the central square with its pond, originally for fire-prevention measures, surrounded by a series of tall churches and other buildings. The description below follows the usual route of Kremlin tours.

The central building is the *Metropolitan's Residence*, (**41**-1), or Samuilov Korpus (entered from the south on the second floor level), a three-story rectangular building from the 16th century, radically remodeled in the 19th as a School of Theology. The exterior was never restored and the upper two floors look like any 19th century neoclassic building, while the lower floor retains some decorative brick work of the earlier period. The building houses the *Museum*, with displays of icons, metal work (chalices, crosses, censers), wood carving, and textiles.

South of the Metropolitan's Residence is the *Church of the Savior "na senyakh," 1674* (**41**-2), the "house chapel" of Metropolitan Iona, which was constructed on the site of a wooden church burnt by lightning in 1671. This church, the tallest in the Kremlin, stands out with its plain white walls, four triangular gables, and single gilt dome. The interior is most impressive, and a little unusual, for the iconostasis has been replaced by a frescoed wall on golden columns on top of a raised stage area which takes up half the church area. The well-preserved frescoes, from the 1670's, have a dominant orange tonality. Particularly interesting is the imaginative depiction of the Last Judgment on the west wall. The round black spots on the frescoes are where the plaster has fallen off of the heads of metal reinforcing spikes in the walls. Larger round holes near the top of the walls are the mouths of ceramic pots built into the walls to serve as acoustic resonators.

To the west of the church is a large enclosed corridor once used for bidding farewell to guests. A stairway leads to the former bakery on the lower level. A portal in the west wall leads into the *White Chambers* (**41**-3), a four-vaulted room with central pillar which houses a decorative arts exhibition.

A doorway in the west wall of the White Chambers leads to a walkway along the wall dividing the main Kremlin area from the garden. To the right is the *Red Chambers, 1670-1680* (**41**-5), built as a guesthouse for important visitors. The building was half-destroyed by the 19th century, when it was used as a salt and wine storehouse. It was rebuilt in 1955 and now houses a Youth Hostel. Its exterior is notable for the window frames, cornice and the magnificent stairway on the east side.

To the south of the wall is the Church of St. George, the interior of which has not survived as well as those of the other Kremlin Churches.

The *Church of John the Divine* (**41**-6) was built in 1683 over the west entrance gate of the Kremlin. This is the most harmonious of the churches and should be viewed from various spots along the wall and from the central courtyard. The church is square in plan with pilaster strips on the facades leading to small pointed gables. The wall surface is also broken by a "belt" of little columns near the top of the walls. The five domes on tall drums add to the height and exquisite silhouette of the church. The church should also be viewed from the west, outside the Kremlin, where the lower part is concealed behind the gate towers and decorative frames and niches of the wall over the entrance arches.

The interior of the church has a frescoed wall in place of an iconostasis, but lacks a raised altar area as found in the Savior Church. The frescoes of 1683, in six bands, are devoted to the life of Christ and to John the Divine. The frescoes have great power in spite of a bad "renewal" job in the 19th century. Just to the north of the church is its small tent-roof belfry on the wall.

In the northwest corner of the Kremlin is the low brick *Odygytria Church*, 1698 (**41**-7), built by Iona's successor, Ioasaf Lazarzvich, in a restrained version of the new "Moscow" style, with red brick walls, pyramidal roof, and paired columns instead of pilasters as wall decoration. The church retains traces of a painted rustication in a triangular pattern, probably influenced by the Refectory of the monastery in Zagorsk. The Odygytria Church now houses a lecture hall, souvenir and postage stamp shop.

Off center on the north wall is the *Resurrection Church*, 1670 (**41**-8), built over the gates leading to the Rostov Cathedral. This five-dome church has plain walls broken only by pilaster strips and a narrow cornice above the windows. From the north the church is framed by two massive round towers flanking the entrance archways and by elaborate frames on the windows of the gallery which surrounds the church on the north, west, and south.

The interior is one large room with two sets of paired ¾ columns on the north and south walls. The altar area is raised four steps and the iconostasis is replaced by a frescoed masonry wall supported by a row of gilt columns. The church frescoes of 1675 have vivid colors of gold, red, and blue, and are forcefully and harmoniously executed. The frescoes of the gallery, more poorly preserved, depict the Creation and Last Judgment.

East of the Resurrection Church, in the corner of the Kremlin, is a two-story building from the 17th century, formerly a *residence hall for monks* (**41**-9). Adjacent to the east entrance into the Kremlin is the former *servants hall* (**41**-10) for the Metropolitan's Residence. On the west side of the Water Tower, with a facade of molded brick, is the so-called *Hierarch's Chambers* (**41**-12), of the 16th century, reconstructed in the 19th. Along the wall to the south is a *Service Building* (**41**-13) from the 16th century, with chimney pots of the 17th century, one of the few remaining examples in Russia of this type of architectural detail. South of the White Chambers and Savior Church are several

small buildings joined on the second floor level, around deep courtyards.

Directly north of the Kremlin is the *Assumption Cathedral of Rostov* (**41**-14), from the 1500's, a large three-apse, five-dome, six-column church. The walls are divided vertically by high-relief pilasters, and horizontally by a column belt and several cornices. The frescoes inside the church, redone several times over the centuries, have not survived well. The baroque iconostasis is from 1730-1740. The original jasper stone floor of this church was removed by Ivan the Terrible and installed in the Annunciation Cathedral in the Moscow Kremlin.

The cathedral stands in a courtyard surrounded by a low wall. To the east is the four-bay *Belfry* (**41**-16), 1682-1687, with bells especially cast at Iona's order. The thirteen bells are known for their harmonious sound. A special recital in 1965 was recorded and a phonograph record is sometimes available.

To the west of the cathedral is the *Holy Gate* (**41**-15) with a large baroque arch and an octagonal upper section which date it from about 1700.

Beyond the wall east of the Belfry is the *Church of the Savior "on the market"* (**41**-17), 1685-1690, a five-dome church in the same style as the Kremlin churches. The church is now in the courtyard of trading rows built in the early 19th century.

Nearer the lake east of the Kremlin is the *Nativity Church* (**40**-3), late 1600's, the only remaining structure of the former Nativity Monastery. This one-dome church with refectory was rebuilt in the 19th century, but preserves frescoes of 1715. The church over-the-gates nearby dates from 1842. Further east is the city park with a fence constructed in the 1830's.

Northeast of the Kremlin, next to the old earthen rampart of the city, is the small *Church of Isidore the Blessed* (**40**-5), (also known as the Church of the Ascension), built in 1566 at the order of Ivan the Terrible, and frescoed in the 1770's. The small Belfry is from the 19th century. Services are still held in the *Tolgskaya Church* (**40**-6), (or, Church of St. John), 1761, a one-dome refectory church, and at the *Church of Nikola*, 1813 (**40**-7), a neoclassical building with four-column porticoes.

Various secular buildings of provincial architecture of the 18th and 19th centuries include the *old Customs House* of 1813 (**40**-8), modeled on the trading rows by the Kremlin; *Emelyanov's House*, before 1779 (**40**-9); *Serebrennikov's House*, 19th century (**40**-10), and the building of the *former Boy's High School*, early 20th century (**40**-11). At 50th October St. #11 is the former Lyons Hotel, a large 19th-century building with a considerable amount of stucco molding on the facade. There is also an interesting wooden house at the corner of Decembrists and Frunze Streets.

Church of John
the Divine
in Rostov Kremlin

walls of this church preserve their original appearance, but the north face is hidden by the Yakov Church, 1725, reconstructed 1824-1837 with a hemispherical cupola on a low drum and a four-column portico on the north side.

The dominant structure of the monastery is the Dmitry Church, 1794, paid for by N. P. Sheremetev and designed by his serf architect Mironov. The church has a massive hemispherical dome, porticoes of Corinthian order, and a variety of wall decor — niches, statues, garland molding, and the like.

The three-tier Belfry, 1780, in the center of the east wall of the monastery, is of brick with limestone details. There is a good view from here of the Metropolitan's Kremlin in the center of Rostov.

Adjacent to this monastery was the Spassky Monastery, founded in the 1200's and disbanded by Catherine in 1764. The *Spassky Cathedral*, 1603 (**40**-13), is the only surviving structure, a large church with a variety of external details added during later remodelings.

A mile or so away, just off the Moscow road, is the village of Bogoslovo, with the wooden *Church of St. John "on the Ishnya,"* 1689 (**40**-14), a small but tall church which harmoniously combines a variety of expressive shapes. The western entrance portal is finely carved in the shape of an ogee arch. The belfry of the church was built in the 1800's.

Toward the eastern end of Rostov on the road to Yaroslavl is the *Kozma and Demyan Church*, 1775 (**40**-15), a five-dome church with a tentroof belfry. Not far beyond it are the remains of the *Avraamievsky Monastery*, founded about 1100 (**40**-16). The oldest structure is the Bogoyavlensky Cathedral, 1553, constructed for Ivan the Terrible to commemorate his victory over the Tartars at Kazan. The plan of the church is very interesting, a central four-column, five-dome cubical section with smaller chapels built at three corners, connected by a gallery. The church was remodeled several times over the centuries, and one of the chapels was converted into a belfry. The church's asymmetrical plan and massing of domes is still striking despite the lack of total restoration.

West of the cathedral is the former main gate of the monastery with two towers flanking the Nikola Church over-the-gates, 1691, reconstructed in a neoclassical style 1826-1837 by P. Pankov, with a portico-pediment surrounding the gateway, and a tall belfry above the church.

The monastery also contains the former Father Superior's Residence, 1830 by Pankov, and the remains of the Vvedenskaya Church and refectory of 1650.

Rostov is "guarded" at each end of town by monasteries. When approaching from Moscow by road, the traveler first sees the splendid panorama of the lake and on its shore the domes of the *Yakovlev Monastery* (**40**-12), from the 14th century. The monastery is surrounded on the north, east, and south by masonry walls. The north and south walls have central gate towers of the 18th century with rusticated lower levels and tall, narrow open-column octagonal structures above, in a neoGothic style. The western edge of the monastery is made up of the Father Superior's residence, late 1700's, and monks cells.

The oldest building in the Yakovlev Monastery is the cubical, four-column, five-dome Zachatievskaya Church, 1686, with frescoes of 1690 and a carved baroque iconostasis of 1762-1765. The east and south

YAROSLAVL

(Map 42)

Yaroslavl, an industrial center with a population of 500,000, is located 160 miles northeast of Moscow on the Volga River. The city was named for Prince Yaroslav the Wise who captured a pagan settlement here in 998 while he was Grand Prince of Rostov. In the early 13th century Yaroslavl began to prosper on the Volga trade routes, but was captured and burned by the Mongols in 1238. Yaroslavl became part of the Moscow princedom in 1463, and grew as an important commercial center in the 16th century after trade with Europe was established through the White sea port of Arkhangelsk. In the 17th century Yaroslavl was second only to Moscow in wealth and prosperity, and it was during this century that the famous Yaroslavl churches were built. After the founding of Petersburg in 1703 and the decline of the trade route to the north, Yaroslavl developed as a manufacturing town.

Yaroslavl's current renown as a tourist center comes from a type of church architecture which developed in the 17th century. Churches in the Yaroslavl style typically have five domes, are surrounded by a gallery on three sides, with one or two attached chapels, and are decorated with molded brick and glazed ceramic tile. The churches were frescoed in a vigorous, imaginative, and expressive style and these frescoes have been preserved in excellent condition.

Yaroslavl developed from a fortified Kremlin on the point of land at the confluence of the Kotorosl and Volga Rivers. The Kremlin fortifications and buildings were destroyed in a fire in 1659, and of the older fortifications only the *Spaso-Preobrazhensky Monastery* from the 12th century remains (**42**-1 and Plan **43**). The oldest structure is the *Spaso-Preobrazhensky Cathedral* (**43**-1), 1506-1516, built at the behest of Vasily III of Moscow, a three-dome church which bore some resemblance to the Archangel Cathedral of the Moscow Kremlin. The church has only partly been restored from later accretions, and a portion of the frescoes of 1564 have been recovered from under refrescoing of 1782.

The south facade of the cathedral is hidden by the *Church of the Yaroslavl Wonderworker* (**43**-2) 1827-1831 by P. Pankov, a neoclassical structure which was remodeled in 1875 with the addition of window frames in the old Russian style. Next to it is the monastery *Belfry* (**43**-3), from the 1500's, with a new pseudo-Gothic top of 1808. The monastery contains a *Refectory* (**43**-4) from the early 1500's, with the often rebuilt *Nativity Church* (**43**-5) on its east, and the *Archbishop's Chamber* (**43**-6), later 1500's, on the west. There are *monks cells* (**43**-9) from the 1680's, and a treasurer's building of 1817.

©Charles A. Ward

SPASO-PREOBRAZHENSKY MONASTERY PLAN **43**

1. Spaso-Preobrazhensky Cathedral
2. Church of Yaroslavl Wonderworker
3. Belfry
4. Refectory
5. Nativity Church
6. Archbishop's Chamber
7. Holy Gate
8. "Water Gate"
9. Monks Cell Building; museum
10. Uglich Tower
11. Bogoroditskaya Tower
12. Present-day entrance
13. Service entrance

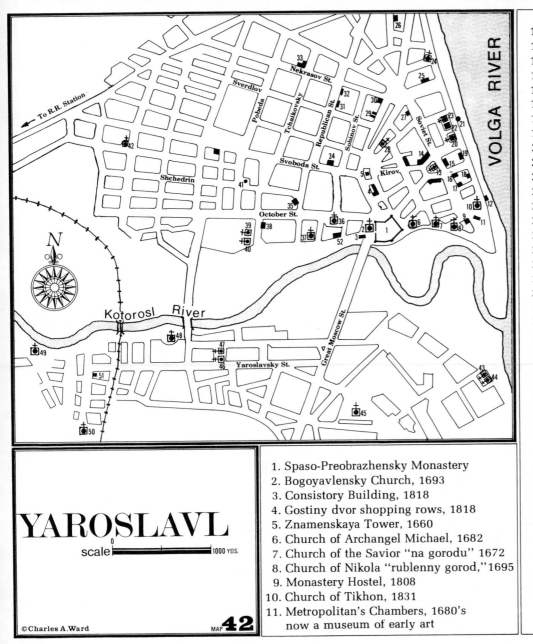

YAROSLAVL

scale |———|———| 1000 YDS.
0   1000

©Charles A.Ward

MAP **42**

VOLGA RIVER

Kotorosl River

To R.R. Station

Nekrasov St.
Sverdlov
Pobeda
Tchaikovsky
Republican St.
Sobinov St.
Svoboda St.
Kirov
Shchedrin
October St.
Soviet St.
Great Moscow St.
Yaroslavsky St.

1. Spaso-Preobrazhensky Monastery
2. Bogoyavlensky Church, 1693
3. Consistory Building, 1818
4. Gostiny dvor shopping rows, 1818
5. Znamenskaya Tower, 1660
6. Church of Archangel Michael, 1682
7. Church of the Savior "na gorodu" 1672
8. Church of Nikola "rublenny gorod," 1695
9. Monastery Hostel, 1808
10. Church of Tikhon, 1831
11. Metropolitan's Chambers, 1680's
    now a museum of early art

12. Volga Tower, 1660's
13. Church of Elijah the prophet, 1650
14. City office Building, 1784; 1820's
15. Sorokina's house, 1816
16. Matveevsky' house, ca. 1800
17. Vakhrameev's house, late 1700's
18. Doctor's Society house, 1700/1820
19. Art Museum
20. Nikola Nadein Church, 1622
21. Rotunda-pavilion, 1840
22. General Dedyulin's house, early 1800's
23. Church of Nativity, and belfry, 1640's
24. Annunciation Church, 1702
25. Kudasov's house, late 1700's
26. Sorokin's house
27. Lopatin's house, 1780's
28. Kazan Monastery Cathedral, 1845
29. Wings of Vakhrameev's house, early 1800's
30. "Passazh" Inn, 1790's
31. Rybkin's house, late 1700's
32. house, late 1700's
33. Pavlov's house, 1780's
34. Nikitin's house
35. Seminary, 1818
36. Dmitry Solunsky Church, 1673
37. Church of Metropolitan Peter, 1657
38. Ivanov's house, 17th century
39. Church of Nikola Mokry, 1672
40. Church of Tikhvin Virgin, 1686
41. Belfry of Nikola Muchenik Church
42. Church of Vladimir Mother of God, 1678
43. Church of St. John Chrysostom, 1654
44. Vladimirskaya Church, 1669
45. Paraskeva-Pyatnitsa Church, 1692
46. Fedorovskaya Church, 1687
47. Nikola Pensky Church, 1691
48. John the Baptist Church, 1687
49. Church of Nikola, 1672
50. Peter-Paul Church, 1742
51. Korytov's house, 1760's
52. Jubilee Hotel

The masonry walls of the monastery were built 1550-1580 at Ivan the Terrible's behest, and were sufficient to withstand a twenty-four day siege by Polish interventionists during the Time of Troubles in 1609. The walls were enlarged, 1621-1646, but were considerably altered in the 19th century. Parts of the east and west wall are original, as are the *Bogoroditskaya Tower*, 1623 (**43-11**) and the *Uglich Tower*, 1646 (**43-10**). The defense towers facing the Kotorosl were replaced by round decorative towers in 1803. This wall still preserves the *Holy Gate*, 1516 (**43-7**), with two vaulted passages and a church with gallery over the gateway. Nearby is the simpler *"Water Gate"*, which was for daily use (**43-8**). The *present entrance* for tourists is from Podbelsky Square through an entrance way made in the 19th century (**43-12**).

Directly west of the monastery is the *Bogoyavlenskaya Church*, 1684-1693 (**42-2**), a cubical church with two rows of kokoshnik gables leading to a flat roof supporting tall decorative drums and onion domes. The exterior makes varied use of glazed tile decoration and the interior, with no columns, is lit by nine windows which excellently illuminate the frescoes of 1692-1693. South of the church is the *Ecclesiastical Consistory Building* (**42-3**) 1815 by Rusca, with paired ionic columns of giant order on the facade facing the river.

To the north of the monastery is a boulevard which replaced the former defense wall of the city. The center of the boulevard contains part of the former *Gostiny dvor shopping rows*, 1814-1818 (**42-4**), and beyond it the *Znamenskaya Tower*, 1660 (**42-5**), a three-story masonry passage tower to which a smaller fourth floor was added in 1884 when the structure was remodeled as a water tower.

Directly east of the monastery is the *Church of Archangel Michael*, 1658-1682 (**42-6**), a large four-column church on a high basement, with a monumental entrance porch ornamented with green ceramic tile. The roof was remodeled sometime later. The frescoes of 1731 are in nine tiers.

A block further east is the *Church of the Savior "na gorodu,"* 1672 (**42-7**), built on an asymmetrical plan with a tent-roof belfry and tent-roof chapel on the north side, and with large drums and domes, a characteristic feature of Yaroslavl churches of the 1670's. Parts of the church were remodeled in 1831 in neoclassic style. The interior has frescoes of 1693. Particularly interesting are the bottom rows of frescoes, and the north wall with scenes of Empress Helen's departure from Byzantium to Jerusalem.

Another block to the east is the *Church of Nikola "rublenny gorod,"* 1695 (**42-8**), a simple, plain-walled refectory church with a single apse, domes on slender drums, and with a harmonious, slender octagonal belfry.

At the edge of the Volga is the *Church of Tikhon*, 1825-1831 (**42-10**), a central-plan church with columned porticoes on all four sides. It was built on the site of a 17th-century church, and is supposedly on the location of the first Christian church in Yaroslavl built in the 11th century. Just to the south are the *Metropolitan's Chambers*, 1680's (**42-11**), built by Metropolitan Iona Sysoevich of Rostov for his visits to Yaroslavl. It is a two-story oblong building with a central stairway entrance. The walls are divided into sections by pilaster strips and are broken by a cornice between the floors and by elaborate window frames on the upper level.

At the edge of the Volga is the *Volga Tower*, 1600-1668 (**42-12**), a massive square defense tower. Its window contours were changed in 1821, and a third floor added in 1842. It now houses a Naval Club.

The central square of Yaroslavl was designed as part of the regularization of the street plan in 1778, during Catherine's reign. The square was constructed around the *Church of the Prophet Elijah*, 1647-1650 (**42-13**), an outstanding building rightly chosen to be the new center of town. The church, built by a rich merchant family, has as its center an unadorned four-column, five-dome cubical church on a high basement level, and is surrounded on north, west, and south by a high, closed-in gallery entered by off-center stairways on north and west. There are small chapels with domes at the northeast and southeast corners of the gallery, a much larger chapel with a very tall tent roof next to the gallery at the southwest corner, and an octagonal bell tower at the northwest corner of the gallery. The walls of the gallery are highly decorated with molded brick and square niches with small ceramic insets. The chapels have decorative window frames and rows of kokoshnik gables. The marvelous harmony of the asymmetrical plan and the varying heights and resolutions of the chapels around the central church are best seen by walking around the church.

The interior is as interesting as the outside, with frescoes of 1680-1681 which have remained astoundingly bright. The frescoes are in six tiers and are endless in their imaginative depiction and exuberance. They are painted not in "frames," but as a continuous narrative band. The gallery is also frescoed, and in addition, on the church wall, has a sort of glazed tile wainscotting of the 1680's. The iconostasis is from the 18th century, but the Tsar's and Patriarch's prayer places are from the late 1600's, moved here from the Nikola Mokry Church. The boldness of plan and the excellence of the frescoes make this church one of the best examples of the Yaroslavl style.

On the west side of the square are the buildings of the former *City Offices*, 1781-1784 (**42-14**), almost totally reconstructed in the 1820's by Pankov. The trading row buildings on October Street also date from the 1790's. On the east side of the square is *Sorokina's House*, 1816 (**42-15**), with an interesting stucco frieze and other ornamentation. In the next block south is *Matveevsky's House*, 1790-1809 (**42**-16), with a central four-column portico and identical side wings. At the end of the block is *Vakhrameev's House*, late 1700's (**42**-17). Across the boulevard to the west one can see the as yet unrestored Afanasievsky Monastery and Spaso-Proboinskaya Church, mid-1600's.

The Volga Quay was reconstructed in the 1820's, at which time the river embankment was relandscaped, forming a very pleasant promenade. Along the way note the house of the former *Doctor's Society* (**42**-18), built ca. 1700, and remodeled in 1820. The basement archway of the earlier structure has been preserved in the newer neoclassical facade. In the next block is the *Art Museum* (**42**-19), in the former governor's palace.

A couple of blocks further along is the *Nikola Nadein Church*, 1620-1622 (**42**-20), one of the oldest churches in town. It was rebuilt in succeeding centuries and has survived with a single dome on a pyramidal roof, and a simple exterior. The frescoes of 1640-1641 were renewed in 1882, and the iconostasis is a baroque work done in 1751. There is a separate Annunciation Chapel on the north side, with rich interior decorations added especially for the merchant who built the church. The belfry received its tent roof in 1695.

Church of the Savior "na gorodu": Yaroslavl

On the quay at this point is a six-column *rotunda pavilion*, built in 1840 (**42**-21). Opposite it is the *former house of a General Dedyulin*, active in the Napoleonic wars (**42**-22). At the corner of February Street is the ensemble of the *Church of the Nativity* and its *Belfry* (**42**-23). The church dates from ca. 1640, with numerous subsequent changes. It is basically a four-column, five-dome church with additional chapels. The east and west facades more or less preserve their original appearance, and the church is slated for eventual total restoration. There is some interesting glazed tile work on the apses and drums. The main attraction of the ensemble is the belfry structure, 1650's, just to the west of the church. The Bell Tower is part of a church "over-the-gates" structure. A double entrance arch supports an open gallery around the church which is surmounted by a large octagonal tent roof belfry. The whole structure is an imaginative mixture of shapes, masses, and decorative detail, and there is nothing else in Russian architecture quite like it.

Three blocks further along, at Volga Quay # 51, is the *Annunciation Church*, 1688-1702 (**42**-24), a small plain church with pleasing proportions. Its domes are from the late 1700's.

There are numerous former private buildings in the central part of the town which are worth a glance if you are in that area. Note the *wings of Vakhrameev's house* on Ushinsky Street, early 19th-century (**42**-29); *Lopatin's House*, 1780's, on Soviet Street (**42**-27); the splendid wooden manor house *(Nikitin's House)*, at Svoboda Street #10a (**42**-34); the *two 18th-century houses* on Republican Street (**42**-31 & 32); or *Pavlov's House*, 1780's, on Tchaikovsky Street (**42**-33). Further to the west is the two-story neoclassical facade of the *former Seminary*, 1818, on Republican Street (**42**-35).

A number of churches were built parallel to the Kotorosl River west of the monastery. The *Church of Dmitry Solunsky*, 1671-1673 (**42**-36), was built of bricks left over from construction of the city defense towers in the 1660's. Over the centuries the domes have been replaced, porches rebuilt, and belfry removed, but interesting frescoes of 1686 survive. The *Church of Metropolitan Peter*, 1657 (**42**-37), a small refectory church, is located a block further west.

At the beginning of Tchaikovsky Street there are three interesting structures. One is the restored 17th-century house of a wealthy burgher, *Ivanov's House* (**42**-38), with a windowless lower level for storage, and living quarters above. Just down the street is the *Nikola Mokry Church*, 1665-1672 (**42**-39), a good example of the developed Yaroslavl style church with five domes and a closed-in gallery ending at tent roof chapels. The three apse windows were given oversize glazed tile frames in the 1690's. The church has excellent frescoes of 1673. Next door is the *Church of the Tikhvin Virgin*, 1686 (**42**-40), a heated church, with a rectilinear apse topped by a dome, a feature rarely found in Russian churches.

Two blocks to the north is a tall octagonal *Bell Tower* (**42**-41), late 1600's, built to accompany the Church of Nikita the Martyr. Several blocks further west is the *Church of the Vladimir Mother of God*, 1670-1678 (**42**-42), built in a former pauper's graveyard. It has three tent roofs on a north-south axis above the main church.

A number of important churches were built in the area beyond the Kotorosl River. One of the most famous is the *Church of St. John Chrysostom*, 1649-1654 (**42**-43), a four-column, five-dome church with a gallery and two tent-roof chapels. The window of the central apse was redone in 1690 with an expanded frame of colored tile, pointed at the top, with a special roof gable to accommodate it. The exterior of the church has molded brick decor, particularly on the gallery. The church contains a carved baroque iconostasis of the 18th century and frescoes of 1732-1733. This church is one of the best examples of the Yaroslavl style and served as a model for other churches, especially the Church of Nikola Mokry.

In 1669 the *Vladimirskaya Church* was built next door (**42**-44), as a heated, winter church. It is almost the same size as the Chrysostom Church, but has a different apse treatment, no gallery or chapels, and has a small refectory to the west.

Between the two churches, somewhat to the west, is the belfry for the ensemble, a 120-foot tall octagonal tower built in the 1680's. The proportion of the height of the tower to that of the tent, the gentleness of the taper, and the slender drum and dome, give the belfry an exceedingly graceful line. About 1700, between the churches and opposite the belfry, an entrance arch topped by a two-tier octagonal tower was built.

There is a slight rise several blocks along Great Moscow Street to the east. This is Tugova Hill (Hill of Sorrows) where the Yaroslavlians lost a bloody battle in an uprising against the Mongols in 1257. The hill became a graveyard and the modest, one-dome *Church of Paraskeva Pyatnitsa* was built in 1692 (**42**-45).

To the west of Great Moscow Street is the Tolchkovo district, once the richest in Yaroslavl. At # 16 Emelyan Yaroslavsky Street is the *Fedorovskaya Church*, 1678 (**42**-46), a five-dome church with a gallery from 1736. The church has very large drums and domes, and a wide brick cornice near the tops of the walls. It contains frescoes of 1715 and a carved gilt iconostasis of 1705. Adjacent is the *Church of Nikola Pensky*, 1691 (**42**-47).

The masterpiece of the Tolchkovo district, and one of the two best churches in Yaroslavl, is the *Church of John the Baptist*, 1671-1687 (**42**-48), a building which summed up the architectural style of the period. The basic four-column, five-dome church is surrounded by a gallery on north, west, and south and has corner chapels next to the apses, rising to the same height as the church. These chapels are topped by five small domes each, so that the massive east wall serves as a pedestal for 15 domes. The walls of the church are highly patterned with decorative kokoshniks, molded brick in a variety of forms, fancy window frames, niches, and glazed tile decoration. The porches and gallery walls are most elaborately decorated.

The church was frescoed in 1694-1700 and is the last word in narrative frescoe technique. The walls have eight and nine bands of frescoes and an enormous number of subjects — all the Orthodox saints, scenes from the Song of Songs, as well as usual Biblical subjects like the Creation. The Kazansky Chapel in the north corner has a carved baroque iconostasis of 1701 with an exquisitely carved central door.

Southwest of the church is a 145-foot tall octagonal belfry, ca. 1700, which reflects elements of the new Moscow style, with white detail work on red brick background.

Further up river is the *Church of Nikola "in Melenki,"* 1668-1672 (**42**-49), a modest church with large domes which provide an impressive silouette when seen from the river. The church was frescoed in 1705-1707.

Nearby is the site of the former Yaroslavl Grand Manufactura, 1722, a cloth factory which became Yaroslavl's leading manufacturing enterprise of the 18th century. Still extant is the factory's *Church of Peter and Paul* (**42**-50), 1736-1742, a western-style rectangular church which resembles the Peter-Paul fortress church in Leningrad. Also nearby is the *Korytov House* (**42**-51), from the 1760's, one of the few secular buildings of this period to survive in Tolchkovo.

Across the Volga and five miles upstream is the Tolgsky Monastery, from the 14th century. The ensemble includes the Holy Gate with Nikolskaya Church, 1672, and adjoining Father Superior's Chambers, 1670's; the Krestovozdvizhenskaya Refectory Church, 1620's, with later reconstruction; and the Vvedensky Cathedral, 1681-1688, a very large church in the Yaroslavl style (five domes, gallery, and chapels), with plain walls and an ornamented gallery. The massive belfry next to it is from 1683-1685. In the northern part of the monastery is the Savior Church, ca. 1700, with hospital chambers, in the new Moscow style. The hospital chambers have highly decorative window frames in the form of large columns and pediments, and the three-tier octagonal drum-dome of the church is surrounded by eight small cupolas.

Ten miles south of Yaroslavl on the road to Moscow is the village of Karabikha. From 1861 it was the home of N.A. Nekrasov, a 19th-century civic poet. His estate was made into a memorial museum in 1947, and its exhibitions were expanded in 1971.

Vladimirskaya Church (left) and Church of John Chrysostom (right): Yaroslavl

VLADIMIR

(Map 44)

Vladimir, an industrial center with a population of 250,000, is located on the high left bank of the Klyazma River 115 miles northeast of Moscow in an area of Russia first settled by Slavs in the 10th and 11th centuries. The town was founded in 1108 by Kievan Prince Vladimir Monomakh, who built a fortress here to guard the northeast area of old Russia. His son, Yury Dolgoruky, moved the Russian capital from Kiev to Suzdal, and largely ignored Vladimir until the 1150's. Because of internecine strife and political troubles in Kiev and Suzdal, Dolgoruky's son Andrey Bogolyubsky, moved the princely throne here in 1157 and made Vladimir the capital of the Rostovo-Suzdal princedom. Vladimir reached the pinnacle of its power during the reign of Andrey's brother, Vsevolod III (1175-1212).

In 1238 Vladimir was captured and burnt by the Mongols. The transfer of former symbols of power to Moscow began in the 1320's when Metropolitan Peter moved to Moscow, continued in 1380 when Dmitry Donskoy took the icon of Dmitry Solunsky to Moscow, and was completed in 1395 when the icon of the Vladimir Mother of God was taken to Moscow (now in the Tretyakov Gallery). From then Vladimir was a provincial town in the Muscovite princedom.

Foreign tourists generally stay at the *Hotel Vladimir* (**44**-1), uphill from the Railroad Station, and the description of the sites of town begins from there. East of the hotel, in the courtyard of Third International Street # 106, is the *Bogoroditskaya Church*, 1649 (**44**-2), a columnless, three-apse church with five tightly clustered domes supported by two rows of receding kokoshnik gables. The walls have pilaster strips and a highly articulated cornice. A small refectory and belfry adjoin to the west.

Opposite the Vladimir Hotel, to the west, is the wall of the *former Rozhdestvensky Monastery* (**44**-3), which was active from the 12th century until 1744. This was an important monastery in the early years, since it was the burial place of Alexander Nevsky (his remains were moved to Petersburg in 1724). The present walls of the monastery, from the early 18th century, enclose former monastery buildings converted to secular use. Along the north wall is the former 18th-century *Church of Nikola*, now used as the *city planetarium* (**44**-4).

Southwest of the monastery is the *Dmitrievsky Cathedral*, 1194-1197 (**44**-5), one of the finest examples of old Russian church architecture. Constructed by Vsevolod III as his palace church, it is a four-column, three-apse, single-dome church of white limestone with walls divided into thirds by semi-detached columns. The plain lower half of the walls was originally hidden by a gallery. The column belt at

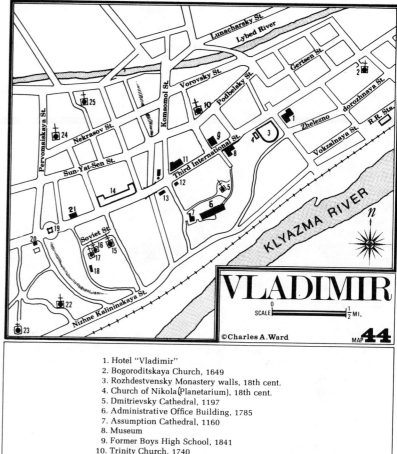

©Charles A. Ward MAP **44**

1. Hotel "Vladimir"
2. Bogoroditskaya Church, 1649
3. Rozhdestvensky Monastery walls, 18th cent.
4. Church of Nikola (Planetarium), 18th cent.
5. Dmitrievsky Cathedral, 1197
6. Administrative Office Building, 1785
7. Assumption Cathedral, 1160
8. Museum
9. Former Boys High School, 1841
10. Trinity Church, 1740
11. Former Nobility Club, 1826
12. Monument to 850th anniversary of Vladimir
13. Former Council Building, 1907
14. Trading Rows, 1790
15. Georgievskaya Church, 1784
16. Church of Savior, 1778
17. Church of Nikola, 17th century
18. City Museum (Water Tower), 19th century
19. Golden Gates, 1164
20. Former Church of Trinity, 1913
21. Restaurant
22. Church of Nikola "v galeyakh", 1735
23. Former Voskresenskaya Church, 1724
24. Nikitskaya Church, 1765
25. Cathedral of Knyaginin Convent, ca. 1500

Vladimir Golden Gate

weakened by a fire in 1185, it was buttressed with a wide gallery on three sides. Large openings were made in the original church wall, so that it became, in effect, a five-aisle, 14-column church. The cathedral was burned by the Mongols in 1238 and again in 1411. After another severe fire in 1536, the cathedral was largely rebuilt. The church was restored in 1888-1891, and at various times in the 20th century, most recently in the mid-1970's. To the north is the Chapel of St. George, 1682, which connects the church to the neoclassical bell tower of 1810.

The interior has a great sense of height, since Vsevolod had the central dome reconstructed to 95 feet, equal to the height of the Sophia Cathedral in Kiev. The early frescoes of 1161 and 1189 are almost totally obliterated, and the magnificent refrescoing of 1408 by Andrey Rublev and Daniil Cherny was damaged in the Tartar raid of 1411, and in subsequent fires. Especially interesting are the scenes from the Last Judgment on the west wall. The baroque iconstasis dates from 1773-1774, but the original Rublev icons have been moved to the Tretyakov Gallery in Moscow. The northeast corner of the gallery contains the tombs of Andrey Bogolyubsky and Vsevolod III.

Third International Street is the main street of old Vladimir. At # 68 is the *Vladimir-Suzdal Museum of History, Art, and Architecture* (**44**-8), from 1958, with old documents, books, applied arts, and historical relics. Across the street (# 35), is the *former Boy's High School* (**44**-9), 1836-1841. A block further north on Podbelsky Street is the *Trinity Church*, 1740 (**44**-10), a cubical church with octagonal second floor. The church belfry has a square base and a cylindrical upper section topped by a spire.

At Third International Street # 33 is the *former Nobility Club*, 1826 (**44**-11), a yellow stucco building with two porticos of white doubled columns. At that intersection is the State Bank with a statue of Lenin before it, 1925. Across the main street is the *monument to the 850th anniversary of the city*, 1958 (**44**-12). To the west of the monument is the *former City Council building* (Duma) (**44**-13), a red brick structure in the pseudo-old Russian style, 1906-1907, by Revyakin. Further along on the north side of the street are the *Trading Rows*, 1787-1790 (**44**-14).

Komintern Street, on the south, leads to the former *Georgievskaya Church*, 1783-1784 (**44**-15), built in a provincial baroque style with stone from the Church of St. George, 1157, which was destroyed by the fire of 1778. The present church is cubical with an octagonal dome. The attached refectory was used in the mid-1970's as a ballet practice room. There is a belfry attached to the refectory. This church is on the site of Prince Yury Dolgoruky's court of the 1150's.

Not far down Soviet Street is the *Church of the Savior*, 1778 (**44**-16), a cubical church with tall sloping roof and slender octagonal drum and

mid-wall is elaborately carved, each little column resting on a carved griffon. Between the columns is a floral frieze and small carvings of saints. The upper half of the walls and the drum are totally covered with relief carving. The main figure of each facade, above the central window, is Biblical King David, surrounded by people and animals who have come to honor him. Vsevolod III is depicted in the east zakomara of the north facade, and Alexander the Great in the east zakomara of the south facade. The church was built at the height of Vsevolod's glory and the implied message of the carvings is Vsevolod's divinely approved reign and his political independence from other Russian towns and princes.

The triple-arch recessed doorways lead to a light, airy interior in which only a part of the fresco of the Last Judgment has survived on the west wall. The church was burned in the 13th, 16th and 18th centuries, and suffered a radical "restoration" in 1837-1839 under Nicholas I.

A walk leading west passes the *Administrative Office Building*, 1783-1785 (**44**-6), a large three-story stucco building now housing the regional Soviet. In the near distance, on the edge of the bluff, rise the domes of the *Assumption Cathedral*, 1158-1160 (**44**-7), constructed for Andrey Bogolyubsky as the main cathedral of the new Russian capital. The church was originally one-dome, six-column, but after being dome. Behind it is the *Church of Nikola*, 17th century (**44**-17), with large window frames, a kokoshnik frieze, refectory, and belfry in the form of a square tower with a spire. This church has been converted to secular uses. Both churches are on the site of Andrey Bogolyubsky's 12th-century palace.

Beyond these churches, on a rise, is the former *Water Tower* (**44**-18), a 19th-century oval-shaped brick structure with a tent roof, which now houses a very well-displayed City Historical Museum, on four floors. The roof of the tower has an observation platform with an excellent panorama of the city. West of the tower across a small ravine is a restaurant designed in the style of old Russian wooden inns.

The former west end of the town is marked by the *Golden Gates* (**44**-19), 1158-1164, a tall limestone structure originally covered with gilded copper sheathing. In present form the gates are much changed, after damage and repairs in 1238, 1469, 1640, and 1785. The central cube of the gates is original; the round buttresses were added in the 18th century when the earthen rampart on the sides was cut away for the road which now skirts the gates. Steps lead up from the southeast corner to a room above the archway which now displays a diorama of the gates and city in 1238. In the gallery around the top of the tower are memorial plaques to Soviet soldiers from Vladimir who were distinguished in World War Two.

Beyond the gates, next to the new Drama Theater, is the former *Old Believers Church of the Trinity*, 1913 (**44**-20), a large brick building in Old Russian style which is now used to exhibit art glass, painted boxes and miniatures, and embroidery. A little further west, across the street, is the new *"Restaurant by the Golden Gates"* (**44**-21).

Beyond the earthen rampart on the sloping hillside descending to the river is the *Church of Nikola "v galeyakh,"* 1732-1735 (**44**-22), a refectory church with a basic cube topped by four octagonal sections of decreasing size. At the west end of the refectory is a well-proportioned belfry.

Further west, on Shchedrin Street, is the *Voskresenskaya Church*, 1724 (**44**-23), from the former Voskresensky Monastery. The church has survived in greatly altered form, and in the mid-1970's housed a shoe factory, though the window frames and wall cornice survive.

Two blocks north of the Golden Gates is the *Nikitskaya Church*, 1762-1765 (**44**-24), a three-story rectangular structure with a massive steeple-belfry in front, and window frames of a provincial baroque style. A block away is the site of the former *Knyaginin Convent*, 1200, founded by Vsevolod III's wife. The remaining *Assumption Cathedral* (**44**-25) dates from ca. 1500, a four-column church with one dome supported by two rows of receding kokoshnik gables. The walls are unadorned excapt for pilasters and ogee zakomaras. A low gallery and chapel were added over the years, but they do not detract from the serene harmony of the church. The church was frescoed in 1647-1648, and was well restored in 1960. The church is not on the usual tours, but there is talk of opening it for view by the late 1970's.

BOGOLYUBOVO

The village of Bogolyubovo, six miles northeast of Vladimir, is the site of Andrey Bogolyubsky's princely palace and stronghold on a hill overlooking the Klyazma River. Of his palace, which was once very extensive, only a stairway tower survives. It now serves as a church belfry, with the addition of a 17th-century tent roof. The belfry adjoins the Nativity Church, 1751, built on the ruins of the previous 12th-century church. The palace ensemble fell into disrepair after Andrey's death, and became the Nativity Monastery. Opposite the tower and church is the huge, squat Assumption Church, 1866, and near it, the entrance gate and Belfry of the monastery, 1841.

Pokrovskaya Church "on the Nerl": Bogolyubovo

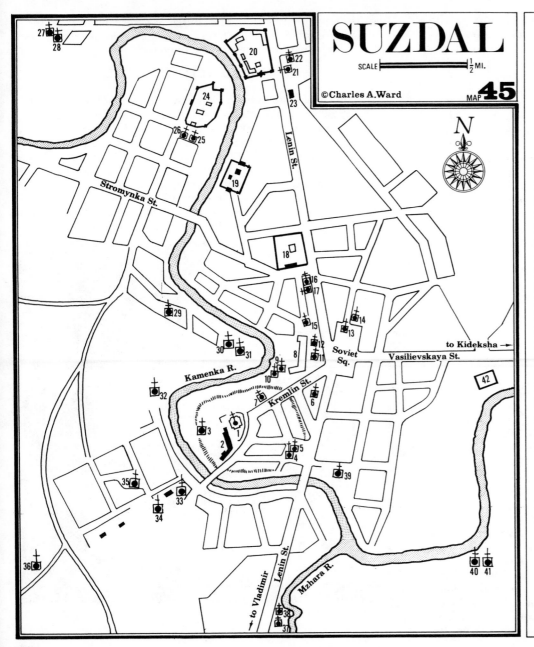

SUZDAL

SCALE |———| ½ MI.

©Charles A.Ward   MAP **45**

N

1. Rozhdestvensky Cathedral, 1225
2. Archbishop's Palace, 18th century
3. Church of Nikola, 1766
4. Nikolskaya Church, 1739
5. Nativity of Christ Church, 1775
6. Church of John the Baptist, 1720
7. Uspenskaya Church, 17th-18th cent.
8. Trading Rows, 1811
9. Entry into Jerusalem Church, 1707
10. Pyatnitskaya Church, 1772
11. Voskresenskaya Church, 1720
12. Kazanskaya Church, 1739
13. Tsar Konstantin Church, 1707
14. Skorbyashchenskaya Church, 1787
15. Kresto-Nikolskaya Church, 1765
16. Church of Lazarus, 1667
17. Church of Antipy, 1745
18. Rizpolozhensky Monastery
19. Alexandrovsky Convent
20. Spaso-Evfimievsky Monastery
21. Smolenskaya Church, 1706
22. Simeonovskaya Church, 1749
23. 17th-century house
24. Pokrovsky Convent
25. Peter-Paul Church, 1694
26. Nikolskaya Church, 1712
27. Kozma & Demyan Church in Korovniki, 1696
28. Bogolyubskaya Church in Korovniki, 1696
29. Tikhvinskaya Church, late 1600's
30. Bogoyavlenskaya Church, 1781
31. Rozhdestvenskaya Church, 1739
32. Ilinskaya Chruch, 1758
33. Transfiguration Church, 1756
34. Resurrection Church, 1776
35. Borisoglebskaya Church, 1747
36. Church in village of Ivanovskoe, 1755
37. Znamenskaya Church, 1749
38. Rizpolozhenskaya Church, 1777
39. Kozma & Demyan Church, 1725
40. Archangel Michael Church, early 1700's
41. Church of Flora & Lavra, 1803
42. Vasiliev Monastery.

About a mile away, on the river Nerl near where it flows into the Klyazma, is the lovely Church of the Intercession "on the Nerl," 1165. The church is reached only by foot, and often is cut off all together by the spring floods. This slender, attractive church is of white limestone, with three apses, one dome, a column belt, and some relief carvings in the upper section of the walls.

SUZDAL

(Map 45)

The small town of Suzdal is located 22 miles north of Vladimir on the Kamenka River. Though Russians settled this area from the 10th century, construction of the Kremlin was begun only in the 1090's by Prince Vladimir Monomakh. In 1096 he built a palace and the Uspensky Church, the first masonry buildings in northeastern Russia. Monomakh's son, Yury Dolgoruky, made Suzdal the capital of old Russia, which it remained until his son, Andrey Bogolyubsky, established the capital in Vladimir in 1157. Like the rest of Russia, Suzdal was captured and burnt by the Mongols in 1238. In the next century the residents of Suzdal and Nizhny Novgorod allied to oppose the growing power of Moscow, but in vain. Suzdal was incorporated into the Muscovite princedom in 1392. The town was off the main trade routes, but remained important as a religious center, with the construction of many churches in the 16th-18th centuries. Large scale church restoration has been going on since the 1950's.

Suzdal contains five monasteries and about fifty churches. The churches date from various centuries, but most of them are early 18th-century. Typically they are small cubical churches with pyramidal roofs, one dome, and a wall cornice of brick courses and a row of kokoshnik arches. The churches are often found in pairs, a smaller, heated church for winter services next to a larger, older, unheated church. The churches often have large octagonal tent-roof belfries of imposing proportions and silhouette. The buildings will be described beginning from the old Kremlin and going to the north edge of town, then counter-clockwise around the center on the far side of the river.

At the center of old Suzdal is the town's oldest church, the *Rozhdestvensky Cathedral*, 1222-1225 (**45**-1), on the site of Vladimir Monomakh's church of 1096, and in the center of the former Kremlin (parts of the earthen rampart remain). The cathedral suffered damage and repairs in 1238, 1445, 1528, and 1750, when the present roof and large onion domes were added. The cathedral was restored in 1964. The church has rough walls of tuff, against which the smooth-cut limestone column-belt on the walls stands out in clear relief. The south and west

facades are the most impressive. The doors in these facades are covered with gold-plated engraved copper panels of 1230. The south door depicts scenes of the Acts of the Archangels and from the Old Testament, while the west doors have scenes from the life of Christ and the Virgin. Inside, some of the frescoes of 1233 remain, particularly in the south apse. The iconostasis of the 17th century still contains some 17th-century icons.

To the south of the Cathedral is its octagonal belfry, 1635, with a small chapel on its east side.

The *Archbishop's Palace*, 15th-18th century (**45**-2), occupies a large area to the south and contains the local Museum, with exhibits of icons and decorative religious arts. There is also a section on the history of the architecture in this area of Russia.

West of the Cathedral is the wooden *Church of Nikola*, 1766 (**45**-3), moved here from the village of Glotovo in 1960. It is a simple structure of two rectangular rooms with a high-pitched roof and a cantilevered porch.

In the area east of the Kremlin is the *Nikolskaya Church*, 1720-1739, restored in 1960 (**45**-4), a cubical church with corner pilasters, a row of small kokoshnik arches above the cornice, and a low sloping roof topped by one dome on a slender drum. The attached belfry to the west has a square base with triangular pediment, topped by a taller octagonal section with various shaped niches separated from the bell arches by a row of colored glazed tile. Above the arches is another ceramic tile cornice and eight little spires at the base of the tall octagonal tent roof.

Adjacent is the *Nativity of Christ Church*, 1775 (**45**-5), with a 19th-century addition, the heated church associated with the older Nikolskaya Church. To the north on Lenin Street is the *Church of John the Baptist*, 1720 (**45**-6), a small one-dome cubical church with an octagonal tent-roof belfry at the west entrance. The walls are plain, with corner pilasters but no cornice, and are broken only by ogee window frames.

To the west on Kremlin Street is the *Uspenskaya Church* (**45**-7), mid-17th century, reconstructed in 1720 and restored in 1958, a small church with cubical base and an octagonal second story. White pilasters and window frames stand out against the red painted walls of the church.

Kremlin Street merges with Lenin Street at Soviet Square, the present center of town. On the west side of the square is the *Gostiny dvor shopping rows*, 1806-1811 (**45**-8). There is a foreign currency souvenir store in the center of the row, and two restaurants at the southwest corner. Opposite the restaurants are two churches. The *Entry into Jerusalem Church*, 1707 (**45**-9), is a modest cubical church with corner pilasters and a cornice with kokoshnik arches. Next to it is the

Cathedral of the
Alexandrovsky Convent:
Suzdal

added in the 19th century. To the northeast is the heated *Skorbyashchenskaya Church*, 1787 (**45**-14), with an attached octagonal belfry.

Just to the north of the Trading Rows is the *Kresto-Nikolskaya Church* (**45**-15), 1765, not fully restored by the mid-1970's. Beyond it is the *Church of Lazarus*, 1667 (**45**-16), a three-apse, five-dome church with a wide cornice and horseshoe-shaped kokoshnik arches. Next to it is the heated *Church of Antipy*, 1745 (**45**-17), a simple rectangular church with a remarkable belfry which has two square sections supporting two octagonal tiers topped by an octagonal tent roof. The belfry has rustication and ornaments painted in tones of red and orange.

Directly north, along Lenin Street, is the *Rizpolozhensky Monastery* (**45**-18), founded in 1207. The oldest structure is the Cathedral, early 1500's, a small columnless church with three domes and plain walls broken only by a row of pentagonal niches as a cornice. In the late 1600's a gallery was built on the west and south sides of the church. The gallery's west facade is particularly rich in molded brick decor. The 235-foot tall belfry of the monastery, the tallest structure in Suzdal, was built 1813-1819.

The main architectural attraction of the Rizpolozhensky Monastery are the Holy Gates in the south wall, 1688, a rectangular structure with two passage arches of differing size, shape, and architectural detail. The face of the structure is decorated with square niches inset with ceramic tiles. Decorative brick courses and a row of tiles set in square frames form a cornice at the top of the wall. Above the gates rise two octagonal tent roofs on low bases with differing details. The present masonry walls of the monastery, more than 800 yards long, were built in the 19th century.

Not far to the northwest on the high bank of the Kamenka River is the *Alexandrovsky Convent* (**45**-19), founded in 1240 by Alexander Nevsky. The convent achieved its greatest fame in the early 1300's, during the reign of Ivan Kalita. The present structures, however, date from the late 17th century. The masonry walls and simple entrance gates in the south and north walls are from ca. 1700. They, as well as the cathedral and belfry, were built by Natalya Kirillovna, Peter the Great's mother. The Ascension Cathedral, 1695, is a large, five-dome cubical church with corner pilasters, symmetrically placed windows and doors with fancy frames, and an elaborate cornice frieze of ornamental brick courses and horseshoe-shaped kokoshnik arches. A chamber on the west of the cathedral served as a heated church. The octagonal tent-roof belfry, on a square base, is restrained in its decor and monumental in its simplicity and size. The convent walls are only partially intact. The convent was disbanded by Catherine the Great in 1764, and has languished over the centuries. There are plans to use the cathedral for art exhibits.

heated *Pyatnitskaya Church*, 1772 (**45**-10), a cubical church with beveled corners and a tall, bowed roof.

Between the trading rows and the square is the *Voskresenskaya Church*, 1720 (**45**-11), a cubical, one-apse church with a fine cornice and fancy two-tier drum supporting the dome. At the northwest corner is an octagonal belfry with spire. The belfry walls have square niches with colored tile insets. The church houses a display of Folk Decorative Wood Carving. Next door is the heated *Kazanskaya Church*, 1739 (**45**-12), open for services.

Across the square is the *Tsar Konstantin Church*, 1707 (**45**-13), with a very wide and elaborate cornice, and with five small domes on slender drums. A small neoclassical chapel with two-column porticoes was

At the northern edge of town on Lenin Street is the *Spaso-Evfimievsky Monastery*, 1352 (**45**-20), the largest in Suzdal. The present masonry walls, 4/5 of a mile long with 12 towers, date from the 1680's. The fortress aspect of the monastery was not lost on Catherine the Great, who converted it into a prison in the 1760's. The main towers are the twelve-sided water tower at the southwest corner, and the massive, square, 70-foot tall Passage Tower in the center of the south wall. The upper part of its walls are covered with rows of decorative niches and frames which give a deceptive lightness to the structure.

To the north of the tower is the Annunciation Church over the Holy Gate, ca. 1600. The church and gate have interesting figured window frames of various designs, and a cornice of decorative brick courses beneath ogee arches.

In the center of the monastery is the Belfry, consisting of a nine-sided tower, early 1500's; an adjacent, taller, square clock tower with tent roof; and next to it, three more arched bell bays of the 16th and 17th centuries. The belfry ensemble, built over 200 years, has a variety of surface decoration, but the harmony of its diverse parts makes it extremely interesting.

Opposite the belfry is the Assumption Refectory Church, 1525, an early masonry tent-roof church which presents its eastern (apse) side to the center of the monastery. The side facades of the church were obscured by the Archmandrites Palace and other later structures.

The Transfiguration Cathedral, 1564, is the largest building in the monastery, a five-dome church with walls decorated by a column belt and exterior wall frescoes of the 18th century. The gallery was added in the 19th century. The chapel on the southeast corner was built about 1510 over the grave of the monk Evfimy, and predates the church. The cathedral was frescoed inside in 1689, but was badly "renewed" in the 1860's and 1870's.

To the east of the church is the grave and a bust of Prince D.M. Pozharsky, one of the leaders of the army which expelled occupying troops from Russia in 1612. The monastery has been undergoing extensive restoration during the 1970's and will house museum exhibits of decorative arts in the former monks cells along the east wall.

Across Lenin Street from the monastery is the *Smolenskaya Church*, 1696-1706 (**45**-21), a cubical, five-dome church with an elaborate cornice of decorative brick and small kokoshnik arches on otherwise plain walls. Of special interest are the north portal and window, with frames of molded brick. The tall, three-tier belfry was built ca. 1800 in late neoclassic style. The heated *Simeonovskaya Church*, 1749 (**45**-22) was greatly remodeled in later centuries. South of these churches, at Lenin Street # 134, is a two-section masonry house of the late 17th century (**45**-23). It was restored in 1971 and contains an exhibit of typical furnishings of a prosperous tradesman's home of the early 18th century.

The *Pokrovsky Convent*, 1364 (**45**-24) lies on the flood plain of the Kamenka midway between the Alexandrovsky Convent and the Spaso-Evfimievsky Monastery. The convent's present form is from the early 1500's when Vasily III of Moscow had it prepared for his first wife, Solomonia, whom he planned to divorce and imprison here. (In the early 1700's Peter the Great's divorced first wife, Evdokia, also lived here.)

The convent walls are from the 16th-18th centuries. The main entrance, in the south wall, is the Holy Gate and Annunciation Church, 1518. The large entrance arch is offset to the east, with a small walkway arch to the west. The tall south wall of the tower has decorative brick courses, and at the top merges with the gallery of the church. The small, one-dome church has ogee zakomaras at the top of the walls, and two subsidiary domes over corner chapels.

The Pokrovsky Cathedral, 1510-1518, in the center of the monastery, is a three-dome, four-column church on a high basement level. An open arcade gallery surrounds the church on three sides, and above it rises the cube of the church with walls divided into thirds by pilasters, and decorated with a column belt. To the southwest stands an octagonal belfry, the lower section from 1515, the bell arches and tent roof from the 17th century. In the 18th century the belfry was connected to the church gallery by a covered walkway supported by two large arches.

North of the cathedral is the refectory Church of the Conception, 1551, a large two-story rectangular masonry structure with a single small dome and an attached hexagonal belfry of the 16th century at the southwest corner. Opposite the south wall of the convent is the *Peter-Paul Church*, 1694, (**45**-25), a large, five-dome church with walls divided into sections by pilasters. It still retains a kokoshnik-arch cornice at the top of the walls. Next to it is the heated *Nikolskaya Church*, 1712 (**45**-26).

Further south along the river is the former *Tikhvinskaya Church* (**45**-29), late 1600's, on the site of the former Andreevsky Monastery. Though the church has lost its belfry and apse, and has been converted to secular use, the basic cube of the church with its window frames and rich cornice remain.

A little to the southeast is the *Bogoyavlensky Church*, 1781 (**45**-30), with rusticated corners and a high, bowed roof supporting a two-tier octagonal dome. Next to it is the heated *Rozhdestvenskaya Church*, 1739 (**45**-31), with a belfry.

To the southwest of the Kremlin area, across the river, is a recent Museum of Wooden Architecture. Most notable are the octagonal *Transfiguration Church*, 1756 (**45**-33), brought here in 1967, and the simpler *Resurrection Church*, 1776 (**45**-34), moved here in 1969. There are two peasant houses of the 19th century, with typical interior furnishings. Ancillary structures include a well, bathhouse, sheep pen, barn, and two windmills.

West of the wooden buildings is the *Borisoglebskaya Church*, 1747 (**45**-35), on the site of the former Borisoglebsky Monastery. The red brick church has features of the baroque style, especially the volutes on the belfry. The church is cubical with an octagonal second story. It was restored in 1961.

South on Lenin Street is the *Znamenskaya Church*, 1749 (**45**-37), on a high base with a stairway to the entrance, and with decorative colored tiles on the domes. Next door is the heated *Rizpolozhenskaya Church*, 1777 (**45**-38), a neoclassic church with four pediments.

East of where Lenin Street crosses the Kamenka is the *Kozma and Demyan Church*, 1725 (**45**-39), on the site of the former Koz-modemyansky Monastery. The church has plain walls divided by pilasters and a low roof leading to a single dome on a drum with ornamental kokoshnik gables. To the west is a large octagonal belfry, and to the south a one-story addition with its own slender drum and dome.

On the east side of town is the *Vasiliev Monastery* (**45**-42), which retains its Cathedral, 1662-1669, a two-column, three-dome church with severe, plain walls. Nearby is the two-story Stretenie Refectory Church, late 1600's.

Three miles east of Suzdal is the village of Kideksha, on the bank of the Nerl River. This former prince's village contains the Church of Boris and Gleb, 1152, the oldest church in northeast Russia. Damaged and neglected over the centuries, the church was badly rebuilt in the 17th century and added to in the 19th, so it is not nearly as well preserved as the Transfiguration Church in Pereslavl-Zalessky, also begun in 1152. Just to the south is the oblong Stefan Church, 1780, and to the west an octagonal tent-roof belfry of the 18th century.

TASHKENT
SAMARKAND
BUKHARA
KHIVA

ARAL SEA

KAZAKH SSR

KIRGIZ SSR

Amu-Darya River

Urgench •
Khiva •

UZBEKISTAN

⊚ Tashkent
• Kokand

CASPIAN SEA

Zeravshan River

TURKMEN SSR

Bukhara ⊚   Samarkand ⊚   • Pendjikent

CHINA

TADZHIK SSR

IRAN

AFGHANISTAN

SCALE 0 — 200 MILES
©Charles A. Ward

MAP 46

Gur Emir: Samarkand

SOVIET CENTRAL ASIA

(Map 46)

For thousands of years the area now known as Soviet Central Asia has been in the path of trade caravans and armies between eastern and western Asia. Until the twentieth century the area was called Turkestan or Transoxiana, the lands beyond the Oxus River (now called the Amu-Darya River) running from the Aral Sea to Afghanistan. After being captured by the Arabs in 712, this area formed the northeast edge of the Baghdad Caliphate. When the Caliphate began to disintegrate in the 9th century, the Samani clan in Bukhara set up an independent Central Asian empire (874-999).

From the 10th century Central Asia was hit by continual waves of Turkic immigration from the far east. In the early 11th century the Samanid empire was taken over by the Karakhanids, a Turkic group which had adopted Islam. One of the Karakhanids was Seljuk, whose followers captured Baghdad in 1055. The coming of Genghis Khan's Mongol horde in 1220 put an end to these Turkic empires.

The Golden Horde's dominance in Central Asia was ended by Tamerlane (1335-1404), a Mongol prince who made Samarkand his capital and established a huge empire during a twenty-five year campaign of military expansion beginning in 1380. After a century of rule, Tamerlane's descendants were displaced in the 1500's by local Uzbeks, the Sheibanids, who made Bukhara the capital of their empire. After being briefly conquered by the Persians in the 1730's, Central Asia developed three local, independent khanates with capitals in Khiva, Bukhara, and Kokand. Though Central Asia became a Russian protectorate in 1867, the local rulers in Bukhara and Khiva continued in power until 1920.

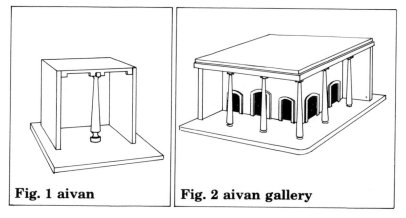

Fig. 1 aivan   **Fig. 2 aivan gallery**

A NOTE ON ARCHITECTURAL TERMINOLOGY

The Islamic architectural monuments of Soviet Central Asia share common features with all Islamic architecture, a style little studied in the West. Though similar structures were built in the Arab countries, in Turkey, and in Persia, the spelling of the names of types of buildings varies from country to country, and for many terms there is no standard English form. The names used in this book are for the most part transcriptions of the Russian forms of the Uzbek version of these terms.

An **Ark** (Arq) is a city fortress or citadel, and in earlier centuries was also the residence of the ruler.

The term **Aivan** (or eyvan) (Fig. 1) refers generally to a space closed on three sides and on top, and open on the front. In Khiva particularly it is a sort of cubical pavilion with one or two columns on the open side supporting the roof. Such porches were used as summer mosques and reception courts. **Aivan galleries** (Fig. 2), a series of columns supporting a roofed gallery, are found mainly on small mosques. In a madrasah, an aivan is a large arched niche in the center of the four sides of the courtyard.

A **Madrasah** (or Medrese) (Fig. 3) is a type of Islamic religious seminary, typically a large rectanglar building with an open courtyard surrounded by one or two stories of cells. The entrance facade is marked by a large central portal, or peshtak. To the right of the entrance vestibule is a mosque, and to the left, a darskhana, or classroom (see plan). These rooms are covered by domes which are often visible from the outside. The corners of the front facade are sometimes marked by round towers called guldasta.

"Kosh" is the term used to indicate madrasahs or other buildings built in pairs, facing each other. Such a relation is found throughout Central Asia.

A **Mosque** is a Muslim house of prayer. A **Djuma Mosque** is a large congregational mosque for Friday prayer. A **Namazga Mosque** is for certain yearly holidays. A **Minaret** is a tower from which Moslems are called to prayer. A **Mihrab** is a prayer niche in the wall of the mosque, and is used to orient the worshipper toward Mecca.

A **Khanaka** is both an inn and a dormitory for holy men.

A **Khauz** is a pool, usually rectilinear, used as a public water supply.

Both **Taki** and **Charsu** are domed trading structures, usually built over the intersection of two or more streets. A **Tim** is a trading structure not over an intersection of streets.

Mausoleums developed as two-chambered structures. The **Gurkhana** is a small room which contained the coffin, and the **Ziaratkhana** is a large anteroom, or "chapel," where pilgrims could pray. Mazar is the local word for mausoleum.

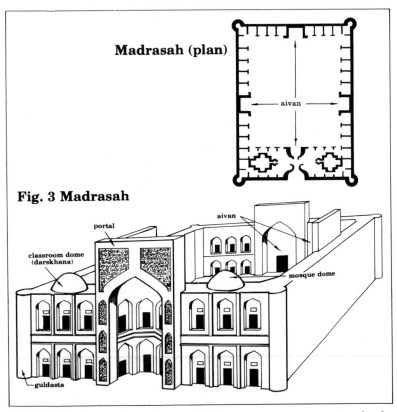

Madrasah (plan)

aivan

Fig. 3 Madrasah

aivan

portal

classroom dome
(darskhana)

mosque dome

guldasta

A **Caravanserai** is an inn and stables where caravans put up for the night. They were usually rectilinear, somewhat like a madrasah, with a large central courtyard, and stalls and rooms around the perimeter for animals, merchants, and wares.

A **stalactite** is a small three-dimensional arch in the shape of half a hollowed-out cube. A series of these arches was used to form the transition from a corner to a round dome above. The decorative ribbing of the arches and their position at the top of walls and entranceways make them resemble natural stalactites.

TASHKENT
(Map 47)

Tashkent ("stone city") arose on caravan routes extending from China and India to Russia and Europe. It shared the fate of the dynasties of Central Asia, being captured by the Arabs in the 8th century, incorpo-

rated into the Samanid empire of Bukhara in the 9th century, and captured by Genghis Khan in 1220. It was part of Tamerlane's empire from the 14th century, and was taken by the Sheibanids, based in Bukhara, in the 16th century. In 1814 it was conquered by the khans of Kokand, a city in the Fergana valley to the southeast of Tashkent. While never the center of an empire, Tashkent was well located on trade routes and always maintained an active level of trade and crafts, even in the 18th century, a period of general decline of Central Asian cities.

Annexed by Russia in 1865, Tashkent became the administrative center of Russian Turkestan in 1867, and of Soviet Turkestan in 1920. In 1924 Turkestan was divided into several republics along ethnic and language lines. The Uzbek Soviet Republic was established in 1925 and Tashkent became its capital in 1930. Tashkent is the administrative center of Soviet Central Asia, and with a population of 1.7 million is the fourth largest city in the Soviet Union (after Moscow, Leningrad, and Kiev).

While Tashkent is a huge city, it was never an Islamic capital and lacks the architectural ensembles for which Bukhara and Samarkand are renowned. Largely rebuilt after a devastating earthquake in April, 1966, Tashkent today is characterized by modern buildings which mix decorative motifs of Uzbek and western architecture, and by an abundance of parks and greenery along wide thoroughfares. In the center of town is a park surrounding the *Navoi Opera Theater* (**47**-1), designed by Shchusev in 1947. The theater is decorated with six foyers in Uzbek national styles. (Alisher Navoi, for whom many streets and cultural buildings in Uzbekistan are named, was an Uzbek poet who lived 1441-1501.) The streets around the theater, especially Marx Street and Lenin Street, contain the main hotels and stores of the city.

Of Tashkent's several museums, the most interesting is the *Museum of Decorative Arts* (**47**-6), at Shelkovichnaya St. # 15, with an extensive collection of ceramics, carved wood, textiles, carpets, metalwork, and other handicrafts. There is also an Art Gallery at Kuibushev St. # 6, and the *Uzbek History Museum* at Kuibyshev Street # 15 (**47**-5).

In the northwest part of town there are several 15th- and 16th-century religious buildings. The 16th century in Tashkent was a time of great cultural flourishing and of grand building projects. The *Kukeltash Madrasah* (**47**-7) is a monumental structure built in the 1560's. Its exterior is of undecorated brick except for a geometric pattern on the upper part of the portal. Near the Kukeltash is a 15th-century Djuma Mosque, totally rebuilt in the 18th and 19th century, and the Hodja Akhrar Madrasah, 1451.

The *Barak-Khan Madrasah*, on Khamza Street (**47**-8), grew from two mausoleum chambers which were later incorporated into the madrasah. The large tomb, built in 1531, has suffered from earthquakes, but

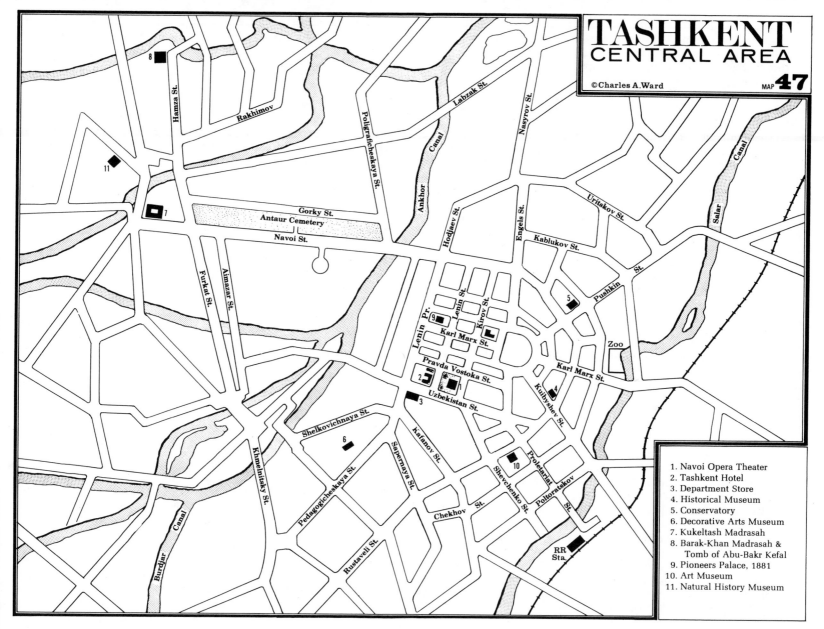

TASHKENT
CENTRAL AREA

©Charles A.Ward

MAP **47**

Hamza St.

Rakhimov

Poligraficheskaya St.

Labzak St.

Nasyrov St.

Ankhor Canal

Solar Canal

Uritskov St.

Gorky St.

Antaur Cemetery

Navoi St.

Hodjaev St.

Engels St.

Kablukov St.

Pushkin St.

Furkat St.

Almazar St.

Lenin Pr.

Lenin St.

Kirov St.

Karl Marx St.

Zoo

Pravda Vostoka St.

Karl Marx St.

Uzbekistan St.

Kuibyshev St.

Shelkovichnaya St.

Khmelnitsky Canal

Pedagogicheskaya St.

Sapernaya St.

Kafanov St.

Proletariat

Shevchenko St.

Poltoratskov St.

Burdjar Canal

Rustaveli St.

Chekhov St.

RR Sta.

1. Navoi Opera Theater
2. Tashkent Hotel
3. Department Store
4. Historical Museum
5. Conservatory
6. Decorative Arts Museum
7. Kukeltash Madrasah
8. Barak-Khan Madrasah &
   Tomb of Abu-Bakr Kefal
9. Pioneers Palace, 1881
10. Art Museum
11. Natural History Museum

elements of its decoration still remain. The smaller mausoleum has survived in better shape. Originally it was to the southwest of the larger, but both were incorporated into the madrasah in mid-century. The madrasah was restored in the early 1900's.

To the north of the Barak-Khan Madrasah is the Abu-Bakr-Muhammed-Kafal-Shashi Mausoleum. The person for whom it was named lived in the 10th century; the mausoleum was built in 1541-1542. The portal leads into a cross-shaped chamber in which only the corner pendentives, the transition from the corner to dome, survive from the original 16th-century building. The remainder has been subjected to later reconstruction. The tomb is small, but of monumental style, constructed on a raised platform base.

The *Sheik-Antaur Cemetery* is in the area between Navoi and Gorky Streets, behind the new buildings along Navoi Street. There are several large mausoleums, including that of Zengi-ata, built by Tamerlane, which still has carved doors of the 15th century; the Mausoleum of Sheik Antaur, of the 16th century; and the mausoleum of Yunus-Khan, late 15th century.

SAMARKAND
(Map 48)

Samarkand, the second largest city of Uzbekistan with a population of nearly 300,000, is situated in the Zaravshan River valley at a height of 2,350 feet above sea level. The area has been settled since about 600 BC, and was conquered by Alexander the Great in 329 BC. It was sacked by the Arabs in 712 and destroyed by Genghis Khan in 1220. Known until 1220 as Maracanda in the West, and as Afrosiab to the local inhabitants, the town was abandoned after the Mongol pillaging. Present-day Samarkand, a mile or two southwest of the Afrosiab site, developed in the 13th and 14th centuries, and expanded greatly when the Mongol leader Tamerlane (Timur) made it his capital in 1370. Flourishing of science, especially astronomy, and further building continued during the rule of Tamerlane's grandson, Ulug Beg, 1409-1449. In the 16th century the capital of this area of Central Asia shifted to Bukhara, and in the 17th century Samarkand became a separate principality of the Uzbek state. In the 1720's as a result of internecine feuds, the town was totally deserted, only to be revived again 50 years later. Samarkand was taken by the Russians in 1868, and soon reflected the influence of industry and Russian culture and architecture. When the Uzbek Soviet Socialist Republic was established in 1925, Samarkand was made its administrative and political capital. Though the capital was moved to Tashkent in 1930, Samarkand continues to be a large city with industry, a university, and modern housing. Its main interest for the tourist consists of outstanding architectural remains from the time of Tamerlane.

The oldest section of Samarkand is on the plateau north of the central city. Here archeological investigations have unearthed the remains of the ancient city of *Afrosiab*, or *Maracanda* (48-1). Digs have been carried out intermittantly since 1874, and there is now a museum on the site displaying recent finds, mainly potshards, coins, and jewelry. Earlier finds are in the Hermitage Museum in Leningrad, and in museums in Moscow.

Northeast of the Maracanda site, across the Afrosiab canal, are the remains of *Ulug Beg's Observatory*, built 1420-1430 (48-2), and totally destroyed in 1451. An excellent astronomer, Ulug Beg had many accomplishments, including the calculation of the length of the year to within one minute, and mapping over 1,000 stars. His observatory was circular, about 150 feet in diameter, and seems to have had three levels. In the center was a giant sextant, a curving stone arc 80 feet long placed in an excavation in the ground. Since this sextant was rediscovered in 1909, it has been covered with a roof and has become the main sight of the observatory. The exact appearance of the original building is unknown, though its three-story walls probably had openings for taking celestial sightings.

The *Khazret-Khyzr Mosque* (48-3), on the slope of the plateau on the west side of the road leading back to town, is an ancient structure rebuilt in the mid-19th century, and radically "restored" in 1915. It is a small asymmetrical mosque marked by harmonious relationships of the low cupola and portal, columned portico along the street side, and a modest minaret in proportion to the rest of the structure.

The most monumental construction of the Timur period in Central Asia was the *Bibi-Khanym Mosque* (48-4 and Plan 49), now in ruins, built by Tamerlane in 1399-1404 with loot from his successful conquest of India. He wanted to build the largest mosque in the world, larger than the one in Delhi. The style is the "djuma" or congregational mosque, which has a domed chamber with mihrab at the end of a large courtyard surrounded by a roofed gallery. The overall dimensions of the structure were 550 feet long and 350 feet across, with a gallery of 480 white marble columns supporting 400 small cupolas. The speed of construction and gigantic size of the building made it succeptible to earthquakes, and deterioration soon set in. Its final destruction came in a severe quake in 1897, which destroyed the entrance portal and the dome of the mosque.

The arch of the entrance portal is gone, but the massive pylons remain, 110 feet tall. The mosque dome is reached through a 100-foot tall arch flanked by tapering octagonal towers. The mosque is square, supporting a dome 130 feet high. Much of the geometric tile decoration remains, and even in ruins the structure is most impressive and dominates the skyline of the city. In the center of the courtyard is a massive marble Koran stand presented to the mosque by Ulug Beg. It was moved to the center of the courtyard in 1875 when there was fear of the mosque

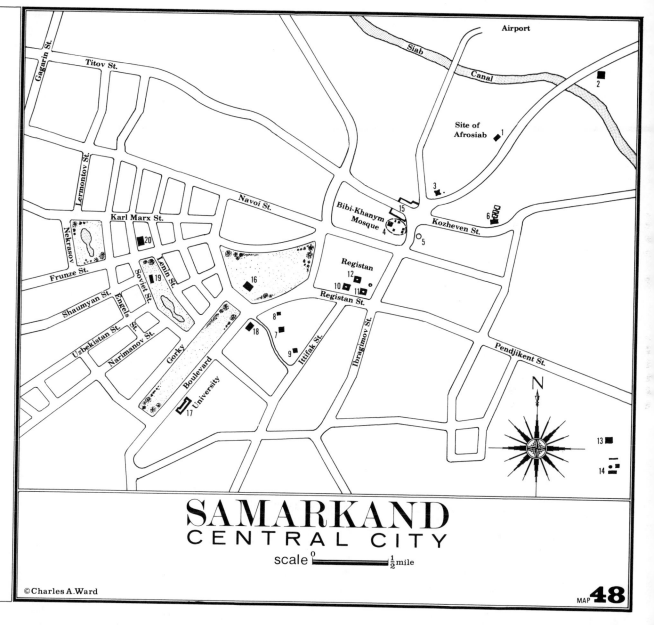

1. Afrosiab Museum
2. Ulug Beg Observatory
3. Kazrat Khyzr Mosque
4. Bibi-Khanym Mosque
5. Bibi-Khanym Mausoleum
6. Shahi Zinda Complex
7. Gur Emir
8. Rukhabad
9. Ak-Sarai
10. Ulug-Beg Madrasah
11. Shir Dor Madrasah
12. Tillya Kari Madrasah
13. Ishrat Khane Mausoleum
14. Hodja Abdi-Darun Mausoleum
15. Bazaar market
16. Opera and Ballet Theater
17. University
18. "Samarkand" Hotel
19. "Zeravshan" Hotel
20. History, Art, & Culture Museum

SAMARKAND
CENTRAL CITY
scale 0 ⊢――――⊣ ½ mile

©Charles A.Ward

MAP **48**

collapsing. (This mosque set the form for congregational mosques in Central Asia. The Kalyan Mosque in Bukhara, though somewhat smaller, is a perfectly preserved example of this type of structure.) Long-range plans call for restoration of the mosque by the late 1980's.

Bibi Khanym, who was one of Tamerlane's wives, built a Madrasah across the street, with a massive portal rivaling that of the mosque. Of the madrasah complex only the octagonal *Mausoleum of Bibi Khanym* has survived to the present (**48**-5).

The *Shahi Zinda Complex* (**48**-6 and Map **50**) is a series of mausoleums arranged on either side of a narrow roadway at the edge of the Afrosiab plateau in the eastern part of the city. The mausoleums, which date from the reigns of Tamerlane and Ulug Beg (1370-1449), arose on the legendary burial site of Kusam-ibn-Abbas, Mohammed's cousin, who came to convert the Uzbeks in the 8th century. Though there is no evidence that Kusam-ibn-Abbas actually ever visited Samarkand, a mausoleum for him was constructed in the 11th century and the area became sacred and a place of pilgrimage.

The complex is entered at the foot of the plateau through a portal built in 1434-1435 (the carved wooden doors are from 1911). The portal leads to a *chartak* (**50**-1), or dome supported on four pillars. To the left is a mosque, which now houses a *museum* (**50**-2). To the right is the small *Davlet Kush-beg Madrasah*, from 1813 (**50**-4). Opposite it is the *summer mosque*, 1911 (**50**-3), an aivan with interesting carved columns and painted ceiling.

Beyond the summer mosque are 36 steps which lead up to the crest of the plateau. To the left of the steps is the *Kazi-Zade-Rumi Mausoleum*, ca. 1437 (**50**-5), with two cupolas. The larger room is the ziaratkhana, with cells in the corners, and the smaller room is the gurkhana, or burial chamber. The vertical emphasis of this tomb distinguishes it from the other monuments of the complex. The building is cubical with an octagonal transition to the tall drum decorated with ornamental Arabic script. The dome is of blue glazed brick. The interiors of the domes, particularly that of the smaller room, have exquisite stalactite arches.

The steps and the chartak at the top were constructed in the 18th century. The first tomb on the right is that of *Emir Hussain*, 1374-1376 (**50**-6). [It is also called after Tuglu Tekin, Hussain's mother.] Generally in disrepair, the tomb has a stunning tile facade facing the walkway. Opposite it is the *Emir Zade Mausoleum*, 1386 (**50**-7), also with elaborate relief terracotta and majolica tiles covering the entire face. The mausoleum is cubical with a cupola on a low octagonal drum.

The next building on the left is the *Shadi-Mulk*, or *Turkan-Aka Mausoleum*, 1373 (**50**-8), which contained the tombs of Tamerlane's sister Turkan and her daughter Shadi-Mulk. It too has outstanding exterior and interior tile decoration in geometrical, floral, and calligraphic patterns.

The second tomb to the right is the *Mausoleum of Shirin Biki-Aka* (**50**-9), built for another of Tamerlane's sisters, who died in 1385. It has a mosaic exterior and elaborately decorated interior (restored in 1940 and 1952).

The third tomb on the right, the *Octagonal Mausoleum*, ca. 1400, (**50**-10), is in great disrepair. Originally a pavilion with eight open arches, some of which were later bricked up, it is decorated with glazed brick and mosaics on the outside, and has a blue and white pattern inside the cupola.

The walkway was once lined with mausoleums all the way to the end. Many of them have disappeared over the centuries, leaving much open space before the final group of buildings.

The *Usto-Ali Mausoleum*, ca. 1400 (**50**-11), named for its builder, has decorative patterns of multicolored geometrical majolica tiles. The side walls have interesting patterns created with unglazed brick.

The first "*Nameless Mausoleum*" (**50**-12) actually bears the name of Ulug-Sultan-Begin. In disrepair, only the portal remains, with fragments of dark blue majolica decor in small geometrical and floral patterns.

The next mausoleum on the left was never finished, but is thought to have been built for *Emir Burunduk*, one of Timur's generals, in the 1380's (**50**-13).

The group of mausoleums at the end of the walkway are centered on the third chartak, built in 1405 by Tuman-aka, one of Tamerlane's wives. To the left is the *Tuman-aka Mosque and Khanaka*, ca. 1390 (**50**-14), an elongated structure with three domed chambers and a mosaic mihrab. Adjoining is the *Tuman-aka Mausoleum*, 1405-1406 (**50**-15), with a facade having mosaic panels of considerable interest. The interior decor includes wall painting, stalactites, and polychrome tiles. The blue dome is on a cylindrical drum.

At the end of the walkway, beyond the chartak, is the portal of the *Hodja Ahmad Mausoleum*, 1360 (**50**-16), decorated with relief terracotta and blue majolica tiles with a stylized vine pattern. The "*Nameless Mausoleum of 1360*" (**50**-17), has a similar portal and tile decoration. It was restored in 1962.

The entrance to the *Kusam-ibn-Abbas Mosque & Mausoleum* (**50**-18), to the right of the Tuman-aka chartak, is through magnificent carved doors from 1404-1405. The present mosque was built in the mid-15th century and remodeled several times since. Beyond the mosque is the *Mausoleum of Kusam-ibn-Abbas*, constructed in 1334 (**50**-19). Most notable is the sarcophagos of Kusam, constructed in the late 1300's, and finished in blue, white, and green tile with gold ornamentation.

In the center of town near the new Intourist hotel is the main tomb of the Timurids, *Gur Emir* (**48**-7), built by Tamerlane for his heir,

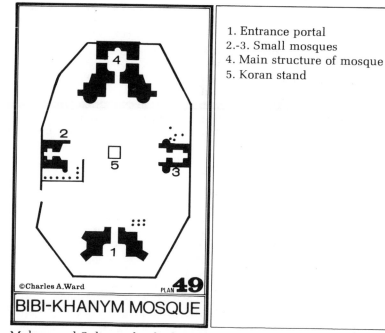

1. Entrance portal
2.-3. Small mosques
4. Main structure of mosque
5. Koran stand

©Charles A.Ward   PLAN **49**

BIBI-KHANYM MOSQUE

The *Rukhabad Mausoleum* (**48**-8), probably from the 1380's, was built over the tomb of a famous mystic, Sheik Burkhaneddin Sagardji. This monumental structure, an unadorned brick cube with massive octagonal transition to a tall conical dome, is located about 400 feet to the north of Gur Emir. The two mausoleums were originally connected by a straight stone path.

The *Ak Sarai Mausoleum*, ca. 1468 (**48**-9), was built southeast of Gur Emir as a tomb for Tamerlane's successors. It was never completed on the outside, so is unprepossessing at first glance. The floor plan represents a new type of many-chambered mausoleum which developed in the 15th century. This tomb is basically cross-plan with a central room and four smaller cells in the corners. Note the system of supporting the main dome and the pendentives of the little cupolas, which form 12- and 16-pointed star patterns. The main room has remnants of decorative panels with fine small-scale mosaic patterns.

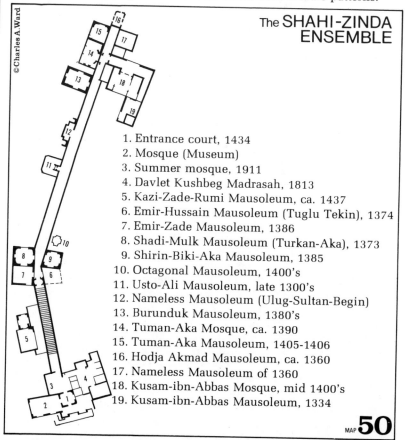

The **SHAHI-ZINDA ENSEMBLE**

1. Entrance court, 1434
2. Mosque (Museum)
3. Summer mosque, 1911
4. Davlet Kushbeg Madrasah, 1813
5. Kazi-Zade-Rumi Mausoleum, ca. 1437
6. Emir-Hussain Mausoleum (Tuglu Tekin), 1374
7. Emir-Zade Mausoleum, 1386
8. Shadi-Mulk Mausoleum (Turkan-Aka), 1373
9. Shirin-Biki-Aka Mausoleum, 1385
10. Octagonal Mausoleum, 1400's
11. Usto-Ali Mausoleum, late 1300's
12. Nameless Mausoleum (Ulug-Sultan-Begin)
13. Burunduk Mausoleum, 1380's
14. Tuman-Aka Mosque, ca. 1390
15. Tuman-Aka Mausoleum, 1405-1406
16. Hodja Akmad Mausoleum, ca. 1360
17. Nameless Mausoleum of 1360
18. Kusam-ibn-Abbas Mosque, mid 1400's
19. Kusam-ibn-Abbas Mausoleum, 1334

MAP **50**

Muhammed-Sultan, who died unexpectedly in 1403. The mausoleum, completed in 1404, was exceptionally well-built, with stone foundations fourteen feet deep, and has survived in good shape to the present. Its striking effect is achieved by the use of simple forms in gigantic scale — an octagonal building with a tall cylindrical drum crowned by a tall ribbed dome in blue glazed brick. This dome, 40 feet high, 48 feet in diameter, with 64 ribs, is one of the most impressive tile domes in all of Islam.

The tomb is reached from the street through a monumental portal, the lower 2/3 of which preserve its original bright mosaic decoration. The large courtyard was flanked by the Muhammed-Sultan Madrasah to the left, and Muhammed-Sultan Khanaka to the right. They fell into disrepair by the 17th century. The interior of the tomb is square, each wall having a door and niche with grilled windows and geometric patterns of various colors. In the center of the marble floor is Tamerlane's jade coffin, presented to the mausoleum in 1425 by Ulug Beg, and other tombs of onyx and marble. Tamerlane was actually buried in the basement beneath his tomb, in a burial chamber discovered only in 1940. Tamerlane's skeleton was found intact (it was identified by an irregularity of his leg bone, which had caused him to be lame).

The *Registan* is the old trading center of town, originally a square lined with mosques, khanakas, trading domes, and caravanserais. Desiring to make it more "official," Ulug Beg built a madrasah on the west side in 1417-1420. As the other structures nearby fell into disrepair, they were replaced by two additional madrasahs in the 17th century, creating the present configuration.

The *Ulug Beg Madrasah*, 1417-1420 (**48**-10), is in the classical madrasah style. The rectangular inner courtyard (175 x 250 feet) has four large aivans and two stories of 28 cells facing the court. The entrance facade has an arch 50 feet wide, and 100-foot tall corner minaret towers topped with stalactite crowns which originally supported a second, smaller tower. The madrasah was extensively damaged over the centuries, especially in the 18th century when the cupolas over the classroom and the upper tier of cells were destroyed. Emergency work in 1932 only just prevented the northwest minaret from falling. The latest round of restoration should be completed by the late 1970's.

The *Shir Dor Madrasah*, 1619-1636 (**48**-11), was built on the east side of the registan as a mirror image of the Ulug Beg Madrasah (the same height, proportions, minarets, and number of cells), but has more elaborate tile decoration, especially the animals on the facade ("shir dor" means "having tigers"). The decorative tile inside and out is of very intense colors and of the greatest variety and interest. Behind the madrasah is the circular Taki-Tilpak Furushon charsu, or headgear bazaar dome, from the early 1800's.

The *Tillya-Kari Madrasah* on the north, 1647-1660 (**48**-12), the last major structure on the Registan, was built to serve the dual function of mosque and madrasah. Three sides of the 150-foot square courtyard are lined by cells, but the fourth (west) is a congregational mosque with columned arcade, built in part to succeed the Bibi-Khanym structure which was already falling into disrepair. The mosque, in the center of the west side, is flanked by domed galleries supported by octagonal columns. The external cupola of the mosque was never constructed, though its tall, elaborately decorated cylindrical drum was built and can be seen clearly. The inner dome and walls are rich in gilt decorative tile ("tillya-kari" means "gilded"). The exterior of the madrasah facing the registan has two stories of cell niches, and the portal has a recessed, three-sided niche. The portal was left undecorated when it was rebuilt after an earthquake in the early 1800's.

The *Ishrat-Khane Mausoleum*, 1464 (**48**-13), was built on the east side of town for women and children descendents of Tamerlane. It has suffered much from weather, man, and earthquakes, particularly that of 1903, but its ruins are still impressive. An example of the many-chambered mausoleum which began to be constructed in the 15th century, it had a large central hall with numerous side rooms on both the first and second floors. The central part is marked by a great portal, and the side sections by the remains of a two-level arched loggia. Fragments of elaborate polychrome tile decoration can still be seen inside.

The *Hodja Abdi-Darun Mausoleum* complex (**48**-14) is located in a cemetery near the Ishrat Khane Mausoleum. First erected in the 11th century, it was rebuilt by Ulug Beg in the early 15th century as a square chamber with pyramidal dome on an octagonal drum. In front of it Ulug Beg built a one-room khanaka which has a large cylindrical drum with calligraphic decoration. In the 19th century a number of other buildings grew up around a pool, including a mosque with aivan-columned gallery.

BUKHARA
(Map 51)

Bukhara, with a population of 110,000, is the second largest city in the Zeravshan River valley. Always an important trade center, the Bukhara area has been mentioned since Darius the Persian conquered it in the 6th century BC. Since the 7th century AD the city has gone through periods of prosperity alternating with periods of military defeat and devastation. Bukhara was conquered by the Arabs in 709, but emerged as an independent state in the 9th century under the Samanid rulers. The empire, founded by Ismail Samani in 874, continued until 999 and encompassed all of Central Asia. The end of this flowering of Bukhara came in 1220 when Genghis Khan devastated the city. Though Tamerlane chose Samarkand as the capital of his Central Asian empire in the 1370's, Bukhara continued to thrive, especially under Ulug Beg (1404-1449), and became a center of Islamic studies. In the 16th century when Bukhara became the capital of the Sheibanid Central Asian empire, many of the architectural monuments which we see today were constructed. The empire split apart again in the early 18th century, and the independent Bukhara which emerged in 1753 controlled only the central Uzbekistan area. Treaties signed in 1868 and 1873 made Bukhara dependent on Russia, though the Emir ruled until 1920.

The central section of Bukhara has been preserved much as it was in the 17th century, with its maze of twisting streets and low mud houses (map 51 shows only the main streets). Thirty-four architectural monuments have been put under government protection and are the main tourist attractions. The former city wall of some six miles in length is mainly gone, though a portion of it with a set of gates remains at the western end of the town. The sites are described geographically, from west to east. There was a strong earthquake near Bukhara in May, 1976, and some of the buildings described here may have been damaged.

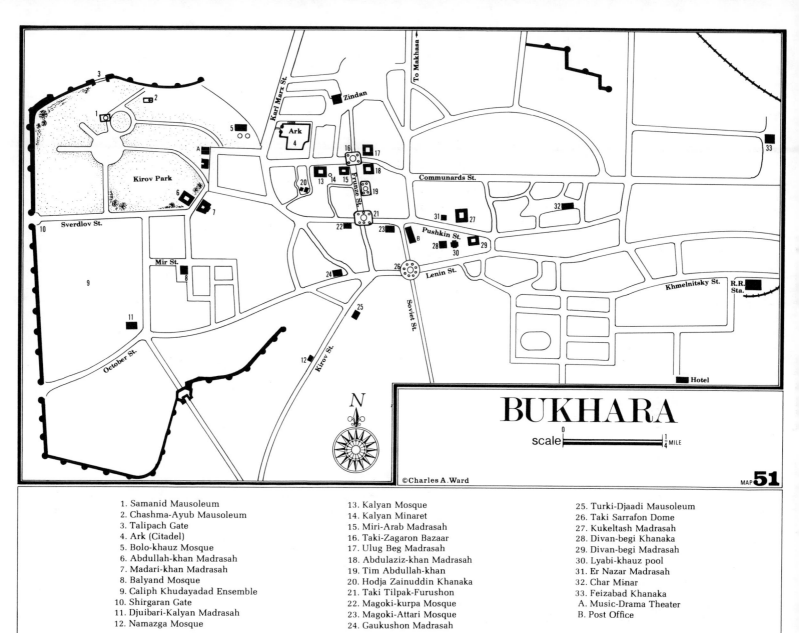

BUKHARA

scale |0 — — — 1/4 MILE|

©Charles A. Ward

MAP **51**

1. Samanid Mausoleum
2. Chashma-Ayub Mausoleum
3. Talipach Gate
4. Ark (Citadel)
5. Bolo-khauz Mosque
6. Abdullah-khan Madrasah
7. Madari-khan Madrasah
8. Balyand Mosque
9. Caliph Khudayadad Ensemble
10. Shirgaran Gate
11. Djuibari-Kalyan Madrasah
12. Namazga Mosque

13. Kalyan Mosque
14. Kalyan Minaret
15. Miri-Arab Madrasah
16. Taki-Zagaron Bazaar
17. Ulug Beg Madrasah
18. Abdulaziz-khan Madrasah
19. Tim Abdullah-khan
20. Hodja Zainuddin Khanaka
21. Taki Tilpak-Furushon
22. Magoki-kurpa Mosque
23. Magoki-Attari Mosque
24. Gaukushon Madrasah

25. Turki-Djaadi Mausoleum
26. Taki Sarrafon Dome
27. Kukeltash Madrasah
28. Divan-begi Khanaka
29. Divan-begi Madrasah
30. Lyabi-khauz pool
31. Er Nazar Madrasah
32. Char Minar
33. Feizabad Khanaka
A. Music-Drama Theater
B. Post Office

The *Ismail Samani Mausoleum* (**51**-1) is located in the Kirov Park, which was laid out in 1950 on the site of a deserted cemetery. The tomb, probably built during Ismail's reign (892-907) was erected over the tomb of his father, Nasr-ibn-Ahmed, who ruled 876-892. The mausoleum is a cube 34 feet square with a hemispherical dome. The structure is made entirely of bricks which are laid with the greatest diversity, creating various surface patterns. The four facades are identical, with arched central portals. The corners have decorative columns topped by small cupolas, and the top of the walls have low galleries with ten arches per side, which hide the transitional arches supporting the dome. The arcade at top and the ornamental brickwork give a lightness to the building which belies its five-foot thick walls. The patterned brick facade provides an interesting play of light and shadow, and the mausoleum is rewardingly viewed at various times of day, as well as at night under a full moon. The mausoleum is an excellently proportioned structure with subtle horizontal lines in the band of bricks at the base and midway up the walls where the portal arches begin. Its charm, in the harmonic interrelation of the structural and decorative elements, has no equal in Central Asia, and it is the only remaining example of this type of pre-Mongol architecture in Uzbekistan.

The *Chasma-Ayub Mausoleum* (**51**-2) is located in Kirov Park not far to the northeast of the Samani tomb. A structure on this site may have existed from the 1100's, but the present building was constructed during Tamerlane's day, in 1379. The central gurkhana is 14 feet square with two side chambers, and its conical dome, which dominates the building, is unique in Bukhara. The entrance vault covers a spring which by legend was caused by Job striking the ground with his staff ("Chasma-Ayub" means "Job's spring"). In the 16th century a sort of hall with a cupola and a vestibule were added, giving the building an elongated east-west orientation (62 x 80 feet), and hiding the older parts of the structure.

Nearby is the *Talipach Gate* of the old city wall (**51**-3), best viewed from the north.

The *Ark* (**51**-4), or central fortress, has existed in some form on this site since the 7th century. It has been alternately destroyed, rebuilt, and enlarged over the centuries, and in its present form is an artificial hill 50-65 feet high covering an area of some seven acres. The ark was both fortress, seat of government, and the residence of the Emir, high officials, and military leaders. It also contained the treasury, a prison, and a mosque. At the beginning of the 20th century about 3,000 people lived in the Ark. Most of its area is now vacant land, except for the Emir's buildings, which house the Regional Historical Museum.

The entrance, on the west, is an ascending roadway which passes through an archway between two round towers. Chambers in the wall on either side of the entrance contained water storage and prison cells. The covered entrance roadway emerges before a mosque built in the early 20th century. From the mosque a narrow road leads to a charsu cupola. To the left of it is the Grand Ceremonial Court, with a mosaic portal, 1604-1606. To the right are the former stables area, behind the entrance towers, and the reception rooms. The reception court is the highest point in the Ark and has a door to a balcony overlooking the Registan, the city's main market square. Public executions formerly took place at the edge of the square where the water tower now stands.

Northeast of the Ark is the Zindan, a former prison built in the 19th century for debtors and political prisoners. The prison had regular cells and special underground cells resembling wells. The Zindan now houses a branch of the Regional Museum, and the well-cells can be viewed.

The *Bolo-Khauz Mosque*, 1712 (**51**-5), at the edge of Kirov Park opposite the entrance to the Ark, is the only structure remaining from a mass of buildings which were once on the Registan Square. The aivan gallery was added in 1917, with interesting oversize stalactite capitals on the columns. A squat minaret and pool (khauz) complete the ensemble.

At the southeast corner of Kirov Park is the Kosh Madrasah. "Kosh" means "paired," and throughout central Asia there was a tendency to build madrasahs and other large structures facing each other. This ensemble is made up of the *Abdullah-Khan Madrasah*, 1588-1590 (**51**-6), to the west, a grandiose building in a striking style with an exterior decor of colored glazed brick and majolica. The cupola of the vestibule, formed by the intersection of four large arches with rib work between them, represents a perfected form of this type of cupola support. The vaults of the galleries and of the mosque have elaborate geometric decorative motifs. The *Madari-Khan Madrasah*, 1566-1567 (**51**-7), to the east is less interesting architecturally. Its entrance portal, with mosaics of glazed brick and majolica, is its best feature.

The *Balyand Mosque* (**51**-8), a little to the south, was built in the 16th century, with the later addition of an "L"-shaped aivan gallery on two sides. The mosque is built on an elevated base ("balyand" means "high") which became a model for small mosques for years to come. The exterior is plain, but the interior is exquisitely and richly done in panels of blue-green tile with gold script. Especially notable are the mosaic work, huge flowery wall panels resembling Persian carpets in design and color, and the carved wooden ceiling.

The *Caliph Khudidad Madrasah* complex (**51**-9), south of Kirov Park, represents a new style of madrasah which developed in the 18th century, a mixture of the older style with local folk traditions. The madrasah has a square mosque with an aivan gallery on two sides, one-story cells, and a khauz and trees in the courtyard.

The *Kalyan Minaret* (**51**-14), a 150-foot tall tower built in 1127-1129, dominates the skyline of Bukhara. While it served to mark the location of the city's main mosque, it also was a prominent symbol of the power of Islam in the town, and a lookout tower for military purposes. The minaret, 29 feet in diameter at the base, tapers slightly as it rises to an overhanging, sixteen-arch rotunda-lantern with a stalactite cornice above and below. The external facade of decorative brick laid in bands of varying patterns rivals the Samani tomb in variety and interest. The decorative bands become wider higher up, a trick of reverse perspective which makes the size of the minaret more impressive from below. Half-way up are the remains of a band of Kufic writing in relief terracotta. Another band in blue glazed tile is just below the stalactite base of the lantern. The minaret has survived centuries of earthquakes, perhaps because of a good foundation, elastic gypsum mortar which stands up to water, and the geometrical relationship of the parts. In the 18th and 19th century the tower was also used as a place of occasional execution. The last such execution was in 1884.

The *Kalyan Mosque* (**51**-13) was built in the late 1400's and is the only large congregational (Djuma) mosque of this era (built on the site of an earlier mosque of the 12th century). It has the same form as the Bibi-Khanym Mosque in Samarkand — a large portal leading to an inner courtyard with mosque and mihrab at the far end, and aivans on the sides. Its overall dimensions are 425 feet long and 260 feet wide, and the courtyard, surrounded by a gallery of 208 columns supporting 288 small cupolas, has held as many as 10,000 worshippers at one time. The building was influenced by the Ulug Beg tradition, with clean lines, distinct form, and restrained decoration. The ornamental script on the drum of the dome can be seen best from outside, behind the mosque.

The *Miri Arab Madrasah*, 1530-1536 (**51**-15) forms a "kosh" ensemble, facing the Kalyan Mosque. The two-story courtyard is lined with 111 cells, which have elaborate grillwork on their windows. Of the courtyard's four aivans, the tall south portal with rich decorative tiles and exposed arches is particularly noteworthy. The madrasah's plan differs from the classic madrasah pattern, with new passageways, corridors, and stairways. The traditional mosque in the entrance facade has been replaced by a tomb for Sheik Miri Arab and his supporters. The classroom (darskhana) has an interesting interior dome with intricate stalactite work, as does the sheik's tomb. The madrasah houses the Soviet Union's only operating Islamic Theological School.

To the west of the Kalyan Mosque is the *Khanaka Zainuddin*, ca. 1550 (**51**-20), an ensemble containing a mosque, khanaka, and khauz. The mosque, built about the same time as the Balyand Mosque, resembles it in the aivan gallery on two sides. The interior has a "floating" dome, with a ring of stalactites leading to the decorative ribbing. The walls are covered with elaborate polychrome decoration from floor to

Samanid Tomb: Bukhara

ceiling, mosaic panels of fine design and bright colors. The layout of the buildings, pool, and the fantastic decor are designed to provide a retreat, a total break from the life outside.

The Trading Domes (charsu or taki) were often built at the intersection of main roads. Those in Bukhara were built in the late 15th century, during the Sheibanid rule. The *Taki Zagaron Dome* (**51**-16), just beyond the Miri Arab Madrasah, has a basic rectangular structure with a large dome on a sixteen-sided drum surrounded by a flock of small cupolas. The radial ribs and concentric set-backs of the dome's structure are left exposed on the exterior. This was originally the jewelers' dome.

Frunze Street leads past the rectangular *Tim Abdulla-Khan*, 1577 (**51**-19), the former silk market, with plain windowless walls and a central dome surrounded by a ring of small cupolas covering the large (56 shops) arcade below. The tim is dark, illuminated only by windows in the main dome and four architectural lanterns in the ring of smaller cupolas.

The *Taki-Tilpak-Furushon Dome* (**51**-21) is over an intersection of five streets which meet at odd angles. The dome is centered on the main street with asymmetrical exits to the others. The dome has always been an area where head coverings are sold.

The *Taki Sarrafon Dome* (**51**-26), at the intersection of Soviet and Lenin Streets, has a dome supported by four massive intersecting arches which are clearly visible from the outside. It was restored in 1947. Here the money changers originally had their shops. The takis are now free-standing structures, cleared of the adjacent buildings which in the past made them spacious shopping areas along the narrow crowded streets of the old city.

Just beyond the Taki-Zagaron Dome on Communards Street are two madrasahs facing each other across the street. On the north is the *Ulug Beg Madrasah* (**51**-17), built in 1417, the oldest surviving madrasah in Central Asia. The building is a typical two-story madrasah with strict, severe proportions. The central portal has simple geometric tile decoration from 1417 and from remodelings in 1586, the 1600's, and restoration in the 1960's.

The *Abdulaziz-Khan Madrasah* (**51**-18) faces the Ulug Beg Madrasah, but was built some two centuries later, in 1598. Comparison of the two shows the development of the ornamental style of architecture. The proportions are heavier and more massive in the later madrasah — the height and size of the entrance portal are out of proportion to the rest of the facade. This is made up for by the ornamental decor, the massive stalactite treatment of the inner surface of the portal arch, the dominant yellow color and use of majolica, brick mosaic, polychrome, mosaic, relief terracotta, and carved marble. The decor even reflects some Chinese motifs (portrayals of birds and dragons), an influence that came with Chinese trade at the time. The use of decorative stalactites is notable. In earlier centuries "prismatic" stalactites were structural, serving as a transition from right angle to curve, or as a buttress for an overhang. In this madrasah we see decorative stalactites used for purely ornamental ends. Most amazing are the inner domes of the darskhana and the mosque, with elaborate star patterns so complex that the line of the dome structure is almost lost. This exuberant decor is astounding in its individual examples, but is achieved at the expense of color harmony and unity of style in the building as a whole. The decoration of the madrasah was never completed (Abdulaziz-Khan went to Mecca before it was finished).

The *Magoki-Attari Mosque* (**51**-23) is one of the oldest buildings in Bukhara, dating from the 800's, and rebuilt in the 1100's. Because of the rise of the level of the city over the centuries, the mosque is now 18 feet below ground level. Only the south portal is visible, excavated in the 1930's. The south facade has interesting decor, a large arched portal with a calligraphic inscription band done in relief, fine columns with a carved vine motif, and panels with decorative geometrical patterns.

The Lyabi-Khauz complex was built around a trading square, with a *large pool* (**51**-30) in the center ("lyabi-khauz" means "edge of the pool"). The square is outlined by the Nadir Divan-begi Khanaka on the west, the Kukeltash Madrasah on the north, and the Divan-Begi Madrasah on the west. The pool, 150 x 115 feet, dates from 1620 and is the largest in Bukhara.

The *Divan-Begi Khanaka*, 1620 (**51**-28) was built on the edge of the pool. It is a tall, cubical structure with tall central portal, one large drum, and round towers on the front corners. Opposite is the *Divan-Begi Madrasah*, 1622 (**51**-29). The fact that it has no mosque or classroom gives credence to the legend that it was originally planned as a caravanserai and converted to a madrasah only at the last stages of construction.

The northern part of the Lyabi-khauz complex is formed by the *Kukeltash Madrasah*, 1568 (**51**-27), one of the largest madrasahs in Central Asia, with 160 cells. The side walls have loggias on the second level outside, a unique break with the tradition of blank outside walls. The main architectural attractions of the building are the dome of the darskhana, supported by four slender intersecting arches; the decor of the darshana and mosque; the dome-crossing in the front archway leading into the courtyard; and the carved wooden doors of the madrasah.

To the west of the Kukeltash is the *Er-Nazar Madrasah* (**51**-31) named for the ambassador of Bukhara to the court of Catherine the Great. Catherine reputedly paid for the madrasah.

Further east, off Pushkin Street, is the *Char Minar Madrasah*, 1807 (**51**-32), also known as the Caliph Niyazkul Madrasah. The small two-story pavilion with four blue-domed corner towers ("char minar" means "four minarets") had on its upper level a library with an open loggia on all four sides. The complex was typical of the 19th-century mixture of styles, for the entrance pavilion led to a one-story cell block arranged in an oblong rectangle which contained a separate mosque with an "L"-shaped aivan gallery on two sides.

The *Faizabad Khanaka*, 1599 (**51**-33) is in the northeast section of the old town. Though in disrepair, its plan is interesting, with a portal and central dome surrounded by two stories of rooms and a one-story gallery. When viewed from the inside, the dome rests on thinly contoured pendentives and has a great sense of lightness.

One-half mile east of the Railroad Station are two mausoleums of considerable interest. The larger is the *Seifeddin Bokharzi Mausoleum*, the only surviving 13th-century monument in Bukhara (little was built after the Mongol conquest of 1220). Bokharzi died in 1261, and the tomb was built soon after. The oldest section is the small gurkhana, or burial chamber, at the back of the current structure. The tomb itself has an exquisite carved wooden coffin cover of the 14th century. In the 1300's the ziaratkhana was built, a larger cubical room adjoining the burial chamber. This was a new feature, a room for the worshippers which isolated the burial place itself, hence making it more "sacred" and not open to everyone who came in to pray. Earlier tombs, like that of the Samanids, had only a single chamber. The ziaratkhana is 38 feet square, a cube with octagonal transition to a dome 65 feet tall inside. The massive portal with its seven-arch "attic" and flanking round towers was built in the late 1400's. The exterior of the tomb is without ornamentation.

Directly behind Bokharzi's tomb is the *Buyan-Kuli-Khan Mausoleum*, constructed over the tomb of a Mongol leader who was killed in 1358. While smaller in scope than Bokharzi's tomb, it is more harmonious in proportion and detail, and was the first building in Bukhara to have polychrome tile decoration. The entrance portal, 28 feet tall, still retains much of its excellent majolica and blue relief terracotta tile. The ziaratkhana has a dome 29 feet tall inside, with walls only one brick thick, which have survived thanks to their glazing inside and out. The gurkhana, or burial chamber, is illuminated by a shaft of light from above. The tile work on the inside is of great interest as well.

The *Namazga Mosque* (**51**-12), in the southwest region of the city outside the old city wall, was originally built in 1119-1120 as a wall with mihrab in the form of a portal. The faithful knelt outside to pray. The mihrab, with a stalactite arch, was attractively decorated with terracotta bricks laid in various patterns, some mosaic insets, carved inscriptions, and blue majolica tiles. The remainder of the building was constructed only in the 16th century.

There are two main ensembles beyond the city. About three miles to the north is MAKHASA (or, Sitori-i-makhi-khasa), the Summer Palace complex of the last Emir of Bukhara. It represents a "decadent" style, a blend of Uzbek and European building styles (the builders were sent to Petersburg and Yalta at the end of the 19th century to study western building techniques). In the new palace the most notable room is the "White Hall," built 1912-1914, of white carved alabaster and mirrors. Note too the dining room and the brightly painted walls of the reception hall. The palace now houses the Applied Arts Division of the Regional Museum, and some of the estate buildings house a worker's sanatorium. The complex includes an entrance portal with crudely done mosaic patterns, a large pool next to the palace with the raised summer pavilion at one end, and a harem building.

The CHAR BAKR ENSEMBLE is located four miles west of Bukhara in a place called Sumitan. It is a group of mausoleums, mosques, and khanakas on the site of the tomb of Abu-Bakr-Saad, from the time of the Samanid dynasty. The present ensemble dates from 1560-1563 when the Sheibanid Abdulla Khan had a mosque, madrasah, and khanaka constructed in a "U"-shaped ensemble facing a group of family tombs. The mosque and khanaka on either side face forward, so their sides form a courtyard with the open madrasah at the back.

KHIVA
(Map 52)

Khiva is in an area known as the Khorezm oasis in the lower Amu-Darya River valley south of the Aral Sea. Cultures have flourished there for thousands of years, but most traces of them were destroyed in the Arab invasion of 712 and by Genghis Khan's Mongols in 1220. Monuments since that time are best preserved in Khiva, and in the ancient capital Kunya-Urgench some 90 miles northwest of Khiva. Sectional strife between Timurids and Uzbeks destroyed most architectural monuments built before the 16th century, when an independent Khiva Khanate emerged. Capture of the area by Persian troops in the mid-1700's was also a disaster for architecture. Khiva became independent again in 1765 under Inak-Muhammed-Amin, and flourished until the 20th century. The area was taken by Russian troops in 1873, occupied by the Red Army in 1920, and incorporated into the Soviet Union in 1923.

Because of its relative isolation, Khiva's old central city, a large rectangle laid out according to the points of the compass, has been preserved without modern buildings. The old city wall is intact and the monumental buildings with their pinkish mud brick set off against brilliant blue, turquoise, and white tiles still present a harmonious, unified atmosphere. Artistically the city is known for its outstanding majolica tile designs and for carved wood aivan columns.

The central city, or ICHAN-KALA, is an area of some 65 acres surrounded by a tapering mud-brick wall 1 1/2 miles long, 25 feet tall, and 18 feet thick at the base. The location of the central city has remained constant since the 10th century, and its walls enclose an area literally crammed with buildings of various centuries. The central city is entered through four gates.

The eastern *Palvan-Darvaza gates*, rebuilt in 1806, are the largest in town (**52**-19). The "gate" is in the form of a closed passage 180 feet long covered by six cupolas. Both sides of the passage are lined with small niches, originally used as the khan's prison, later coverted to trading stalls.

The *Bagcha-Darvaza gateway*, on the northern wall (**52**-35), is a closed passage about 15 feet wide and 32 feet long, covered by two cupolas. Semicircular towers 30 feet tall stand at the entrance. The *Tash-Darvaza* (**52**-36) is on the southern wall. The *Ata Darvaza* (**52**-6),

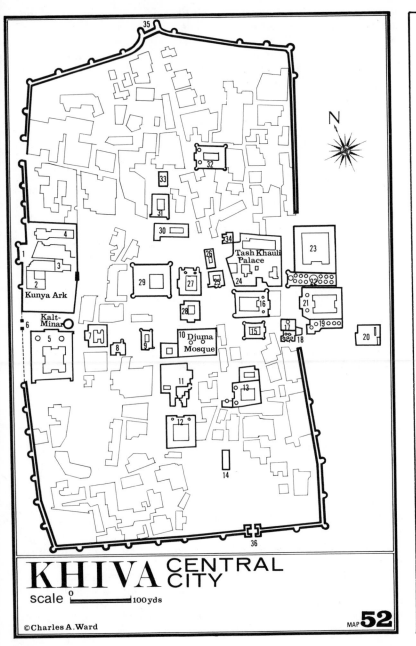

1. Ashik-baba Mausoleum
2. Reception Court (Kunya Ark)
3. Summer Mosque (Kunya Ark)
4. Former mint (Kunya Ark)
5. Mohammed-Amin-Khan Madrasah, 1852-1855
6. Ata Darvaza, west gates, rebuilt 1975
7. Divan-Begi Madrasah
8. Seyid Allauddin Mausoleum, 1303
9. Kazi-Kalyan Salim Madrasah, 1905
10. Djuma Mosque, rebuilt 1788
11. Pahlavan Mahmud Mausoleum, 1835
12. Shirgazi-khan Madrasah, 1719-1728
13. Islam Hodja Mosque, Madrasah, Minaret, 1908-1912
14. Bagbanla Mosque
15. Hodjamberdyby Madrasah, 1688
16. Kutlug-Murad-Inak Madrasah, 1804-1812
17. Ak Mosque, 1674-1677
18. Anusha-khan baths, 1657
19. Palvan darvaza gates, 1806
20. Seyid Bey Madrasah and Mosque, 1842
21. Allakuli Khan Madrasah, 1834-1835
22. Allakuli Khan Tim (Sarai Bazaar), 1832-1835
23. Caravanserai, 1832-1835
24. Tash Khauli Palace, 1828-1838
25. Muhammed-Amin-Inaka Madrasah, 1765
26. Arab Muhammed Madrasah, 1616-1800's
27. Arab Khan Madrasah
28. Matpana Bey Madrasah, 1905
29. Muhammed Rahim-Khan Madrasah, 1871
30. Yusup Yasaul Bashi Madrasah, 1906
31. Musa Tyure Madrasah, 1841
32. Emir Tyure Madrasah, 1870
33. Kash Begi Mosque
34. Uch-Avliya Mausoleum, 16th century
35. Bagcha-Darvaza
36. Tash-Darvaza

the western gates, are between the Kunya Ark and Muhammed-Amin-Khan Madrasah. They were demolished in 1920 to make way for traffic, but were reconstructed in 1975.

The buildings within the Ichan Kala are numerous and are arranged without much order. Though the city gates are on the four walls there is no clear road pattern connecting them, and the narrow roadways and walkways twist and turn among the buildings. As part of the program of restoration and rebuilding, numerous small structures of no particular significance have been, and are being, demolished to improve sightlines to the main buildings.

Just north of the gates in the west wall is the KUNYA ARK or "old fortress," a large rectangular compound along the city wall, surrounded by its own crenellated wall. A mound on the outer city wall is the ruins of the ancient stronghold and location of a sanctuary structure called *Ashik-baba* (**52**-1). It is also the highest point in the Ichan Kala and provides the best view of the whole central city.

The Kunya Ark, rebuilt and fortified in the 1680's, was the residence of former rulers. The entrance, on the east, leads to the *Reception Court* (**52**-2), a two-column aivan with carved wooden columns on marble bases (one of which is dated 1855). Two grilled windows and a door lead through the back wall of the aivan porch into a large hall in which the khan's throne stood (the throne is now in the Armory Museum of the Moscow Kremlin). The aivan is well-proportioned and has excellent wall decorations of navy, turquoise, and white majolica tile. The *Summer Mosque* (**52**-3), to the right of the main entrance, is an aivan similar to the Reception Hall, with majolica decor of 1838. At the north end of the fortress is the *old Mint* (**52**-4) and the aivan hall of the harem.

Opposite the south end of the Ark is the *Muhammed-Amin-Khan Madrasah*, 1852-1855 (**52**-5), a large two-story madrasah notable for its size and entrance portal. In the later 1970's the madrasah was being converted into a tourist hotel. The madrasah is also known for its minaret, called Kalt Minar, a 79-foot tall cylinder 45 feet in diameter at the base, and covered with blue glazed brick. The minaret was built at a time of Khiva-Bukhara rivalry, and was planned as the tallest minaret in the Islamic east. It was left unfinished after the death of the khan.

The *Seyid Alauddin Mausoleum*, 1303 (**52**-8) is located just behind the small Divan-Begi Madrasah east of Kalt Minar. The mausoleum is the oldest structure in Khiva and consists of two square chambers. The gurkhana, or burial room, is small and unlit, and contains two coffins with remarkable relief majolica decoration in a free floral pattern. This work exerted influence on Samarkand craftsmen after Tamerlane captured Khiva, and is approached in excellence only by the tomb of Kusam-ibn-Abbas in the Shahi Zinda complex in Samarkand. This type of tile work was soon lost for centuries in Khiva, though it lived on in Samarkand. The mausoleum was restored in 1957.

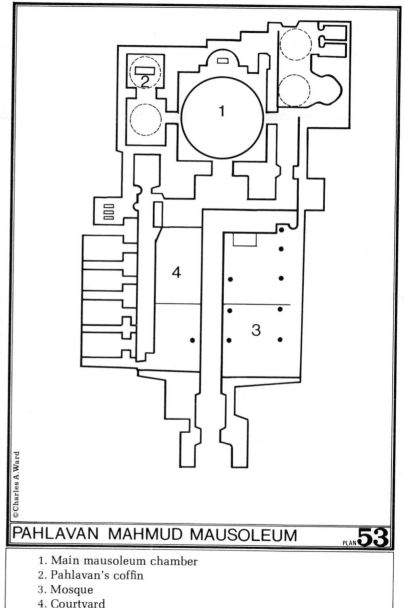

©Charles A. Ward

PAHLAVAN MAHMUD MAUSOLEUM PLAN **53**

1. Main mausoleum chamber
2. Pahlavan's coffin
3. Mosque
4. Courtyard

Further along in the center of the Ichan Kala is the *Djuma Mosque* (**52**-10), dating from the 10th century, but enlarged and remodeled in 1788. It is a low building with a flat roof supported by 17 rows of 13 columns, totaling 218 carved wood columns. Most of the columns are recent replacements, but 12 of them are originals of the 11th-16th century, and are carved at the bottom as a palmetto leaf overlapping a sphere. The columns rest on a variety of stone bases, one dated 1316, another 1510. The main entrance is to the north, down a few steps (the ground level has risen around the mosque over the centuries). The minaret was constructed in the 18th century.

South of the mosque is the *Pahlavan-Mahmud Mausoleum* (**52**-11 and Plan **53**), built in memory of Pahlavan Mahmud, a 14th-century soldier and poet who became a sort of patron saint of the city. The first tomb over his grave, built in 1664, was demolished in 1810 and replaced by the present buildings in 1835. The tomb complex is entered from the south through carved doors of 1701. Beyond a little courtyard of trees, a well, and a summer mosque on slender columns is the main mausoleum building, entered through a tall brick portal with majolica tile decoration in various patterns. The large hall is clearly articulated and contains tombs of political leaders. Off to the left is a smaller tall domed room entirely covered with patterned majolica tile (done in 1836), the main sight of the mausoleum. The dome of the main tomb on the outside is covered with turquoise glazed brick and surmounted by a golden sphere, and it is the largest cupola in Khiva. A new structure on the west side of the court, built in 1913, reflects some influence of Russo-European architecture. It also contains tombs in the westernmost section, and good majolica work.

Across the street from the entrance to the mausoleum is the *Shirgazi-Khan Madrasah*, 1718 (**52**-12), in a state of disrepair. It was one of the first theological seminaries in Khiva.

East of the Pahlavan Mausoleum is the *Islam Hodja Madrasah, Mosque, and Minaret*, 1908-1912 (**52**-13). The minaret, 145 feet tall and 29 feet in diameter at the base, is the tallest and finest in Khiva, with bands of brick alternating with narrower bands of green and blue ceramic tile. The first secular school in Khiva was opened in the Islam Hodja Madrasah.

North of the Islam Hodja complex is the *Hodjamberdyby Madrasah* (**52**-15), a small one-story madrasah from the 17th century. The left half of the building has an ornamental carved portal with elaborate detail work. Above the door is a marble plaque with the date of construction, 1688.

Just north of Hodjamberdyby is the *Kutlug-Murad-Inak Madrasah*, 1804-1812 (**52**-16), at one time the main theological school of the city. The portals inside the courtyard are decorative and the eastern court facade contains a summer mosque with a wooden balcony on the

second floor level. The arches of the galleries are framed in majolica and patterned terracotta tiles. The carved entrance gates of the madrasah are outstanding examples of wood carving. The courtyard contains an underground cistern which was the main water supply of the town in the 19th century.

North of the madrasah is the *Tash Khauli Palace* (**52**-24 and Plan **54**), built in the 1820's-1838 by Allakuli Khan as his residence. It is a completely preserved residential palace and is less fortress-like than the Ark, even though it is surrounded by a high brick wall with crenellations and semicircular towers. Main entrances on the south and west lead to eight courtyards of various sizes with aivan porches and elaborate tile panels on the walls. The Reception court and Harem court are a feast for the eyes with carved two-story aivan columns on massive carved marble bases, and wall designs of navy, turquoise, and white majolica panels resembling oriental carpets. The Historical Museum of the city is located in the former Harem courtyard and adjacent rooms.

Northwest of the Tash Khauli Palace is the small *Uch Avliya Mausoleum* (**52**-34), or "tomb of three dervishes."

A series of buildings stretch along the eastern wall of the inner city. Just east of the Hodjamberdyby Madrasah is the small *Ak Mosque*, 1677

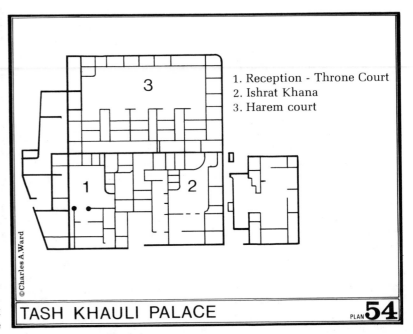

1. Reception - Throne Court
2. Ishrat Khana
3. Harem court

©Charles A. Ward

TASH KHAULI PALACE PLAN **54**

(**52**-17), a one-cupola structure with slender columns supporting an aivan gallery which surrounds the mosque on three sides. Behind the Ak Mosque are the *Anusha-Khan Baths* (**52**-18), built in 1657, a modest building representative of secular architecture of the 17th century. The entrance is through a vestibule with a small dome.

The Palvan Darvaza Gates are just beyond the Ak Mosque. They adjoin the *Allakuli-Khan Madrasah*, 1834-1835 (**52**-21), which has Khiva's tallest and prettiest portal, richly decorated with blue tile and white Arabic inscriptions. The inside of the madrasah is of no special interest.

The *Caravanserai* (**52**-23) and *Tim Allakuli Khan* (or Serai Bazaar) (**52**-22), 1832-1835, were built at the height of Khiva's trade with Bukhara, Persia, and Russia. The Caravanserai is a large rectangular building with one-story rooms around the perimeter, covered by small vaults. The Tim Allakuli Khan or Serai-bazaar, was built next to the Caravanserai to handle trade. It is a long passage with fourteen domes and domed niches along the sides. From its central dome a passage leads into the Caravanserai. It also serves as a passageway into the Ichan Kala from the outside.

Outside the Palvan Darvaza gates is the *Seyid Bey Mosque* (**52**-20), built in 1842. Its minaret is in line with that of the Djuma Mosque and the Kalt Minar, forming a marked east-west axis in the Ichan kala. The Seyid Bey minaret is one of the most attractive in Khiva, with delicate bands of brick laid in contrasting patterns.

The DISHAN KALA is the name given to the city beyond the central city. It arose in the 17th and 18th centuries as a suburb for craftsmen and was divided into five sections on the basis of the craft pursued. The Dishan Kala was enclosed in 1842 by a wall over four miles long, 22 feet high, with towers every 56 feet. It had ten gates, eight of which survive today. The main architectural attraction of the Dishan Kala is the Nuralabey Palace, constructed at the beginning of the 20th century by the last khans of Khiva.

APPENDICES

APPENDIX A: *Bibliography*

Despite increased interest in Russia over the past two decades, the amount of useful descriptive literature in English remains small and often difficult to locate. The best reference book has only recently appeared, Victor and Jennifer Louis's *The Complete Guide to the Soviet Union* (New York: St. Martin's Press, 1976). It describes all the Soviet cities open to foreign travelers and has a large number of accurate maps. The Nagel Series' *U.S.S.R.* (Geneva, 1970) is an encyclopedic guide with a great deal of information, and also a considerable number of typographical and factual errors. The most readily available is the *Soviet Union* volume of the Fodor Guide series (New York: McKay, various editions), with long articles on Russian history and culture, but less than detailed description of many of the major sights. The Nagel series' *Moscow* and *Leningrad* (Geneva, 1969), have the most extensive coverage of those cities. More readily available is *Smith's Moscow* by Desmond Smith (New York: Knopf, 1974).

The best work on Russian art is George H. Hamilton, *The Art and Architecture of Russia* (Baltimore: Penguin Books, 1954; 2nd edition, 1976). The book *Early Russian Architecture* by Hubert Faensen (New York: Putnam, 1975) has pictures and description of all major Russian buildings before 1700. *The Palaces of Leningrad* by Audrey Kennett (Putnam, 1973) illustrates and describes the main baroque and neoclassical structures of the former capital. Derek Hill's book, *Islamic Architecture and its Decoration* (London: Faber & Faber, 1967) has many photographs of Central Asian buildings, as well as those in other areas of Islam. Publishing houses in the Soviet Union occasionally issue works on major tourists cities in English, but these do not find their way into many U. S. libraries.

While in preparing this work I have drawn on my own notes, photographs, and recollections, this book would have been impossible without reference to many Russian sources. The most important, but by no means all, are listed below, arranged in the order that the cities are presented in the book. The abbreviations M. and L. stand for Moscow and Leningrad.

Arkhitekturnye pamyatniki Leningrada, ed. A. N. Petrov (L., Lenizdat, 1972).

Leningrad: Kratky putevoditel'. V. E. Mushtukov (L., Lenizdat, 1970).

Petrodvorets. N. I. Arkhipov, A. G. Raskin (M.-L., "Iskusstvo," 1961)

Parki Petrodvortsa. N. N. Fedorova (L., Lenizdat, 1966).

Muzei i parki v Pushkine. E. S. Gladkova, et. al. (L. Lenizdat, 1964).

Pavlovsk. A. M. Kuchumov (L. Lenizdat, 1970).

Novgorod veliky. M. K. Karger (M.-L., "Iskusstvo," 1966).

Tallinn. P. Bruns, R. Kangropool (M.-L., "Iskusstvo," 1971).

Kiev. G. Logovin (M., "Iskusstvo," 1967).

Iz istorii moskovskikh ulits. P. B. Sytin (M., "Moskovsky rabochi," 1952).

S putevoditelem po Moskve. F. Kurlat, Yu. Sokolovsky (M., "Moskovsky rabochi," 1975).

Moskva. M. Ilin (M., "Iskusstvo," 1970).

Kolomenskoe. M.A. Gra, B. Zhiromsky (M., "Iskusstvo," 1971).

Kuskovo. I. M. Glozman, L. V. Tydman (M., "Iskusstvo," 1966).

Ostankino. N. R. Elizarov (M., "Iskusstvo," 1966).

Arkhangelskoe. V. V. Poznansky (M., "Iskusstvo," 1966).

Novo-devichi monastyr. Yu. Ovsyannikov (M., "Iskusstvo," 1968).

Troitse-Sergieva Lavra, ed. N. N. Voronin V. V. Kostochkin (M., "Iskusstvo," 1968).

Pereslavl-Zalessky. I. Purishev (M., "Iskusstvo," 1970).

Rostov. Uglich. V. Ivanov (M., "Iskusstvo," 1975).

Kreml' Rostova velikogo. V. Banige (M., "Iskusstvo," 1976).

Yaroslavl. Tutaev. E. Dobrovolskaya, B. Gnedovsky (M., "Iskusstvo," 1971).

Vladimir. Bogolyubovo. Suzdal. Yuriev-Polskoy. N. N. Voronin (M., "Iskusstvo," 1965).

Samarkand. Bukhara. G. A. Pugachenkova (M., "Iskusstvo," 1968).

Vydayushchiesya pamyatniki arkhitektury Uzbekistana. G. A. Pugachenkova, L. I. Rempel' (Tashkent, 1958).

APPENDIX B: Russian rulers mentioned in this book, and the dates that they reigned.

Vladimir I, Christianizer of Russia; Prince of Novgorod, 969-979; Prince of Kiev, 979-1015.

Yaroslav I "The Wise," (son of Vladimir), Prince of Rostov, 998-1010; Prince of Novgorod, 1014-1019; Prince of Kiev, 1019-1054.

Vladimir Monomakh (Yaroslav's grandson), Prince of Chernigov, 1073-1113; Prince of Kiev, 1113-1125.

Yury Dolgoruky (Monomakh's son), Prince of Rostov-Suzdal, 1125-1155; Prince of Kiev, 1155-1157.

Andrey Bogolyubsky (Dolgoruky's son), Prince of Rostov-Suzdal, 1157-1174.

Vsevolod III "Big Nest," (Bogolyubsky's brother), Prince of Rostov-Suzdal, 1176-1212.

Alexander Nevsky (Vsevolod's grandson), Prince of Novgorod, 1236-1251; Prince of Vladimir-Suzdal, 1252-1263.

Ivan I "Kalita," (Nevsky's grandson), Prince of Moscow, 1328-1340.

Dmitry Donskoy, Prince of Moscow, 1363-1389.

Ivan III "The Great," Prince of Moscow, 1462-1505.

Vasily III, 1505-1533.

Ivan IV "The Terrible," Tsar of all the Russias, 1533-1584.

Fedor Ivanovich, 1584-1598.

Boris Godunov, 1598-1605.

Mikhail Fedorovich Romanov, 1613-1645.

Aleksey Mikhailovich, 1645-1676.

Peter and Ivan, 1682-1698.

Peter I "The Great," 1698-1725

Anna Ioannovna, 1730-1740

Elizabeth Petrovna, 1741-1761

Peter III, 1761-1762

Catherine II "The Great," 1762-1796

Paul, 1796-1801

Alexander I, 1801-1825

Nicholas I, 1825-1855

Alexander II, 1855-1881

Alexander III, 1881-1894

Nicholas II, 1894-1917

Soviet leaders

Lenin, 1917-1924
Stalin, 1924-1953
Khrushchev, 1953-1964
Brezhnev, 1964-

APPENDIX C: *Architects mentioned in this book.*

Alevisio Fryazin (or, Aloisio da Milano), Milanese builder active in Moscow from 1494-ca. 1515.

Argunov, Fedor Semenovich (1732-1768), serf-architect of Count Sheremetev, active at Kuskovo.

Argunov, Pavel Ivanovich (1768-1806), serf-architect of Count Sheremetev, active at Ostankino.

Bazhenov, Vasily Ivanovich (1717-1799), Russian architect.

Benois, Nikolay Leontevich (1813-1879), Russian architect.

Beretti, Aleksandr Vikentevich (1816-1895), Russian architect active in Kiev (son of V.I. Beretti).

Beretti, Vikenty Ivanovich (1781-1842), Russian architect, born in Petersburg, active in Kiev after 1837.

Blank, Karl Ivanovich (1728-1793), Russian architect associated with Moscow.

Bove, Osip Ivanovich (1784-1834), Russian architect, active in Moscow.

Brenna, Vincenzo (1745-1820), Italian architect; worked in Russia from 1780.

Bryullov, Aleksandr Pavlovich (1798-1877), Russian architect, active in Petersburg.

Cameron, Charles (ca. 1740-ca. 1812), Scottish architect, active in Russia from 1779.

Charlemagne, Iosif Ivanovich (1782-1861), Russian architect, active in Petersburg and Petrodvorets.

Chevakinsky, Savva Ivanovich (1713-late 1760's), Russian architect, pupil of Rastrelli.

Chichagov, Dmitry Nikolaevich (1836-1894), Russian architect.

Efimov, Nikolay (1799-1851), Russian architect, active in Petersburg.

Fioravanti, Rudolpho (1415-1486), Italian architect from Bologna, worked in Russia from 1474.

Fontana, Giovanni Maria, dates unknown; Italian architect active in Russia, 1703-1716.

Geste, Vasily Ivanovich (William Hastie), an English architect who worked in Russia from 1783-1825.

Gonzago, Pietro (1751-1831), Venetian stage designer, brought to Russia by N. B. Yusupov in 1790.

Grigorovich-Barsky, Ivan Grigorevich (1713-1785), Kievan architect.

Kavos (Cavos), Albert Katerinovich (1801-1863), Russian architect.

Kazakov, Matvey Fedorovich (1733-1812), Russian architect active in Moscow.

Klein, Roman Ivanovich (1858-1924), Russian architect associated with Moscow.

Kokorinov, Aleksandr Filippovich (1726-1772), Russian architect.

LeBlond, Alexandre (1679-1719), French architect, brought to Russia by Peter the Great in 1716.

Lidval, Fredrik Ivanovich (1870-1945), Russian architect, associated with Petersburg.

Melensky, Andrey Ivanovich (1760-1833), Ukrainian architect.

Menelaws, Adam Adamovich (1753-1831), English architect, worked in Russia from 1784.

Michetti, Niccolo, died 1759; Italian architect who worked in Russia 1718-1723.

Michurin, Ivan Fedorovich (1700-1776), Russian architect associated with Moscow.

Mikeshin, Mikhail Osipovich (1836-1896), sculptor.

Mikhailov, Andrey Andrevich (1773-1849), Russian architect.

Mironov, Aleksey (1745-1809), serf-architect of Count Sheremetev.

Monighetti, Ippolito (Ippolit Antonovich) (1819-1878), Russian architect.

Montferrand, Auguste Ricard de (1786-1858), French architect, worked in Russia from 1816.

Neelov, Ilya Vasilievich (1745-1793), Russian architect.

Neelov, Vasily Ivanovich (1722-1782), Russian architect and park designer; active at estate in town of Pushkin.

Parland, Alfred Aleksandrovich (1842-1920), Russian architect, associated with Petersburg.

Pomerantsev, Aleksandr Nikanorovich (1848-1918), Russian architect.

Quarenghi, Giacomo (1744-1817), Italian architect, worked in Russia from 1779.

Rastrelli, Bartolomeo (1700-1771), Italian-Russian architect, lived in Russia from 1715.

Rinaldi, Antonio (1709-1794), Italian architect, worked in Russia from 1752-1790.

Rossi, Karlo Ivanovich (1775-1849), Russian architect associated with Petersburg.

Ruffo, Marco, Milanese builder active in Russia after 1481.

Rusca, Luigi (1758-1822), Italian architect, worked in Russia 1782-1818.

Schaedel, Gottfried (1680's-1752), German architect active in Russia from 1713.

Scotti, Giovanni Battista (Ivan Karlovich) (1776-1830), Italian-Russian decorator.

Shchusev, Aleksey Viktorovich (1873-1949), Russian architect.

Shekhtel, Fedor Osipovich (1859-1926), Russian architect, active in Moscow.

Sherwood (Shervud), Vladimir Osipovich (1832-1897), Russian architect.

Sokolov, Egor Timofeevich (1750-1824), Russian architect associated with Petersburg.

Solario, Pietro Antonio (ca. 1450-1493), Italian architect from Milan, active in Moscow from 1480's.

Stakenschneider, Andrey Ivanovich (1802-1865), Russian architect.

Starov, Ivan Egorovich (1743-1808), Russian architect.

Stasov, Vasily Petrovich (1769-1848), Russian architect.

Thomon, Thomas de (1754-1813), French architect, worked in Russia from 1799.

Thon (Ton), Konstantin Andreevich (1794-1881), Russian architect.

Tressini, Domenico (1670-1734), Swiss-Italian architect, came to Russia in 1703; associated with Petersburg.

Ukhtomsky, Dmitry Vasilievich (1719-1774), Russian architect, associated with Moscow.

Vallin de la Mothe, Jean-Baptiste Michel (1729-1800), French architect, worked in Russia 1759-1775.

Velten (Felten), Yury Matveevich (1730-1801), Russian architect, associated with Petersburg.

Vitali, Giovanni (1794-1855), Russian sculptor.

Volkov, Egor Ivanovich (1755-1803), Russian architect.

Voronikhin, Andrey Nikiforovich (1759-1814), Russian architect, serf of Count Stroganov.

Zakharov, Adrian Dmitrievich (1761-1811), Russian architect associated with Petersburg.

Zarudny, Ivan Petrovich, died 1727; Ukrainian architect, active in Moscow from 1701.

Zemtsov, Mikhail Grigorevich (1688-1743), Russian architect, associated with Petersburg.

Illustration 1: Entry of the Bolshoy Theater in Moscow, showing typical neoclassical elements.

Tent Roof

Ogee Zakomara

Bell Arch

Drum

Column Belt

Apse

Open Gallery

Basement Level

Illustration 2: Pokrovsky Cathedral in Suzdal, showing architectural elements.

APPENDIX D: Glossary of architectural terms used in this book.

Apse — a semi-circular extension protruding from the east wall of Russian churches (illustration **2**).

Basement Level — in Russian churches, a high lower room which raises the first floor above ground level. The line between basement and first floor is often marked on the exterior by a protruding brick course (illustration **2**).

Blind Arcade — a type of wall decoration in the form of a row of arches supported by pilasters.

Capital — the projecting top end of a column. The neoclassic style had three main types of capitals, (1) Doric, with a round projection at the top, (2) Ionic, decorated with a curving scroll shape (illustration **1**), and (3) Corinthian, with decorations in the shape of acanthus leaves.

Column Belt — in old Russian churches of the northeast, a row of small attached columns at mid-wall (illustration **2**).

Cornice — a projecting horizontal molding, usually at the top of a wall (illustration **1**).

Drum — a vertical cylindrical structure used to raise a dome above the roof line (illustration **2**).

Entablature — in neoclassical architecture, the horizontal section which rests on a row of columns (illustration **1**).

Frieze — a decorative horizontal band at the top of a wall (illustration **1**).

Fresco — a type of wall painting done on wet plaster.

Gallery — a covered, sometimes totally enclosed passageway around several sides of a church or other building (illustration **2**).

Iconostasis — a screen between the sanctuary and altar of a Russian Orthodox church. It consists of a wooden frame which supports several rows of icons (illustration **3**).

Kokoshnik — a small semi-circular or ogee-shaped gable, originally used in several tiers to support a drum.

Ogee Arch or Gable — an arch with a double curve (illustration **2**); it represents the shape of the silhouette of an onion dome.

Pilaster — in neoclassical buildings, a rectangular column with base and capital, which projects only slightly from the wall (illustration **1**). In old Russian churches, walls were divided by **pilaster strips**, which usually were without base or capital.

Pendentive — an overhanging, concave triangular section which serves as a transition from a right angle to a dome above.

Portico — on neoclassical buildings, a series of pilasters or columns supporting a pediment, either on the face of a building, or free-standing (illustration **1**).

Pediment — in a portico, the triangular gable supported by a row of columns (illustration **1**).

Refectory — the dining room in a monastery.

Refectory Church — a church with the addition of a room on the west side. The room had a variety of uses (waiting for the service, etc.), and was not necessarily a place for meals.

Rustication — a type of wall treatment where deep seams are made to give the appearance of construction from large rough blocks of stone. In Russia, usually found on the lower floor of a neoclassical building (illustration **1**).

Tent Roof — a steep-pitched roof with four, six, or eight sloping sides. The height is at least 1½ times the base diameter (illustration **2**).

Zakomara — a semicircular or ogee-shaped gable which forms the top of a section of a wall in old Russian churches. The zakomara usually coincided with the end of a ceiling vault, but in later development was also an ornamental feature (illustration **2**).

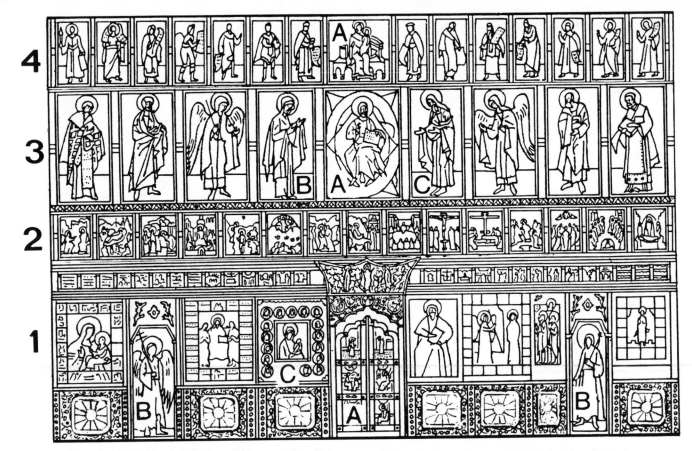

The **Iconostasis**, a wooden frame supporting rows of icons, developed in Russia from a low altar screen. By the 14th century the size and arrangement of the iconostasis had reached its present form. Though the size and number of rows varied from church to church, most iconostases extended the full width of the church and consisted of at least four rows of icons, arranged in a particular order.

1. The lowest row is the Veneration Tier, those icons which could be reached by the worshipers. In the center is the Tsar Door (**1-A**), which leads to the altar. It is often decorated with six panels representing the four Evangelists and the Annunciation. The Eucharist is sometimes portrayed above the central door. To the left is always a large icon of the Virgin and Child (**1-C**). To the right, either Christ or the Saint to whom the church is dedicated. The two side doors in the iconostasis often depict the archangels Michael and Gabriel (**1-B**).

2. The next tier of smaller, square icons, usually depicts Church Holy Days. The number of icons varies, but from left to right usually includes the Annunciation, Nativity, Presentation at the Temple, Baptism, Transfiguration, Entry into Jerusalem, Last Supper, Crucifixion, Descent from the Cross, and Ascension.

3. The Deesis Tier is the main row of icons. In the center is Christ enthroned (**3-A**), with the Virgin on the left (**3-B**), and John the Baptist on the right (**3-C**), flanked by archangels and saints. The figures are depicted standing, and are usually life-size or larger.

4. The Prophet's Row has an icon of the Virgin and child in the center (**4-A**). The prophets are depicted holding scrolls. Large cathedral iconostases sometimes have two tiers of prophets.